BLACK PANTHER

REFRAMING
HOLLYWOOD

BLACK PANTHER

INTERROGATING A CULTURAL PHENOMENON

TERENCE McSWEENEY

University Press of Mississippi / Jackson

The University Press of Mississippi is the scholarly publishing agency of
the Mississippi Institutions of Higher Learning: Alcorn State University,
Delta State University, Jackson State University, Mississippi State University,
Mississippi University for Women, Mississippi Valley State University,
University of Mississippi, and University of Southern Mississippi.

www.upress.state.ms.us

The University Press of Mississippi is a member
of the Association of University Presses.

First printing 2021
∞

Library of Congress Cataloging-in-Publication Data

Names: McSweeney, Terence, 1974- author.
Title: Black Panther : interrogating a cultural phenomenon / Terence
McSweeney.
Other titles: Reframing Hollywood.
Description: Jackson : University Press of Mississippi, 2021. | Series:
Reframing Hollywood | Includes bibliographical references and index.
Identifiers: LCCN 2021031878 (print) | LCCN 2021031879 (ebook) | ISBN
978-1-4968-3608-3 (hardback) | ISBN 978-1-4968-3609-0 (trade paperback) |
ISBN
978-1-4968-3610-6 (epub) | ISBN 978-1-4968-3611-3 (epub) | ISBN
978-1-4968-3612-0
(pdf) | ISBN 978-1-4968-3613-7 (pdf)
Subjects: LCSH: Black Panther (Motion picture : 2018) | Africans in motion
pictures. | Superhero films.
Classification: LCC PN1997.2.B5815 M35 2021 (print) | LCC PN1997.2.B5815
(ebook) | DDC 791.43096—dc23
LC record available at https://lccn.loc.gov/2021031878
LC ebook record available at https://lccn.loc.gov/2021031879

British Library Cataloging-in-Publication Data available

Dedicated to Chadwick Boseman (1976–2020)

Contents

Acknowledgments

To be able to give a film like *Black Panther* the focus it deserves in a book dedicated to it and it alone has been one of the most thrilling experiences of my academic career. My thanks go out to Craig Gill for his faith in the project and the support of the team at University Press of Mississippi, especially Emily Bandy. I was very fortunate to be able to write *Black Panther: Interrogating a Cultural Phenomenon* at a time when interest in the superhero genre had never been greater, which gave me the opportunity to present some of the ideas contained in this book at a range of locations, both within the realm of academia and outside of it. Thank you to the British Film Institute for the invitation to present to the public (alongside my colleague Dr. Claire Hines) as part of their "New Writings" series in December 2018. I would also like to thank the wonderful staff and students at my own institution, Solent University, and those at the Lilly Library, Indiana University, where I was fortunate enough to be the recipient of their generous Everett Helm Fellowship. The archives at the Lilly Library provided an invaluable insight into the tapestry of the history of the United States, which formed, and continues to sustain, the superhero phenomenon. Special mention should also be reserved for the staff and my colleagues at the IAS (Institute of Advanced Studies) at UCL, where much of this manuscript was written during my tenure as Visiting Research Fellow in the academic year 2018–19. Finally, during the final stages of the preparation of this book Chadwick Boseman, T'Challa, aka the Black Panther him-self, tragically passed away from cancer at the age of forty-three, denying fans future stories continuing the character's adventures that will now never be made. In *Black Panther* and his other screen appearances, his spirit will live on for contemporary audiences and those from generations to come.

BLACK PANTHER

A "defining moment for Black America" or Just a Movie?

Black Panther is a defining moment for Black America.

CARVELL WALLACE, *New York Times Magazine*, February 12, 2018

In this sense, black superheroes . . . are not only fantastic representations of our dreams, desires, and idealised projections of ourselves, they are also a symbolic extension of America's shifting political ethos and racial landscape.

ADILIFU NAMA, *Super Black: American Pop Culture and Black Superheroes* (2011, 1)

What does it mean to be African? That was the question I had been wondering since before I can remember. My parents described Africa to me as best they could. I knew that although I was living in America, my ancestors came from a different place—a place far away where we assume they were free of some of the struggles that we faced as a people here in the States, until one day they were captured, enslaved, and transported thousands of miles from their homeland. But the truth was, how could I know anything about a place that I, and no one I knew, had ever been. As I got older, I came to understand that Africa was the birthplace of human life. But the representations of Africa in the media were rarely positive and always incomplete. I had learned to take great pride in my family and my neighbourhoods, but

the images I saw about Africa often filled me with a sense of shame.
I knew these images couldn't be the whole truth about Africa. . . . As
for the question of what it means to be African, I found the answer in
this project. . . .

RYAN COOGLER, quoted in Eleni Roussos, *The Art of Marvel Studios: Black
Panther* (2018, 9)

I.

There are few films in the last decade that have had as much of a
cultural impact as Ryan Coogler's *Black Panther*, released in February 2018 as the eighteenth film in what is widely referred to as the
Marvel Cinematic Universe (MCU), a franchise which had started
almost exactly ten years before with the release of *Iron Man* in 2008.
As the first film in the MCU with a Black protagonist and indeed the
first superhero film with a Black character named in the title since
Hancock (2008), *Black Panther* was eagerly anticipated by many, but
none could have foreseen the levels of financial success it achieved
and the acute social and cultural significance it acquired. On its way
to earning a remarkable $1.3 billion around the globe, the film broke
several records and achieved many consequential "firsts" indicative
of this impact: from having the biggest February American box-
office opening of all time ($202 million), to being the first film since
Avatar (2009) to spend five weeks at number one (February 16–18 to
March 16–18), to having the largest pre-ticket sales of any film not
in the Star Wars franchise (1977–). It also had the largest opening
weekend box office for a Black director in film history, became the
highest grossing superhero film in the US of all time ($700 million)
and, perhaps most significantly, became the first superhero film ever
to be nominated for an Academy Award for Best Picture.[1]

Kevin Feige—the architect behind Marvel's transition from
comic book publisher to fully fledged film studio and home of
the most financially successful film series ever produced, com-
fortably surpassing rival franchises like James Bond (1962–) and
Star Wars (1977–), even though they have existed for decades

longer—suggested that *Black Panther* was the "best film we've [Marvel] ever made" (quoted in Fuster and Gonzalez 2018). Feige was not alone in holding this opinion through 2018 as a huge number of critics echoed these sentiments: many read along the lines of Bryan Bishop, writing at *The Verge*, who described it as "gripping, funny, and full of spectacle, but it also feels like a turning point, one where the studio has finally recognized that its movies can be about more than just selling the next installment" (2018), or Peter Travers at *Rolling Stone*, who wrote that it "raises movie escapism very near the level of art: You've never seen anything like it in your life" (2018). As unscientific as they are, review aggregator sites like Metacritic and Rotten Tomatoes also testify to how widely the film was embraced, with the latter having *Black Panther* at 97 percent "fresh," putting it in unlikely company with *La Grande Illusion* (1937), *Psycho* (1960), *Alien* (1979), and *Boyhood* (2014). Carvell Wallace, in the epigraph used for the introduction above, called *Black Panther* "a defining moment for Black America," a phrase which was regularly returned to in descriptions of the film (see also Prouix 2018). Others referred to it as a "watershed" (see Pitts Jr. 2018; Robbins 2018; Turner 2018) or a "milestone" (see Smith 2018; Mock 2018). These reactions were not only to be found in the United States, but spread around the globe too: in France in *Le Figaro*, the film was described as "a turning point in the representation of black people on screen" (anon. 2018), Pedro Moral in the Spanish newspaper *El Mundo* said it was nothing less than "a movie to change the world" (2018), and Kenyan writer Abdi Latif Dahir, writing for *Quartz Africa*, declared: "This might sound very hyperbolic but I have never been more proud of being black and African" (quoted in Kazeem, Chutel, and Dahir 2018).

Why a superhero film, *of all genres*, prompted such reactions is one of the central questions this book seeks to explore. After all, aren't films from the genre merely crudely reactionary tales featuring (mostly) men and women in tights vanquishing simplistic and stereotypical bad guys? How could a mere superhero film move audiences in such a way? It is a genre frequently lambasted by journalists and industry professionals with comments along the lines of "is the superhero craze destroying the movies?" (Gillmore 2016) or "comic book movies are killing the movie industry" (Last 2016). Academy Award-winning director Alejandro González Iñárritu referred to the superhero film as "poison, this cultural genocide, because the audience is so overexposed to plot and explosions and shit that doesn't say anything about the experience of being human" (quoted in Fleming Jr. 2014), renowned graphic novelist Alan Moore, creator of *Watchmen* (1986–87) and *V for Vendetta* (1983–85), suggested that the wave of superhero films made during the first two decades of the twenty-first century should be regarded as a "cultural catastrophe" (quoted in Flood 2014) and acclaimed actress-turned-director Jodie Foster continued the environmental disaster metaphor with her comments in January 2018 discussing the genre when she remarked "Going to the movies has become a theme park . . . studios making bad content in order to appeal to the masses and shareholders is like fracking—you get the best return right now but you wreck the earth . . ." (quoted in Hodges 2018a). In October 2019, esteemed director Martin Scorsese referred to films from the genre as "not cinema," continuing, "Honestly, the closest I can think of them, as well made as they are, with actors doing the best they can under the circumstances, is theme parks. It isn't the cinema of human beings trying to convey emotional, psychological experiences to another human being" (quoted in Bell 2019).

It was not just critics that *Black Panther* seemed to resonate with; ordinary audiences were drawn to the empathetic T'Challa (Chadwick Boseman), the film's eponymous protagonist, in his journey from prince to king of the mysterious fictional African country of Wakanda. *Time* had previously declared that T'Challa was not just the richest superhero, but "almost undoubtedly the wealthiest fictional character of all time" (see Davidson 2015) with a fortune estimated at $90.7 trillion, largely derived from Wakanda's access to the extraordinary substance known as vibranium described as "the rarest metal on earth" by Howard Stark (Dominic Cooper) in *Captain America: The First Avenger* (2011).[2] Its antagonist was also able to connect with viewers in ways that those from other films in the MCU hadn't; a character who goes by three names over the

Chadwick Boseman as T'Challa, aka the Black Panther, the first Black character as a protagonist in the MCU and a rare example of a Black superhero on the cinema screen.

course of *Black Panther*, arguably indicative of the crisis of identity he experiences. Played with a brooding intensity by Michael B. Jordan, the Wakandan name given to him by his father, Prince N'Jobu (Sterling K. Brown), is N'Jadaka, which is the name he seems to self-identify as and to which this book will primarily refer to him, but his American name is Erik Stevens and the nickname he is given during his time in the American military, both the Navy SEALs and JSOC (Joint Special Operations Command), for his talent and propensity for violence, is Killmonger.[3] The character was described by many as the best villain in the Marvel Cinematic Universe (see Wittmer 2018; Schwerdtfeger 2018), "the most complex villain in the post-[*The*] *Dark Knight* cycle of superhero blockbusters" (Vishnevetsky 2018), and even "the film's true hero" by no less a cultural arbiter than Slavoj Žižek (2018; see also Faruqi 2018). The star of the film, Chadwick Boseman, suggested that he too empathized with N'Jadaka/Killmonger and that the character should be considered as symbolic of the broader social and political concerns of the African American community in ways we will see frequently echoed by audiences and academics too often to dismiss purely as hyperbole. He remarked, "I don't know if we as African-Americans would accept T'Challa as our hero if he didn't go through Killmonger . . . Because Killmonger has been through our struggle, and I [as T'Challa] haven't" (quoted in Liao 2018).

These audiences and those who wrote and spoke about *Black Panther* are the object of study for this book almost as much as the film itself, with their reactions compiled from broadcast interviews, online reviews, commentaries, articles, and message boards, many of whom returned to similar ideas in their efforts to explain why the film had meant so much to them. According to the Motion Picture Association of America's (MPAA) "Theme Report" of 2017, while African Americans comprised 12 percent of the total population of the United States, they made up on average only 10 percent of cinema ticket-buyers during the same year, but for *Black Panther* a remarkable 37 percent of its total domestic audience was African American.[4] In connecting with so many, and not just African Americans, the film dispelled the notion that so called "Black-themed" films cannot be financially successful in the US and abroad, an idea that Scott Mendelson has called "the lesson that Hollywood refuses to learn" (2018). This was something that the actor Don Cheadle, himself no stranger to the Marvel Cinematic Universe, having played the character of James Rhodes/War Machine since *Iron Man 2* (2010), discussed on the release of his directorial debut *Miles Ahead* (2016), when he speculated

> Is it really true that black movies don't sell overseas? If you don't sell them, sure. I know people who sell movies overseas who say, "When I've got the films in my briefcase and one of them is whatever movie that's got the black cast I don't even pull that one out because the presumption is they're not going to buy it." It becomes a fait accompli and a self-fulfilling prophecy. (quoted in Rees 2016)

A young woman by the name of Ilona Williams, interviewed by Philadelphia television channel 6ABC Action News in a segment entitled "Philly audiences find deeper meaning in *Black Panther*" (2018), commented on the very same topic: "I'm just as excited about this movie as about when Barack Obama became the first African American president for the United States, I have that same exhilaration because I can hand down this to my grandchildren, they can see that it is possible for us to have black heroes." Ilona Williams was not the only one to express this sentiment, as exaggerated as it might sound, as contributor for CNN Issac Bailey wrote something similar, that *Black Panther* was "for film what Barack Obama was for the presidency" (2018), and on 6ABC Action News, she was followed by another woman, this time unnamed, who stated, "It's incredibly powerful for black people to see a film where we're the superheroes finally. I've spent my whole life watching films with people who look nothing like me saving the day time and time again, and we get to be the sidekick . . . and this time *we were everything*." This idea was also returned to by members of the cast and crew of the film. In an interview in *Entertainment Weekly*, Sterling K. Brown, the actor who plays the character of Prince N'Jobu, expressed his pride and satisfaction that "I get to take my kid to see a black superhero movie and he gets to see an image of himself as *the man*, and when I was a kid I got a chance to see Christopher Reeve [as Superman], I got a chance to see Michael Keaton [as Batman], but I didn't get a chance to see Chadwick Boseman [as Black Panther]. Chadwick Boseman looks like me, *he looks like my son*" (2018). Around the time of the film's release, New Yorker Frederick Joseph launched the #BlackPanther-Challenge, raising more than $40,000 for children from Harlem to see the film at cinemas. Joseph said, "All children deserve to believe they can save the world, go on exciting adventures, or accomplish the impossible. I am grateful that all of you have answered the call and are taking action to help more kids watch their heroes on the big screen" (quoted in Edwards 2018).

What this diverse range of people collectively articulate is not an abstract concept nor an anecdotal one, as empirical studies by a range of individuals and institutions have documented the lack of diversity within the American film industry for decades. Furthermore, while there is a general consensus that we are currently living in an age in which diversity is more widely accepted and promoted than ever, this is not the case in terms of *actual* representation in the culture industries. While there have been several notable Black superheroes in comics over the years: for example, the likes of Black Panther himself (first appearance, July 1966), Falcon (September

The power of the world of Black Panther: fans dress up as their favourite characters in cosplay (photograph by Pat Loika).

1969), the John Stewart iteration of Green Lantern (December 1971/ January 1972), Luke Cage (June 1972), Blade (July 1973), and Spawn (May 1992), cinematic incarnations of Black superheroes have been considerably less frequent and less impactful. Indeed, as mentioned above, in the ten years prior to the release of *Black Panther*, there was only a single high-profile superhero film with a Black actor as lead, *Hancock* (2008), starring Will Smith. Going back even further does little to improve these numbers, as in the ten years before *Hancock* we are left only with the disastrous Halle Berry vehicle, *Catwoman* (2004), and Wesley Snipes as Blade in the trilogy of films of *Blade* (1998), *Blade II* (2002), and *Blade Trinity* (2004): twenty years of the superhero genre, with the total number of films featuring African American leads able to be counted on the fingers of one hand.[5]

Outside of the superhero genre, in the American film industry as a whole things are slightly better, but not by much, as was revealed in a study of representation in popular films taken over eleven years entitled "Inequality in 1,100 Popular Films: Examining Portrayals of Gender, Race/Ethnicity, LGBT & Disability from 2007 to 2017" (2018), led by Dr. Stacy L. Smith at the University of Southern California (USC), part of the Annenberg Inclusion Initiative. The study found that only 12.1 percent of speaking characters in the top one hundred films of 2017 were Black, the lowest since 2012, with 2011 as the nadir in the time studied with just 9.1 percent. For Black women, the statistics are even more depressing, with forty-three of the top hundred films released throughout 2017, not too far away from half, featuring no Black female characters *at all*. Smith et al. conclude with a comment that the authors choose to present in bold for emphasis, "Overall, the findings reveal that no meaningful change has occurred in the percentage of Black/African American, Hispanic/Latino, Asian, or Mixed Race/Other characters during the years studied" (2018, 15). Moving behind the camera, this disparity continues, and across the entire eleven years and the 1,100 films studied only 5.2 percent were helmed by a Black/African American director.[6] Another startling study led by Marc Choueiti called "Critic's Choice 2: Gender and Race/Ethnicity of Film Reviewers Across 300 Top Films from 2015–2017" (2018) revealed that this inequality was even more prevalent on the fringes of the industry, noting that in the time studied 78.7 percent of reviews were written by white males, with only 13.1 percent of critics being male and of color, and 3.7 percent women of color. Marc Choueiti et al. similarly conclude:

In the three years examined, there was no meaningful change in the percentage of female critics or reviewers from underrepresented racial/ethnic groups working across all reviewers or as Top critics. . . . Overall, this study adds to our knowledge regarding the inequity that exists in film criticism. As a key part of the filmmaking ecosystem, it is clear that the conversation is dominated by white male voices. What does it mean for audiences to have their impressions of a film filtered through this skewed group of reviewers?" (17/19)

With this context provided it is entirely understandable that many African American audiences would react in such a way to a film like *Black Panther*, which is directed, written, and features a cast of African American or African performers, with only two of its main roles occupied by Caucasians: Everett K. Ross (Martin Freeman) and Ulysses Klaue (Andy Serkis).[7] Around the time of its release a popular twitter feed called #whatblackpanthermeanstome was set up by Kayla Sutton, director of online marketing for *Black Girl Nerds*, after her young son had reportedly remarked to her about the character of Black Panther: "He's awesome, he's like the coolest in all of the comic books and all of the stuff. And he's black like me" (quoted in Childs 2018). The complicated discourse at play here was rarely engaged with in any depth by the media, either in print or online, but was something expressed very clearly in an article by Jamil Smith which appeared in *Time*, "The Revolutionary Power of Black Panther":

> If you are reading this and you are white, seeing people who look like you in mass media probably isn't something you think about often. Every day, the culture reflects not only you but nearly infinite versions of you—executives, poets, garbage collectors, soldiers, nurses and so on. The world shows you that your possibilities are boundless. Now, after a brief respite, you again have a President. Those of us who are not white have considerably more trouble not only finding representation of ourselves in mass media and other arenas of public life, but also finding representation that indicates that our humanity is multifaceted. Relating to characters onscreen is necessary not merely for us to feel seen and understood, but also for others who need to see and understand us. When it doesn't happen, we are all the poorer for it. (2018)

This cursory engagement with just a few studies (and there are numerous others which come to very similar conclusions) has been largely rejected by many in a backlash which has labeled a discussion of these very real issues as an obsession with "identity politics," with many of those who comment on the topic being dismissed as either SJWs (Social Justice Warriors) or found guilty of what is now described as "virtue signalling" (see Bartholomew 2015; Young 2016).

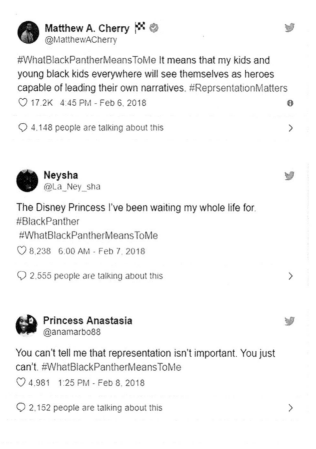

Matthew A. Cherry
@MatthewACherry

#WhatBlackPantherMeansToMe It means that my kids and young black kids everywhere will see themselves as heroes capable of leading their own narratives. #ReprsentationMatters

♡ 17.2K 4:45 PM - Feb 6, 2018

○ 4,148 people are talking about this

Neysha
@La_Ney_sha

The Disney Princess I've been waiting my whole life for. #BlackPanther #WhatBlackPantherMeansToMe

♡ 8,238 6:00 AM - Feb 7, 2018

○ 2,555 people are talking about this

Princess Anastasia
@anamarbo88

You can't tell me that representation isn't important. You just can't. #WhatBlackPantherMeansToMe

♡ 4,981 1:25 PM - Feb 8, 2018

○ 2,152 people are talking about this

Amber Sessoms @sessoms1011 · 18 Feb 2018

Bearing witness to major motion picture with predominately Black cast! WE are no longer invisible! Message brings to question: How are we going to COLLECTIVELY change the perpetual narrative of marginalized groups and center their voices? **#WhatBlackPantherMeansToMe** #BlackPanther

○   ↻ 1   ♡ 13

The popularity of #whatblackpanthermeanstome offers an indication of what *Black Panther* came to mean to fans all over the world.

II.

In what ways should we understand a superhero film emerging from the Hollywood film industry like *Black Panther* as being a political text? It was referred to as being very much political by those at opposite ends of the ideological spectrum throughout 2018, even "the most political movie ever produced by Marvel Studios" by Jamelle Bouie (2018). However, its politics were alternately described as "toxic" by Nonso Obikili (2018), "radical" by Mark Powell (2018), "revolutionary" by Jamil Smith (2018), and even "racist" by Christopher Lebron (2018).[8] It is hard to imagine how *Black Panther* can be all of these things *at the very same time*, but that is how it seemed in 2018. There is a dynamic body of work produced during the second half of the twentieth century into the twenty-first which persuasively argues that all popular culture texts should be considered as emphatically political in ways general audiences rarely acknowledge: from Roland Barthes's work on wrestling in *Mythologies* (1957) to Henry Giroux and Grace Pollock's on Disney's animated films in *The Mouse That Roared: Disney and the End of Innocence* (1999) to Jack Zipes's work on fairy tales in his definitive study of the form, *Fairy Tales and the Art of Subversion* (2006). As different as these three studies are, they each articulate the problems of considering popular culture distinct from ideology in similar ways to how this book will assert that the superhero film is an intrinsically and unequivocally political genre. Whether we turn to Jason Dittmer's groundbreaking study of the superhero in his book *Captain America and the Nationalist Superhero: Metaphors, Narratives, and Geopolitics* (2012), where he maintains that because of their pronounced connection to and embodiment of the values of the country they were created in, that "superheroes are not reflections of, but are instead (along with many other elements) co-constitutive of the discourse popularly known as American exceptionalism" (10), or Dan Hassler-Forrest, in his *Capitalist Superheroes: Caped Crusaders in the Neoliberal Age* (2012), who argues that given that the vast majority of popular American films are created and embedded within capitalist, corporate-owned enterprises, it should come as no surprise that the films habitually adopt and inculcate dominant ideological perspectives on issues of ethnicity, gender, and sexuality. What is certain for scholars of the screen is that *every* film is ideological regardless of its genre or subject matter, as Comolli and Narboni memorably argued in *Cahiers du cinema* in 1976 when they wrote, "every film is political, inasmuch as it is determined by the ideology which produces it" (24–25), even those used to sell toys, pyjamas, and Happy Meals, or perhaps *especially when they are.*

Tanner Mirrlees convincingly demonstrates how the first film in the MCU, *Iron Man*, reinforces three separate but interconnected aspects of American hegemonic power: "US economic power (as a Hollywood blockbuster and synergistic franchise), US Military power (as a DOD-Hollywood co-produced militainment) and cultural power (as a national and global relay for US imperial ideologies)" (2014, 5). The politics of *Iron Man* are readily apparent for those looking for them, but absent (and perhaps even more impactful as a result) for those who are not. *Iron Man* provides a mythologised portrait of American technological, military, and moral superiority in 2008, a year in which more than 600 US soldiers and 12,000 civilians were killed in the ongoing wars in Iraq and Afghanistan (where a large part of the film is set), just as the original incarnations of Superman and Captain America, as Chris Rojek maintains, "present idealized representations of American heroism and the defence of justice" (2001, 25) on the eve of America's entry into World War II. The character of Iron Man (who first appeared in comic book form in March 1963) was, according to Matthew Costello, "born under the mushroom cloud of potential nuclear war that was a cornerstone of our four-decade bipolar division of the world between the United States and the USSR" (2009, 1).[9] *Iron Man* is one of a range of the MCU's mythopoetic narratives that legitimize enduring fantasies of American exceptionalism in the post-9/11 era; in doing so these films participate in the perpetuation and consolidation of configurations of American identity not just within the US but, given their international reach, all around the globe.

For a variety of reasons, *Black Panther* is a more complicated case study than a film like *Iron Man*. The character himself is one who has been explicitly political from the moment he first graced the pages of *Fantastic Four*, vol. 1, no. 52, in July 1966, created by Jack Kirby and Stan Lee, in a comic book published in the year after the assassination of Malcolm X (February 1965), the Selma to Montgomery marches (March 1965), and the Watts riots in Los Angeles (August 1965), and just three months before the founding of the Black Panthers by Huey Newton and Bobby Seale in Oakland, California (October 1966). This final event, the creation of the real-life African American revolutionary organization, has often been connected to the fictional superhero who bears the same name. Huey Newton himself was (and still is) a divisive figure, revered by some and reviled by others, with the diversity of responses to him summed up in the title of his obituary in the *New York Times*: "Hero, Criminal or Both: Huey P. Newton Pushed Black Americans to Fight Back" (Hassan, 1989/2016). These connections were what motivated Marvel Comics to briefly change Black Panther's name to Black Leopard starting with *Fantastic Four*, vol. 1, no. 119 (February 1972), but due to negative fan responses, the company reversed course and returned to the original title only nine months later in *Avengers*, vol. 1, no. 105 (November 1972).[10]

Since that time, Black Panther has functioned as a remarkable barometer and even cultural battleground on the page, often providing a commentary on the shifting coordinates of American race relations and attitudes since the mid-1960s. While Marc Singer was entirely correct when he wrote "comic books, and particularly the dominant genre of superhero comic books, have proven fertile ground for stereotyped depictions of race" (2002, 123), during the 1970s, Black Panther even sometimes fought against the KKK (Ku Klux Klan) in *Jungle Action* nos. 19–24 (January–November 1976), was shown to visit Rudyarda, a thinly veiled substitute for South Africa in *Fantastic Four*, vol. 1, no. 119 (February 1972), and a place that Ben Grimm, aka The Thing, says "divides its own people into 'Europeans' and 'coloureds.'" In 1989, *Panther's Quest* actually featured South Africa, where T'Challa went to rescue his stepmother

Ramonda just a few years before apartheid was formally abolished, and in the following year in *Panther's Prey* (September 1990–March 1991), a crack cocaine epidemic swept through Wakanda around the same time that President George H. W. Bush called the drug "the greatest domestic threat facing our nation today" (quoted in Harwood 1989). The Reginald Hudlin era of Black Panther comics (2005–2008) saw the protagonist marry Storm and the creation of Shuri as his sister, a character who is central to Ryan Coogler's film, but also had Black Panther meet Skrull versions of civil rights leaders Malcolm X in *Black Panther*, vol. 4, no. 32 (January 2008) and Martin Luther King Jr. in *Black Panther*, vol. 4, no. 33 (February 2008), and saw several of Marvel's Black superheroes team up to help in the aftermath of Hurricane Katrina in *Black Panther*, vol. 4, no. 12 (March 2006). Hudlin commented, "The Black Panther, Cage, Blade, and a whole host of black heroes come together to help save a black city. It was just fun to do because I said, 'Well, why doesn't this happen?' Six white superheroes get together all the time and it's not a racial issue. They just happen to be six white people. So why can't six black people come together and save people just as well?" (quoted in Johnson 2018).

Moving into the twenty-first century, having already seen the remarkable impact of *Black Panther* on viewers and critics and at the box office, it seems relatively uncontroversial to assert that the character and the film in which he appeared seemed to be more relevant than ever to audiences as the film's fictional characters and themes spoke to real-life fears, anxieties, hopes, and dreams concerning identity, borders, belonging, and geopolitical accountability, which resonated particularly for American audiences in the wake of Donald Trump's election victory in 2016. Critics like Manohla Dargis at the *New York Times* wrote that "in its emphasis on black imagination, creation and liberation, the movie becomes an emblem of a past that was denied and a future that *feels very present*" (2018, italics added), and Tim Grierson, at *Screen International*, described the film as one "rooted in a desire to speak meaningfully about racism, global culture clashes, and the tension between hiding behind one's borders and helping outsiders in need" (2018). These writers, and many others, saw the film resonating in the "Age of Trump," a malleable phrase that means something very different depending on the political perspectives of those who use it, finding in *Black Panther*'s thematic motifs and even in specific lines of dialogue connections to issues at the very core of American political discourse in 2018 ("In times of crisis the wise build bridges . . ."; "You let the refugees in, they bring their problems with them"). So when one of the film's actors, Bambadjan Bamba, who played Militant Leader in the film's Nigeria set opening scenes, was revealed to be a recipient of DACA (Deferred Action for Childhood Arrivals), a program established by Barack Obama to grant temporary residential status to nearly one million immigrants brought to the US as children, an act that Trump was steadfastly against, the film became embroiled in that discussion in very public ways (see Lopez 2017). These moments—and there are many more—add a tapestry to the film that lingers within its fictional diegetic frames and reaches beyond them in tangible ways into the real world.

While it is clear why the film resonated in such a way with audiences in February 2018, this book will remain wary of making simplistic causal connections between *Black Panther* and the social and political environment in which it was released, an arena that is much more complicated than many scholars, journalists, and online commentators have traditionally acknowledged. Thus, while many understood *Black Panther* as a product of the Trump era, it is important to recognize that the film was conceived and written during the second term of the Obama presidency (2012–16), with its first day of principal photography on January 21, 2017, the day after Trump was inaugurated as the forty-fifth president of the United States of America (see Pearson 2018; Eeles 2018). It is more accurate—and, as we will see, more productive—to consider it as a product of the Obama era released during the Trump presidency, even as an example of "Obama Cinema" (see Hoberman 2012; Izo 2014), embracing the complicated discourse that this results in at the same time as interrogating why such diverse audiences saw their own political ideologies reflected in the film or even attacked by it when it was released during the second year of the Trump administration.[11]

The *Black Panther* comic con panel from July 2016. From left to right: Kevin Feige, Ryan Coogler, Lupita Nyong'o, Michael B. Jordan, Danai Gurira and Chadwick Boseman. Photograph by Gage Skidmore.

III.

Despite the overwhelming praise for the film, a range of writers and commentators have expressed concerns about *Black Panther* from almost as diverse perspectives as those who embraced it. We will return to these voices and their criticisms, many of whom raise valid issues, in more detail throughout this book, but some were disappointed that a film praised for being such a landmark in representations of Black people would only offer what they perceived as reductive representations of African Americans, with the film's single notable African American character, Erik "Killmonger" Stevens, being a cold-blooded murderer bent on revenge and seeking to kill "oppressors" all over the world "and their children." These concerns were articulated by academics like Délice Williams who expressed "reservations about the film's treatment of Black Americans" (2018, 27) in particular Killmonger, who she argues is defined by his "violent, shortsighted egotism and hyper-masculine megalomaniacal aggression" (2018, 29); critics like Christopher Lebron, in an article entitled "*Black Panther* is Not the Movie We Deserved" who wrote, "In 2018—in a world home to both the Movement for Black Lives and a president who identifies white supremacists as fine people—we are given a movie about black empowerment where the only redeemed blacks are African nobles. They safeguard virtue and goodness against the threat not of white Americans or Europeans, but a black American man, the most dangerous person in the world

... [who is a] receptacle for tropes of inner-city gangsterism" (2018); and audience members like the YouTuber who goes by the name of "Sal" who suggested, "I went to school with Killmonger, I worked jobs with Killmonger, I went to college, high school with Killmonger, played football with Killmonger.... Go to the barber shop I see Killmonger! These are people that I see, and I see him every day in my life. And to see the movie make him out to be crazy was kinda sad ... *this is a dangerous movie*" (2018). Others were critical of the film's refusal to portray non-heterosexual relationships as had been the case with *every* MCU film prior to it, especially when there had been a high-profile example in the recent Black Panther comic series with characters featured in the film. In *World of Wakanda* (November 2016–), written by Roxanne Gay and Yona Harvey, Ayo (played in the film by Florence Kasumba), a member of the Dora Milaje, has a relationship with another female Dora Milaje called Aneka. It had been rumored that in the film Okoye (Danai Gurira) would be romantically connected to Ayo, but nothing of this remains in the final version aside from a brief ambiguous exchange between the two. If Okoye and Ayo had been shown as partners they would have been the MCU's first explicitly framed non-heterosexual characters and the first gay relationship in the franchise (see Yang 2018). Others lamented T'Challa's uncomplicated relationship with CIA agent Everett Ross considering the often-destructive role the CIA played on the continent of Africa in the second half of the twentieth century and beyond (see Stockwell 1978; Mwakikagile 2000 and 2001; Paramore 2018).

Is it necessary to outline the cultural significance of the cinematic medium in a book such as this, which is more than likely being read by those interested in film beyond its superficial pleasures? However, for many, even though an overwhelming body of work argues the contrary, many still insist that "popular culture, or at least the part of it transmitted by the mass media, tends to "go in one eye and out the other" (Gans 1999, xiii). Writers like John Shelton Lawrence and Robert Jewett, in their ground-breaking *The American Monomyth*, called this lingering belief in the superficiality of popular culture the "bubblegum fallacy" (1977, 1–22). It is very easy to cite specific texts that transcend this interpretation of the relationship between film and society, whether we regard those that are able to represent the cultures and the times in which they are made or those who are able to have some sort of direct and discernible impact: should we discuss D. W. Griffith's *The Birth of a Nation* (1915) and its documented influence on support for the KKK not just at the time of its release but for decades after (see Martin 2019)? Or Oliver Stone's *JFK* (1992) and how it fundamentally transformed the public's perception of the Kennedy assassination despite its myriad of speculative narrative interpretations (see Scott and Thompson 2006; Seitz 2016)? Michael L. Kurtz suggested that "with the exception of *Uncle Tom's Cabin* [1851–52] ... *JFK* probably had a greater impact on public opinion than any other work of art in American history" (2000, 174). Or should we discuss *Saving Private Ryan* (1998) and its pronounced impact on how World War II has come to be remembered as the conflict moved towards the fringes of living memory, a film seen by millions more people around the globe than will ever read A. J. P. Taylor's *The Origins of the Second World War* (1961), John Keegan's *The Second World War* (1997), or Antony Beevor's *The Second World War* (2012).[12] This book places *Black Panther* alongside these texts despite the fact that it is *just a superhero film*, proposing it should be considered first and foremost as a richly affective cultural artifact in ways similar to them, each of which have resonated with audiences and found themselves both *embedded* into and *impacted on* cultural discourse. In addition to providing the prerequisite kinaesthetic demands of the superhero genre, *Black Panther* dramatizes and explores some very pertinent themes related to contemporary African and African American discourse: whether we view it through the prism of debates concerning the stereotypical portrayals of Africans and African Americans perpetuated by the American film industry (see Guerro 1993; O'Brien 2017); the personal and cultural traumas across generations of African Americans deprived of connections to their ancestral homelands in Africa (see Eyerman 2001; Alexander et al. 2004); the weight of the past on the African continent discussed in diverse schools of inquiry like decolonial ethics (see Mignolo 2011) and postcolonialism (see

Images of Africa in the superhero genre: as problematic "then" as "now" in the exotic tribes of the Gotham Botanical Gardens in *Batman & Robin* (1997), the tribal warlords of the fictional Nairomi in *Batman v Superman: Dawn of Justice* (2016) and the citizens of Lagos, Nigeria, who are placed in the background, literally and figuratively, of *Captain America: Civil War* (2016).

Loomba 1998; Ashcroft, Griffith, and Tiffin 1995); a discussion of gender and identity in African women (see McKittrick 2006); or the shifting coordinates of Black masculinity in contemporary United States (see Sexton 2017).

In this sense we should understand *Black Panther* in a range of ways, but primarily as a richly significant wish-fulfillment fantasy, one of the central tenets of the superhero genre, which operates on both personal and cultural levels. The superhero film offers us powerful individual fantasies about who we *could be*: stronger, faster, more virile, and more attractive (attributes that are literalized within the diegesis in the cases of Peter Parker, Steve Rogers, and Scott Lang), but also fantasies of empowerment on the global stage, whether it is the United States as it is throughout the majority of the films in the MCU, or the fictional African country of Wakanda, as it is in *Black Panther*. Carvell Wallace combined these two dimensions of wish-fulfillment when he asserted that the film should be regarded as "a vivid re-imagination of something black Americans have cherished for centuries—Africa as a dream of our wholeness, greatness and self-realization" (2018). It is not a coincidence that *Black Panther* opens with the line, "Tell me a story, Baba"; as it has a vivid story of its own to tell, a vibrant and very particular fantasy which the superhero film and the American film industry as a whole has never attempted to tell before. It is an avowedly Afrofuturist fantasy, to use the neologism coined by Mark Dery in 1994, and defined as "an intersection of imagination, technology, the future, and liberation" which reformulates "culture and notions of blackness for today and the future" by combining "elements of science fiction, historical fiction, speculative fiction, fantasy, Afrocentricity, and magic realism with non-Western beliefs" by Ytasha Womack, in her *Afrofuturism: The World of Black Sci-Fi and Fantasy Culture* (2013, 9). *Black Panther* taps into the ability of the superhero film "to imagine empowering social and political roles for marginalized people" (Marlene D. Allen 2018, 20), but from very particular perspectives by providing an allohistorical narrative, with its central "what if" undeniably that of a diaspora's fantasy: What if Europeans had not colonized Africa? What if Africans had found a remarkable source of energy? What if one African country had remained a secret and developed into the world's most advanced and powerful nation? Yet it is a fantasy, as Jelani Cobb argues in his article "*Black Panther* and the Invention of 'Africa'" (2018), that should be understood as "no more or less imaginary than the Africa conjured by [David] Hume or [Hugh] Trevor-Roper, or the one canonized in such Hollywood offerings as Tarzan [1918–]. It is a redemptive counter-mythology." Cobb here refers to the infamous expressions used by historians and philosophers to describe the supposed inferiority of African nations and their peoples that were commonplace in previous centuries, referring explicitly to the Scottish philosopher David Hume's 1753 controversial footnote to his "Of National Characters," in which he wrote,

> I am apt to suspect the negroes, and in general all the other species of men (for there are four or five different kinds) to be naturally inferior to the whites. There never was a civilized nation of any other complexion than white, nor even any individual eminent either in action or speculation. No ingenious manufactures amongst them, no arts, no sciences.

Cobb also refers to the British historian Hugh Trevor-Roper, who in 1963, only three years before the first *Black Panther* comic was published, wrote, "Perhaps, in the future, there will be some African history to teach. But at present there is none, or very little: there is only the history of the Europeans in Africa. The rest is darkness" (quoted in Mazrui 1978, 94). But Cobb could just as easily have quoted from many more equally esteemed philosophers or historians, even the likes of Immanuel Kant, who wrote, "Humanity is at its greatest perfection in the race of the whites. The yellow Indians do have a meagre talent. The negroes are far below them" (1802, 316). Of course, one would prefer to categorize these abhorrent ideas as distant relics of the past, and in some sense they are, but unfortunately there are far too many contemporary examples which make it problematic to do so, both inside the United States and outside of it. Here, for the sake of brevity, three will have to suffice, each of which took place in the first three months of 2018, just before the release of *Black Panther*, and illustrate that we are not as far removed from the comments of Hume, Trevor-Roper, and Kant as we would like to think. In January 2018, Republican state representative Steve Alford was asked about the legalization of marijuana in his home state of Kansas and answered, "What you really need to do is go back in the '30s and when they outlawed all types of drugs in Kansas [and] across the United States. What was the reason why they did that? One of the reasons why—I hate to say it—it's the African Americans, they were basically users and they basically responded the worst off those drugs just because their character makeup, their genetics, and that" (quoted in Lopez 2018). A few weeks before the release of *Black Panther*, Nigerian author Chimamanda Ngozi Adichie was asked by a journalist, "Are there any bookstores in Nigeria?" (quoted in Musila 2018), and in the same month Donald Trump reportedly referred to a number of African countries as "shitholes." When the cast of *Black Panther* were asked to comment about Trump's remarks, the most memorable came from veteran actor John Kani, who plays T'Challa's father T'Chaka (the former king and Black Panther). Kani said

> Africa has survived for centuries; today Africa stands strong. We are not going to spend time discussing it. We are not a shithole country—we're the greatest kingdoms of the world. I am a descendant of great kingdoms. My grandfather and my great-great-grandfather were kings and princes. When someone says something that really displays extreme ignorance, it doesn't warrant my second thinking about it. (quoted in Outlaw 2018)

The purpose of this book, then, is to explore and interrogate the *Black Panther* phenomenon and to provide a critical framework for an analysis of its production and reception. It will be approached, as this introduction aims to have shown, from a diverse range of perspectives: political, historical, cultural, ideological, and cinematic. As Adilifu Nama states in his *Super Black: American Pop Culture and Black Superheroes*, representation of Black superheroes onscreen is an area that has not been explored as much as it should have been, he argued, "Despite the symbolic significance of black superheroes in American popular culture, the topic remains, for the most part, unexamined" (2011, 1). Since Nama wrote those words, few other critical book-length studies have contributed to this topic for reasons that are hard to discern, although it must have been influenced by the lack of Black superhero films being made, except for the important *Black Comics: Politics of Race and Representation* (2013), edited by Sheena C. Howard and Ronald L. Jackson II, which focuses on, as the title suggests, the comic book medium rather than on film. This book builds upon and draws from these and others of note by Brown (2001; 2013) and Denison and Ward (2015) in an attempt to contribute to this discourse.

My central assertion is that *Black Panther* is a particularly resonant text and should be considered as a cultural battleground around which a war of representation and interpretation has been waged. That *Black Panther* was a phenomenon seems hard to disagree with, but worthy of further sustained critical analysis is why, how, and what the implications of its emergence are. As this book will reveal, its contours illuminate both the limitations and the potentialities of modern blockbuster cinema, and what it offered audiences in 2018 and what they found in it are discussed in the pages that follow.

CHAPTER 1

"Tell me a story, Baba"

What is the State of Wakanda?

It's all a front. Explorers searched for it for centuries. El Dorado. The Golden City. They thought they could find it in South America, but it was in Africa the whole time. A technological marvel. All because it was built on a mound of the most valuable metal known to man. Isipho, they call it . . . "the gift."

ULYSSES KLAUE (ANDY SERKIS), *Black Panther*

Speculative science fiction that treats African-American themes and addresses African-American concerns in the context of twentieth century technoculture—and more generally, African-American signification that appropriates images of technology and a prosthetically enhanced future—might, for want of a better term, be called "Afrofuturism." The notion of Afrofuturism gives rise to a troubling antinomy: Can a community whose past has been deliberately rubbed out, and whose energies have subsequently been consumed by the search for legible traces of its history, imagine possible futures?

MARK DERY, "Black to the Future: Interviews with Samuel A. Delany, Greg Tate, and Tricia Rose" (1994, 180)

I.

While *Black Panther* is the first time Wakanda has been featured at length in the MCU, the secretive African nation had been both alluded to and mentioned more than once in the seventeen films in the franchise made prior to it since 2008. Two years before, the Black Panther himself, T'Challa, had been introduced in *Captain America: Civil War* (2016) attending a meeting of the United Nations in Vienna with his father, T'Chaka, in order to ratify the Sokovia Accords, during which the elder statesman was killed by an explosive device his son was unable to save him from, a failure that haunts T'Challa throughout *Black Panther. Captain America: Civil War* had concluded with a post-credits scene in which T'Challa granted shelter to Bucky Barnes, the man originally accused of killing his father, in Wakanda, the first time the country had been physically seen in the series, with its final brief shot pushing deeper into an imposing and misty jungle terrain, revealing a giant statue of the panther goddess Bast, a figure who would play a significant role in *Black Panther.* Even before that, in *Iron Man 2* (2010), Tony Stark (Robert Downey Jr.) had been shown sitting in front of a digital S.H.I.E.L.D. (Strategic Homeland Intervention, Enforcement and Logistics Division) map of the world that seemed to reveal the location of Wakanda. In *Avengers: Age of Ultron*, Ulysses Klaue (Andy Serkis), who also features prominently in *Black Panther,* is shown to have a cache of vibranium that he stole from Wakanda that he sells to the malevolent sentient A.I. Ultron. Indeed, Steve Rogers, Captain America himself, had carried with him a piece of Wakanda in every film he was featured in, his iconic red, white and blue shield made from vibranium built by Howard Stark, Tony Stark's father, in *Captain America: The First Avenger* (2011) in 1944.

Black Panther itself goes back even further than the middle of the twentieth century with the first of its two short world- and character-building prologues, both of which establish the film's diegetic setting, history, and some of the thematic motifs that will define its narrative. The first begins with the voice of a young American-accented boy who asks his father, "Tell me a story, Baba." The film that follows is very much concerned with the *act* and *impact* of storytelling: of the stories we tell to others and ourselves to make sense of the world, both within its diegetic frames and beyond, responding, as we have already seen, to the demand from African American audiences for tales that reflect themselves in a genre that historically has, at best, marginalized and, at worst, erased their experiences entirely.

The story that the father responds with is one of the earliest chronological moments in the MCU and shows a vast meteor made of vibranium striking the surface of the African continent millions of years ago.[1] On first viewing it is not exactly clear who the boy asking for a story is, as he has just three lines of dialogue and is not shown on screen; this led many to assume, perhaps understandably, that it was a young T'Challa asking his father, the then-king, T'Chaka. This would make sense given that T'Challa emerges as the film's main character and he is the eponymous Black Panther of the film's title, and also that this would be a fairly conventional way to open a film as something similar happens in *Thor* (2011), which began with Odin (Anthony Hopkins) narrating a similar story to his young sons, Thor and Loki. In fact, the boy is a young N'Jadaka asking his father, N'Jobu, for a tale about their ancestral homeland, Wakanda, from which, we will learn, they are both disconnected. N'Jobu is a prince and also a War Dog, that is, a Wakandan spy on assignment in the United States. His young son, who is half-American and half-Wakandan, has never been to his father's country and only ever heard tales of its beauty, customs, and traditions. N'Jadaka, or Erik "Killmonger" Stevens as he is also referred to later in the film, is one of the only characters in *Black Panther* with an American accent, which offers a striking contrast here in the prologue to his father's clipped Xhosa-inflected (an Nguni Bantu language spoken widely across Africa discussed in more detail in chapter two) English. This will also distinguish him from many other characters when he is an adult and played by Michael B. Jordan. It is important to note that N'Jobu is telling his story to *us, the audience*, as much as he is to his young son, creating a context and a world for the film we are about to see. He says:

‧Millions of years ago, a meteorite made of vibranium, the strongest substance in the universe, struck the continent of Africa, affecting the plant life around it. And when the time of man came, five tribes settled on it and called it Wakanda. The tribes lived in constant war with each other until a warrior shaman received a vision from the Panther Goddess Bast, who led him to the Heart-Shaped Herb, a plant that granted him superhuman strength, speed and instincts. The warrior became king and the first Black Panther, the protector of Wakanda. Four tribes agreed to live under the king's rule, but the Jabari Tribe isolated themselves in the mountains. The Wakandans used vibranium to develop technology more advanced than any other nation. But as Wakanda thrived, the world around it descended further into chaos. To keep vibranium safe, the Wakandans vowed to hide in plain sight, keeping the truth of their power from the outside world.

In interviews, Nate Moore, the film's producer, stated that this introductory scene was not one originally conceived by the film's cowriters Ryan Coogler and Joe Robert Cole; on the contrary, it was added late in the production following test screenings. He remarked, "Audiences really liked the film but found there to be a barrier to understanding exactly what's happening because they didn't quite understand how Wakanda worked, something which is entirely understandable given the size and scope of what *Black Panther* creates as part of its narrative" (quoted in Mithaiwala 2018).

The images shown on the screen, which bring to life N'Jobu's story, are also recreated in a way which seems peculiar on first viewing, with the animation being formed with a textured, even sand-like quality. Only later, without ever being told explicitly, will we realize that the story was rendered in a granular form of vibranium (which the script calls "sand vibranium" [Coogler and Cole 2018, 1]) that shifts, undulates, and reforms itself into a range of shapes in order to visualize N'Jobu's brief history of Wakanda. Thus, the images are created with the very substance that he is referring to, the substance that has marked Wakanda out as different from every other country

N'Jobu's story to his son of "home" is rendered on the screen in granular vibranium and reveals why Wakanda has remained hidden for millennia.

around the globe. Vibranium as a symbol of Wakandan power, heritage, and identity emerges as central to *Black Panther* and is interwoven into Wakandan culture in ways that draw attention to it in the film and also in its background: it is used both to build and to fuel its futuristic cities, to create advanced vehicles and weaponry, stitched into clothing in intricate designs, and even onto the bodies of its citizens as tattoos.

The prologue covers more than a million years in just a couple of minutes, showing not only the meteor strike, but the derivation of Wakandan religious beliefs, the creation of the vibranium-infused herb that gives powers to those who imbibe it, but also introduces the first king of Wakanda and the original Black Panther, Bashenga, who will have a mountain named after him that is the country's primary source of vibranium. As the sequence moves chronologically through time, it shows a range of images indicative of the historical events that have prompted the Wakandans to "hide in plain sight," an idea that will be one of the film's central motifs. We see images of Africans being kidnapped, forced into slavery, and transported all over the world, an act which, according to many historians and social psychologists, still has a profound impact on Africans and African Americans to this day in ways which are rarely acknowledged (see Snyder 2015; DeGruy 2005). The legacy of slavery in the country where *Black Panther* was conceived, produced, and filmed was described by Rochelle Riley as "America's open wound.

It is the painful injury that a third of America lives with and the rest of the country attempts to ignore" (2018). As time moves forward in the sequence, we see images from World War II (1939–45), which ends with a visual representation of the detonation of the atomic bomb. These images suggest, quite powerfully, the reasons why the Wakandans have chosen to hide themselves from the world, although importantly the ramifications of this decision are not yet explored and they will be shown only as the film progresses. The scene concludes with two further questions from the boy: "And we still hide, Baba?" to which his father answers, "Yes." This is followed by: "Why?" It is a question which is absolutely fundamental to *Black Panther*, one that many of the film's characters will have strikingly different perspectives on.

II.

The film moves forward chronologically, but not yet to the present for its second prologue, set in a very specific time and place, an apartment in a tenement block in Oakland, California, in 1992. Two men, N'Jobu and his trusted friend James (Denzel Whitaker), stand over a table bestrewn with guns and plans, with schematics and maps pinned behind them on the wall. We never learn in the film what it is they are actually planning to do as they are about to be interrupted, but in interviews Ryan Coogler revealed it was to secure the release of N'Jobu's imprisoned partner, the boy's mother, from the California National Guard. He said, "The idea was when you see those guys talking over the paperwork in the beginning of the film, they're talking about a way to break her out of jail. The idea was they never got her out, and she passed away in prison, so Killmonger didn't come up with a mom either" (Coogler quoted in Holmes 2018). The walls of the apartment are decorated with an array of African and African American accessories and art in the form of drapes, tapestries, sculptures, and vases. Additionally, there are posters on the wall of the groups NWA (1987–91) and Public Enemy (1985–), artists from a genre of music that, as George

Ciccariello-Maher stressed, provides a "series of perspectival first-person narratives that illustrate the reality of life as a young black male in a country where they can only be viewed—as Public Enemy's name reflects—as a threat" (2007, 188).

Ciccariello-Maher's "first-person narratives" of the Black experience is something that *Black Panther* itself offers audiences, not just in the scenes set in Oakland but throughout the film. Oakland is not a location chosen at random, but one hugely significant for the film and those responsible for its creation for a number of reasons. Oakland has no historical connections to the comic book iteration of the character of Black Panther, but has a palpable resonance both textually and extra-textually since it is where the director Ryan Coogler grew up, the place featured in his early student film *Locks* (2009) and his feature film debut *Fruitvale Station* (2013), the latter about the real-life shooting of Oscar Grant in 2009. Indeed, the scene thus far could even be from one of those early films with the men talking in American accents, even though they are both soon revealed to be of Wakandan origin, and Oakland-born rapper Too Short's "In the Trunk" (1992) from his album *Shorty the Pimp* playing on the soundtrack. About these two men who open the film, Coogler observed,

> The interesting part about being black is until you open up your mouth, people don't know where you're from. . . . I thought it would be cool if you start on the scene in Oakland. You have these two black dudes, they talk and [audiences presume], "Oh, it's two black dudes from Oakland." And then at some point the guy switches and starts talking with the African accent. "Oh shit, wait, this dude's from Africa?" You realize, "Oh yeah, I can't tell the difference. He [looks like] the same people you know." (quoted in Lussier 2018)

Oakland was also the birthplace of the Black Panther political party formed in 1966, and a picture of the group's co-founder, Huey Newton (who was also killed in Oakland in 1989), can be seen on the wall in the iconic image of him sitting on a rattan throne chair holding a rifle in one hand and a spear in the other taken in 1967 and attributed to Blair Stapp. The camera scarcely lingers on the image, but it is one which has had a significant afterlife in debates concerning Black representation. Discussing the photo, Jo-Ann Morgan wrote, "The image was and remains among the most iconic in American culture, inspiring reverence and evoking nostalgia, embodying the ideology of Black Power and self-determination with a compelling immediacy" (2014, 129). In the photograph, an empowered Newton gazes directly at the camera in a composition that challenges the iconography and conventions of colonial-era portraits, reclaiming and restating his identity from those who would stare at him as some sort of object. The image can only be seen for a few seconds, but its use and placement could not be more deliberate by Coogler and production designer Hannah Beachler, who won an Academy Award (shared with Jay Hart) for her contribution to the film. Later, in scenes featuring the throne of Wakanda, many saw parallels between the photograph of Newton and how the throne was designed and framed (see Budds 2018).[2]

A shot of television news playing in the background dates the scene even more precisely as it is footage filmed in the aftermath of what are commonly referred to as "the Rodney King riots" or "the 1992 Los Angeles riots," which occurred between April 29 and May 4, 1992, after the acquittal of four officers of the Los Angeles Police Department charged with using excessive force on a young African American man even after videotapes of the event had been widely broadcast that appeared to categorically confirm their guilt. Later that same year, Spike Lee would open his *Malcolm X* (1992) with footage of the beating itself and an image of the American flag burning until it formed an X. The early 1990s were a significant period for African American cinema, not just because of *Malcolm X*, the third film in a remarkable series of almost annual releases from Lee that continued throughout the whole of the 1990s, beginning with *Mo' Better Blues* (1990) and *Jungle Fever* (1991), and ending with *Summer of Sam* (1999). Yet Lee's films were a few of many, including *Juice* (1992), *South Central* (1992), *New Jack City* (1991) and *Boyz n the Hood* (1991) described as "honest, intelligent portrayals

N'Jobu and James aka Zuri share the frame with T'Chaka in the apartment in Oakland in 1992, a place *Black Panther* will unexpectedly return to twice more.

of both modern African-American life and US history from a black perspective—the type of stories only black film-makers could tell" (Rose 2016b). Not coincidentally, when *Black Panther* premiered in Oakland at the Grand Lake Theatre in 2018 with Coogler himself in attendance, he told the audience that his father had taken him to see "whatever movie he thought a Black father and Black son should come see together," one of which was "*Boyz n the Hood* when I was like four years old or three years old or something crazy like that. . . . I sat right here in this back row right there and cried like crazy at the end of the movie" (quoted in Yandolli 2018).[3]

When N'Jobu hears a noise at the door the two men quickly pack away their weapons and he looks out the window to see a group of young boys playing basketball "Tim Hardaway style," a reference to the Golden State Warriors player and NBA All-Star three years in a row (1991–93), on a milk crate court below. James asks, "Is it the feds?" as they quickly hide away their "straps" behind a concealed panel, but N'Jobu somehow knows that it is not. In fact, it is his brother T'Chaka, the king of Wakanda, who appears in full Black Panther regalia with two of his imposing female guards (James comments that they are "Grace Jones-looking chicks"), the Dora Milaje, with their outfits inspired by the Turkana tribe of Kenya and shaven heads reminiscent of the Masai peoples in Kenya and Tanzania, incongruous in the rather mundane setting of an Oakland apartment. T'Chaka is much younger than we had seen him in *Captain*

America: Civil War, where he was played by the septuagenarian John
Kani. Here he is played by Kani's actual son Atwanda Kani, who also
acted as the film's cultural consultant on issues of Xhosa language
and culture. When asked "ungubani?" or "who are you?" in Xhosa,
a question that will be asked very often of characters throughout
the film and becomes rich with metaphorical significance, N'Jobu
immediately shifts from American-accented English into Wakandan and Wakandan-inflected English, pulling back his bottom lip
to reveal a glowing purple vibranium-infused tattoo as proof of his
Wakandan heritage, a plot point which will return for his son much
later in the film's present.

The two slip between Xhosa and English with their cordiality
seeming genuine even though both are aware it is a pretence. The
tone abruptly shifts as T'Chaka informs his brother that a quarter
of a ton of vibranium has been stolen from Wakanda by the South
African terrorist Klaue (he shows him a 3D holographic image,
something that is advanced in 2018, but illustrative of how innova-
tive Wakandan tech is even in 1992) and that many Wakandan lives
have been lost after Klaue detonated a bomb at the border.[4] When
James reveals himself to not be American at all, but also secretly
of Wakandan origin and sent by T'Chaka to monitor N'Jobu's
operations in Oakland, N'Jobu becomes distraught. James, whose
real name is Zuri, hands over a large vial of the stolen vibranium
they have been hiding in the apartment, proving N'Jobu's complic-
ity. T'Chaka demands of his brother, "Tell me why you betrayed
Wakanda." N'Jobu replies, "I did *no such thing*." At this point, it seems
that N'Jobu is denying his involvement in the act of stealing vibranium, but later, when the scene is returned to again, it is clear that
he means that he *was involved*, but that his act is one he feels justi-
fied in having done and therefore, in his mind, he has not betrayed
Wakanda in the way the king asserts. T'Chaka tells N'Jobu that he
will return home to face Wakandan justice, and the scene, for now,
ends leaving several pieces of information absent that it will provide
audiences with in a surprising flashback about an hour later. It is a
pivotal scene for many reasons that the audience does not yet know
about, and it is of such central significance that *Black Panther* will

return to it twice more, from very different perspectives. It turns out to be a defining day for almost all of the film's main characters, even those that are not present in the room like N'Jadaka/Erik or even in the country, like T'Challa. Its final shot is of the young boys playing basketball at the foot of the apartment block looking up into the sky, with one of them lingered on in particular, as they happen to see a futuristic Wakandan jet, a Royal Talon Fighter, gliding silently through the clouds as it disappears. At this point in the narrative there is so much we the audience do not know: we do not know that the boy, until now only identified by his basketball playing friends as "E," is N'Jadaka/Erik, and it is he who asked for the film's opening story and the question "why?"

III.

The young N'Jadaka's question is still relevant in the film's present more than twenty years later, as T'Challa is shown returning to Wakanda after the death of his father featured in *Captain America: Civil War* for his coronation as the new king. As the jet, constructed in the same shape as the one seen moments before in the prologue, flies over the African landscape, Wakanda is revealed to us for the first time, no longer realized in granular vibranium technology, but in sweeping panoramic shots of its spectacular and diverse landscape: we see its jungles, mountains, valleys, deserts, and rivers. Three young shepherds wave at the jet as it passes above providing a striking contrast between old and new that the film will frequently return to, a juxtaposition even embodied in the jet itself which is constructed with highly advanced futuristic technology, but is shaped like a traditional African tribal mask. The scene is accompanied by the plaintive vocals of Senegalese musician Baaba Maal in a track called "Wakanda" composed by Ludwig Göransson, who won an Academy Award for his work on the film. Even for those of us who do not understand the Fula language that Maal sings in, Pulaar, spoken throughout Senegal, Mauritania, the Gambia, and western Mali, the song is an emotive one based only on its threnodic melody

"We are home": Wakanda revealed to the audience for the first time with the name of the country written in the futuristic BEYNO font.

and the context in which it is placed. The words of the song itself though are significant to the story, a lamentation to the ancestors informing them of the loss of an important person metaphorically through the death of a great elephant. In the jet are T'Challa, Okoye (Danai Gurira) a Wakandan general, head of the Dora Milaje and T'Challa's childhood friend, and Nakia (Lupita Nyong'o), his former partner and now a Wakandan War Dog herself. As important as the panoramic shots of the Wakandan landscape are, just as significant are the close-ups of each of their faces which wordlessly accentuate the deep feelings they have for their motherland, not coincidentally the film's secret working title.[5] As they gaze out at the Wakandan sunrise, Okoye tells them, "*We're home.*"

It is only then, as the jet seems to be flying over a dense jungle and with T'Challa's suggestion that "this never gets old" that the craft moves through an invisible barrier, described in Jim McCann's novelization of the film as a "hologram projected across thousands of miles of land" (2018, 16–17). It is this hologram which has kept Wakanda's true identity as the world's most advanced civilization a secret for so many years. With this move Ludwig Göransson's score also makes a melodic transition as it blends together Maal's traditional African music and more contemporary sounds in a way which has characterized the Senegalese musician's work throughout his career and will similarly define the soundtrack of the film. When interviewed around the time of the film's release, Maal said, "I'm very traditionalist, but also very modern in the way that I love electronic sounds and the way technology changes culture.... The way it comes across in the film is that the culture is ancient, but also it talks to the future as well" (quoted in Perry 2018).

Inside the invisible barrier we are introduced to the capital city of Wakanda, Birnin Zana, sometimes referred to as the Golden City, which reveals a culture that has clearly thrived in its isolation from the rest of the world, but also remained deeply connected to its past. These connections are not only manifested in Ludwig Göransson's score, but also in Wakanda's architecture: in its huge modern skyscrapers with traditional African rondavel conical thatched rooftops; in the way the buildings seem to emerge from the natural landscape; in its geometrical rather than angular shapes; and in the repeated use of earth tones and naturally occurring materials and landscape features. As urbanist and city planner Brent Toderian remarked in an interview with *Architectural Digest*, "Unlike most superhero movies, where cities are filled with futuristic glass-and-steel towers reaching into and above the clouds, Wakanda's architecture comes in all shapes, sizes, and materials" (quoted in Malkin 2018). The fact that a superhero film was discussed in such a journal might itself be considered as emblematic of the cultural reach of *Black Panther*. Toderian continued: "There's density in Wakanda, but it doesn't seem oppressive. I immediately saw urbanism at all scales. I saw tall towers, I saw midrise towers, and I saw human-scale urbanism. It looks like regional architecture as opposed to this anywhere-ness that we seem to have in our global architecture these days. I saw architectural expression that was not only organic, but of its place and of

Drawing extensively from real African countries, Birnin Zana, the capital of Wakanda is a city of the future, but one very much informed and inspired by the past.

its culture" (Malkin 2018). In Ronald L. Smith's novel *Black Panther: The Young Prince* (2018), which does not take place in the MCU but uses many of the same locations and characters, the author describes the city in the same way as it appears in the film: "Towering structures loomed up out of the forest. They weren't just skyscrapers. They curved and swooped, twisted and turned, and seemed to defy the laws of physics. . . . It would be a strange picture for someone unfamiliar with the landscape—a futuristic city rising up out of the jungle—but this was no ordinary place" (8–9).

The creation of Wakanda on such a scale must have been a considerable challenge for Coogler, Beachler, and their team. Certainly, those responsible for many films in the MCU have created (and recreated) diverse environments throughout its existence: some real (New York, Kolkatta), some fantastical (Xandar, Asgard), and others in a slightly ambiguous position somewhere between (Gulmira, Afghanistan in *Iron Man*, Novi Grad, Sokovia in *Avengers: Age of Ultron*, and Kamar Taj, Nepal in *Doctor Strange*). However, the requirements for *Black Panther*, creating an entire fictional country replete with its own history, urban and social structures and aesthetic, all of which was to be seen onscreen, might be considered unprecedented in the MCU and one that, as producer Nate Moore suggested, was designed to "feel like a place that could exist on Earth rather than being a fantasy land" (quoted in Wilkins 2018, 16). The Wakanda the team set about generating draws on a disparate range of real-world African countries, customs, traditions, clothes, art, and architecture to such an extent that in the commentary recorded for the Blu-ray release of the film, Beachler revealed that a 500-page "bible" had been put together for *Black Panther* which was just the start of the creators' elaborately detailed history of the country. Writing in *The Art of Marvel Studios: Black Panther* (2018), adopting the rhetorical device of Wakanda being a real place, Eleni Roussos expressed this idea distinctly:

> A balance between old and new. We are in the infancy of public knowledge regarding Wakanda. As facts slowly emerge, it is impossible not to be enthralled by what is revealed. Tribal customs have been preserved, affording anthropologists a rare glimpse at traditions and ceremonies relatively unaffected by the passage of time. But these ancient traditions have not blocked their civilization's technological advancement. Wakanda's ground-breaking scientific progress far exceeds other countries' advancements in the fields of robotics, mechanics, and telecommunications. (2018, 7)

Although Ryan Coogler's remarks about the film's production designer, Hannah Beachler, with whom he had worked with both on *Fruitvale Station* and *Creed*—"She was able to bring about images that don't exist" (quoted in Roussos, 9)—might be applied to anyone responsible for the creation of a fictional world onscreen, it could be argued that the state of Wakanda presented a very particular case for a number of reasons, because as filmmaker and contemporary of Ryan Coogler, Ava DuVernay, stated, "Wakanda itself is a dream state . . . a place that's been in the hearts and minds and spirits of black people since we were brought here [the United States of America] in chains" (quoted in Wallace 2018). What Coogler, Beachler, and Moore articulate here, without using the term itself, is one of the central tenets of Afrofuturism, a concept first used by Dery in 1994 (two years after the Oakland-set prologue) but refined and developed by Ytasha Womack in her *Afrofuturism: The World of Black Sci-Fi and Fantasy Culture*. She wrote, "Whether through literature, visual arts, music, or grassroots organizing, Afrofuturists redefine culture and notions of blackness for today and the future. Both an artistic aesthetic and a framework for critical theory, Afrofuturism combines elements of science fiction, historical fiction, speculative fiction, fantasy, Afrocentricity, and magic realism with non-Western beliefs. In some cases, it's a total reenvisioning of the past and speculation about the future rife with cultural critiques" (2013, 9). Womack's wide-ranging study of the concept moves fluidly between a dynamic variety of artistic media: from literature (Octavia Butler; Samuel Delany) and painting (Jean-Michel Basquiat; Angelbert Metoyer), to music (Sun Ra; Afrika Bambaataa) and visual artists (Renee Cox). In feature films, however, given the financial requirements of the medium, cinematic examples of Afrofuturism have been rare with only the likes of *The Brother from Another Planet* (1984), *Brown Girl Begins* (2017) and DuVernay's own *A Wrinkle in Time* (2018) said to have been able to explore some aspects of the movement (see Clarke 2015). Yet what Womack describes seems precisely what *Black Panther* sets out to achieve, leading to it emerging as the most comprehensive cinematic embodiment of Afrofuturism ever produced by the American film industry. In its centralization of the lives and experiences of those who live in a futuristic African country that has not suffered from the legacy of slavery, *Black Panther* does what Womack argues is one of the defining elements of Afrofuturism utilizing "black characters or aesthetics to deconstruct images of the past to revisualize the future" (2013, 22). Thus Afrofuturism, while concerned with the future as its name suggests, is intimately connected to how the past informs this vision of futurity as Olalekan Jeyifous, a Brooklyn-based Afrofuturist artist observed of the film: "It's a fictional Africa, and there's spaceships, but there are also aspects that hearken back to pre-agrarian times" (quoted in Mikael-Debass 2018).

Whatever image of Africa is offered in *Black Panther*, it is certainly a far cry from those proposed by David Hume or Hugh Trevor-Roper that we saw in our introduction or that of Immanuel Kant, who wrote of Africa in 1822:

> All our observations of African man shows him as living in a state of savagery and barbarism, and he remains in this state to the present day. The negro is an example of animal man in all its savagery and lawlessness, and if we wish to understand him at all, we must put aside all our European attitudes. . . . We cannot properly feel ourselves into his nature, no more than into a dog.

Black Panther might be considered, in some ways, as a response to comments like these and the perpetuation of stereotypes about Africa in American film and television which Coogler himself considered "rarely positive and always incomplete" (quoted in Roussos 2018, 9) and even the lack of Black superheroes brought to the screen since *Superman* (1978). As Adilfu Nama conjects, writing about the comic book iteration of the character but with comments that could just as well be applied to the film, "Consequently the Black Panther not only symbolized a politically provocative and wildly imaginative convergence of African tradition with future technology, but he also stood as a progressive racial symbol and anti-colonialist critique of the economic exploitation of Africa" (2011, 43).

IV.

T'Challa has returned to Africa to participate in a ceremonial ritual which is designed to end with his succession to the throne and him becoming both the king of Wakanda and the Black Panther in a sequence which provides us with further examples of how far the film is immersed in traditional African customs and traditions. In what is obviously a hugely significant day for the country, it seems like a very large part of Wakanda has turned up to participate in the event which takes place at Warrior Falls, a huge waterfall on the fictional Amanzi Kwakhona Umlambo river which runs through the country. Many of those Wakandans attending would not have seen an event like this before as the previous king, T'Chaka, had a long reign stretching back to when T'Challa was a child, at least before 1992.

It is here at the towering waterfall, which Wakandan technological advances allow them to halt the flow of its current in ways not possible in the real world, that we are reintroduced to the four tribes of Wakanda which were originally mentioned in the prologue, each of which are based on a variety of real-life African tribes.[6] First among them is the Merchant tribe, who trade in Wakandan-produced clothing and art, with their representative, or elder, an imposing presence, a mature matriarchal figure played by octogenarian Dorothy Steel. Both she and the young warrior at her side wear clothes based on the Tuareg people in Saharan and Sahelian regions, with their large Fulani earrings and turbans adorned with Tuareg symbols. They are followed by the Border tribe, who appear to be shepherds and farmers but are in reality fierce warriors and the primary defenders of the borders of Wakanda. They are also dressed in traditional garb based on the Basothan and Lesothan peoples, with blanket coats that have vibranium woven into their fabric adorned with richly significant Adinka symbols. Among them the camera briefly lingers on W'Kabi (Daniel Kaluuya), a character who is later revealed to be one of T'Challa's childhood friends and the partner of Okoye. Then comes the River Tribe with clothing and customs drawn from the Tsamai and Suri tribes in southern Ethiopia and the Wagenia fisherman in the Congo. Their unnamed tribe elder (played by Isaach de Bankolé) is shown to have a magnificently realized lip plate like those of the Mursi or Surma peoples of Ethiopia, worn to suggest wealth or social status. Standing next to him is Nakia, T'Challa's former partner and one of the film's central characters. The final group are the Mining tribe, based on the Samburu tribe in Kenya and the Dinka of South Sudan, wearing

The four tribes of Wakanda on the day of the ceremonial ritual: from top to bottom, the Merchant tribe, the Border tribe, the River tribe, and the Mining tribe.

the striking red colors of the ovaHimba tribe in Namibia. Their tribal elder, another mature female, wears the distinctive hairstyle of ovaHimba women, one that is "sculpted in otjize paste, made of butter, fat, red ochre and scented with herbal aromatics, ovaHimba plait or twist their hair into thick locks, often leaving ends to puff" (Lynsey Chutel and Yomi Kazeem 2018).

It is a remarkable and vivid collection of African tribal customs and traditions the likes of which have never been shown in such detail in a mainstream American film before. Even so, some expressed concerns about the centralization and appropriation of these tribal identities for an American blockbuster and Disney film, regarding them as symptomatic of western culture's fixation with patrimonial African practices, a reductive and too frequently turned-to stereotype in depictions of the continent. It is possible to see both sides here certainly, with numerous Africans understandably pleased to see their own rich cultural traditions rendered on the screens of an American film, but also the sincerity of others more critical of exactly the same thing, wary of an American cinema that has historically featured crude representations of Africa on its screens throughout its long history. Larry Madowo recognized the film's power but at the same time categorized its influences as something of an "African bingo" (2018), with Van R. Newkirk II concurring, asserting that its African-ness "can be read as a hodgepodge, or it can be read as the African American syncretic embrace of a motherland lost" (2018).

It is not just the tribes of Wakanda who are there to witness the ritual, but members of the royal family and other representatives of the state. The queen—T'Challa's mother, Ramonda (Angela Bassett)—is shown wearing a ceremonial costume and a disk-shaped headdress known as an *isicola*, drawn from Zulu culture. Standing beside her is her daughter—T'Challa's sister, the Princess Shuri—who looks distinctly uncomfortable in her traditional ceremonial corset replete with bone jawline, offering a stark contrast to how the film will position her as a modern, youthful, and dynamic progressive figure. The royals are attended by the Dora Milaje, the all-female bodyguards we had earlier seen in the film's prologue. The

Dora Milaje were originally introduced during Christopher Priest's tenure as writer of the comic book series, taking the position of not only protectors of the king but also potential wives, although this element has been entirely erased in their MCU iteration. While a fictional creation they too have real-world precedents such as the female warriors of the Fon Minos in the nineteenth-century Kingdom of Dahomey in modern-day Benin, otherwise known as the Dahomey Amazons (see Alpern 1998).

The ceremonial ritual about to be conducted at the foot of the now-dry waterfall is both a governmental and a religious one as the king of Wakanda is the head of state as well as its religious leader. In addition to being a monarch, he becomes a representative of the Wakandan goddess, Bast, who is mentioned several times throughout the film and similarly intimately connected to African tribal customs. Intriguingly in *Black Panther*, the Wakandan religion and its customs are certainly much more present in the narrative than Christianity has ever been in the MCU where it has been marginalized, erased, or becomes the subject of humor, resulting in religious scholars writing about the superhero film from a theological perspective having to seek it in subtext or allegory (see Bell 2017). The MCU's most explicit and memorable references to religion outside of *Black Panther* are indeed humorous ones: like the Joss Whedon-scripted line given to Captain America in *The Avengers*, "There's only one God, ma'am, and I'm pretty sure he doesn't dress like that," or in *Avengers: Infinity War*, in which Peter Quill, aka Star-Lord, asks, "What master do I serve? What am I supposed to say, *Jesus*?"[7] Given this example as representative of broader tendencies in popular film and media, which it indeed is, one might speculate as to why in a country where 75 percent identify as Christian, according to a 2015 poll, mainstream films now tend to elide that which used to be commonplace. At the same time we might also understand why those who do identify as Christian feel that their faith is no longer proportionally represented in popular culture and when it is, is often the target of criticism or humor not directed at other faiths (see Newport 2015). Bast will be mentioned seven times throughout the film in total; another god, the Indian deity Hanuman, will be mentioned once, too. On all of these occasions, the Wakandan religion, both the people who follow it and its practices, are portrayed with sincerity and reverence, never questioned by anyone on the screen, joked about or derided, and the religious beliefs of the Wakandans actually play a central role in the film as it progresses, whether that might be its embrace of what appears to be a real and literal physical afterlife, respect for religious customs and ceremonies, or the belief that the powers of the Black Panther were bestowed upon Bashenga many years before by an actual godddess, Bast herself.

The ceremonial ritual is conducted by the state's other senior religious representative, the purple-clothed wise man, tribal elder, and spiritual leader, high shaman Zuri (Forest Whittaker). The name Zuri had been mentioned very briefly in the film's Oakland prologue as the character of James's real name, but this happens so quickly that one might imagine most audiences had not picked up on the connection (which is saved for a subsequent dramatic reveal). As with the other characters, Zuri's clothes are immersed in very real tribal customs which fuse technology and spirituality, like his flowing, wide-sleeved Agbada robe, traditionally worn throughout the Sahelian and Saharan regions of Africa, most frequently in Yoruba and Dagomba cultures. Zuri carries the spear of Bashenga, not referred to in the film by name but the one held by the first king of Wakanda in the film's animated prologue. Whether this might be considered an "Easter egg," that is, a moment included for fans to delight in spotting and pore over in repeated viewings of the film, a practice which has become habitual in modern blockbuster cinema, or just a small part of the densely textured tapestry that Coogler has designed, is up to audiences to decide. *Black Panther* features many more such moments in the form of objects, characters, and references to the wider world of the MCU or the comic books on which the films are based. For example, when Shuri later opines, "Another white boy for me to fix!" for some in the audience it will mean nothing significant, but for those participating in Marvel's ongoing experiment they know she is referring to James "Bucky" Barnes, the erstwhile Winter Soldier, to whom T'Challa offered shelter at the end of *Captain America: Civil War* and who will later return in the post-credits coda of *Black Panther*; or Stan Lee's cameo, one of his last before his death in November 2018, as a gambler in the South Korean casino; or when characters repeat lines from previous moments in the comics, like T'Challa's "Every breath you take is mercy from me!" to Klaue, originally spoken to Prince Namor of Atlantis in *New Avengers*, vol. 3, no. 22 (2014). These pass by unacknowledged by casual audiences but have emerged as one of the central pleasures of the superhero genre for more devoted fans and further evidence of what Henry Jenkins described as "participatory culture" in his *Convergence Culture: Where Old and New Media Collide* (2006, 3), noting that audiences demand more active experiences from their entertainment products than they have ever done before.

T'Challa is shown to be very close to Zuri, later saying of him, "He was like a father to me." The character emerges as a shaman and something of a griot—that is, a community storyteller in the west African tradition and oral historian.[8] At a key point later in the film, he will tell a story that changes the way T'Challa perceives his father's past, and in doing so, given their shared kingly status, the future of the entire country. As part of the ceremony, each of the tribes are offered the opportunity to challenge T'Challa in combat, but all four present decline. Zuri then asks, "Is there any member of a royal blood who wishes to challenge for the throne?" Shuri raises her hand, provoking gasps from the crowd, but it is only another opportunity for the character to light-heartedly bristle at tradition: "This corset is really uncomfortable . . . so could we all just wrap it up and go home?" However, at the same time it is also an Easter egg for fans who might be aware that in the comics she does actually become the Black Panther and it also prefigures a real challenge from someone of royal blood about an hour of screen time and just a few diegetic days later.

It is then, that the ceremony is disturbed by rhythmic, guttural sounds of something, or rather someone, emerging from a dark tunnel at the base of Warrior Falls that turns out to be the representatives of the Jabari tribe, led by the towering figure of M'Baku (Winston Duke), who wants to mount a challenge for the throne. The mountain tribe of the Jabari had been mentioned in the film's

M'Baku, chief of the Jabari, starts off as a fierce and antagonistic figure but becomes an ally of T'Challa by the time the film ends.

animated prologue, where they were shown choosing to disconnect themselves from the rest of Wakanda, and the film remains ambiguous as to their reasons, but in the history of the comics it has been more explicit, as the Jabari have turned their back on vibranium in favor of a technology free existence in the mountains.[9] The Jabari are just as connected to real-world African tribes as those we have already seen—in this case, the Karo tribe in Ethiopia and the Dogon tribe in Mali. In the comics, M'Baku became known as Man Ape, wearing the skin of a giant white gorilla mutated by prolonged exposure to vibranium, which some understandably speculated might have proved too racially coded and problematic to be used in a contemporary adaptation (McMillan 2018). In *Black Panther*, the character is rewritten in a much more sympathetic and decidedly less contentious fashion, as even though he opens the film as an antagonist to T'Challa, he ends it as a trusted ally and advisor.[10] M'Baku informs those watching the ceremony that "we [the Jabari] have watched and listened from the mountains! We have watched with disgust as your technological advancements have been overseen *by a child*! [gesturing towards Shuri]."

M'Baku's challenge of T'Challa is a potent one, not just due to his considerable size and evident power but also because his words directed towards the prince seem to be a manifestation of T'Challa's own fears that he is indeed a man "who could not keep his own father safe" and is "just a boy not fit to lead." Before their combat begins, the film shows T'Chaka being stripped of his powers, as he can have no unfair advantage over his opponent during a challenge and if he wins, it must be by skill alone. The ensuing battle establishes a template that the rest of the film will follow by which action sequences not only fulfill the prerequisite kinaesthetic demands of the genre, but are also designed to develop character and theme at the same time. In the case of this fight between T'Challa and M'Baku, the former is shown as determined but also empathetic, as at his moment of victory he offers M'Baku words of commiseration and the opportunity to save face in front of his people and the rest of Wakanda by telling him, "You have fought with honor, now yield, *your people need you*," and it is this that inspires the Jabari leader to recognize T'Challa's qualities and later save his life and fight by his side in the film's climactic battle. There is a key moment during their fight when T'Challa appears to be losing and, to highlight his discombobulation, the camera turns upside down in a way it will only do on one other occasion during the course of the film. As he is seemingly about to be defeated, T'Challa sees his mother and she yells to him, her voice distorted and the image blurred, "Show him who you are!" to which he responds, "I am prince T'Challa, son of king T'Chaka," before fighting back and overcoming M'Baku as one would expect the protagonist of a superhero film to do.

V.

T'Challa's reward for victory over M'Baku is twofold: the first is his anticipated accession to the throne and it is Zuri who proclaims him king in front of all those Wakandans present, each of whom had witnessed their king defeat M'Baku. Chadwick Boseman, it should be observed, was no stranger to portraying real-life iconic figures in Black history, having played baseball legend Jackie Robinson in *42* (2013), music icon James Brown in *Get on Up* (2014), Thurgood Marshall, the first African American Supreme Court justice in *Marshall* (2017), and even an African god, Thoth, in the critical and commercial disaster that was *Gods of Egypt* (2017). The role of

T'Challa is a noteworthy one in ways we have already observed, as a rare African American lead in the superhero genre and in a big-budget studio film, but just as important is how the character offers broader dimensions than many roles afforded to African Americans in mainstream American films: he is not just a king and a leader, which would be significant in itself, but also a brother, a son, a friend, and a former lover, and each of these dimensions are given screen time, adding further layers to the character.

T'Challa's second reward is the opportunity to participate in another ritual where he drinks the heart-shaped herb in the Wakandan holy underground temple called the City of the Dead. By taking this substance and being buried in the temple's dark red sand, he is allowed to visit what the film calls the ancestral plane and be reunited, if only for a brief time, with his ancestors. This ancestral plane had been mentioned in *Captain America: Civil War* as T'Challa sat on a bench outside of the United Nations building in Vienna near Black Widow/Natasha Romanoff in the aftermath of his father's murder, a scene that saw him holding his father's ring (an object that becomes an important plot point in *Black Panther*) and informing her that "in my culture death is not the end, it's more of a stepping off point, to reach out with both hands and Bast and Sekhmet they lead you into the green veldt where you can run forever."[11]

It is not entirely clear whether the scenes taking place in the ancestral plane, of which there are three in the film, are actually real or a figment of the imagination, but for those who participate in it, *it seems to be real*. Furthermore, the way they are presented onscreen seem to ask the audience to accept them as having actually happened for those characters both alive and dead. Certainly, it is a wish-fulfillment fantasy that many of us might desire—to be reunited with our lost loved ones—and it is one of the foundational beliefs of many world religions. Its presentation here is definitely connected to African cultural practices too in the way it is constructed, with ancestral veneration being central to many African societies in its dramatization of the prevailing beliefs that the boundaries between the living and the dead are much more porous than many cultures would have us believe. For T'Challa, as

T'Challa is reunited with his beloved father, T'Chaka, on the ancestral plane.

one might expect, his desire is to be reunited with his beloved father who was taken away from him so abruptly and in such traumatic circumstances in *Captain America: Civil War*. It is to this place that T'Challa is transported and the transition is shown through sepia-tinted flashes of memories, with their edges blurred and accompanied by distorted non-diegetic sounds. He wakes up in an idyllic location among verdant grassland on the veldt as he had mentioned to Black Widow in *Captain America: Civil War*, with aurora borealis visible in the purple sky above. In the distance is an acacia tree with many literal black panthers sitting among its branches, suggestive of his ancestors going back thousands of years. One panther drops to the floor, transforming into T'Chaka, enabling father and son to be reunited. The first thing T'Challa tells his baba is "*I'm sorry*" as he drops to his knees and begs him for forgiveness, adding, "I am not ready to be without you." T'Chaka asks him, "Have I ever failed you?" to which T'Challa replies, "*Never,*" with a marked certainty in his line delivery. But T'Challa's unequivocal veneration of his father will emerge as problematic, as no person, whether monarch, father, or both, could live up to such an idealized image. Later in the film, T'Challa will see a more complete and ambiguous picture of his father, one which will challenge his unblemished image of him to such an extent that when he returns to the ancestral plane again not only will he not drop to his knees, but he will raise his voice at him and all his other ancestors present, a taboo in African cultures. Unbeknownst to T'Challa, T'Chaka's mistake, which was only hinted at in the film's Oakland-set prologue, is one that has remained secret for decades and is about to return to Wakanda with T'Challa and not T'Chaka forced to deal with its ramifications in the present. In doing so, he will have to reconcile himself to the fact that his father was not as perfect as he thought and that many of his own long-held assumptions about Wakanda might also have been wrong.

CHAPTER 2

A Black Panther for the New Millennium

Geopolitics in the Marvel Cinematic Universe

Klaue is leaving out that door with me. You've been warned . . .
T'CHALLA to CIA Agent Everett Ross in *Black Panther*

An advanced African civilization, thriving in isolation, untouched by war or colonialism . . . an African nation that could serve as a beacon of hope—curing diseases, offering foreign aid, accepting refugees—across the continent and beyond.
CHRISTOPHER ORR, *"Black Panther* Is More Than a Superhero Movie," *The Atlantic*, February 16, 2018.

I.

In MCU films prior to *Black Panther* the audience and those who reside within its diegesis know very little about Wakanda, to the extent that even the genius Bruce Banner (Mark Ruffalo) is unable to pronounce it correctly in *Avengers: Age of Ultron* ("Wakanada?"), and a group of teenagers on the streets of Oakland in *Black Panther* can be heard asking, "What is a Wakanda?" In *Captain America: Civil War*, a reporter from MSNBC states that the country has been "traditionally reclusive," and on BBC's *Global News* in *Black Panther* real-life presenter Lucy Hockings is shown informing the audience, "Though it remains one of the poorest countries in the world, fortified by mountain ranges and an impenetrable rainforest Wakanda does not engage in international trade or accept aid." Later, CIA agent Ross in the same film suggests the country is best known for its "shepherds, textiles . . . cool outfits." These three descriptions are ones the Wakandans have been happy to promulgate throughout their country's history, to keep people away from its borders and ignorant of the secrets within them.[1] As we have seen, while it is a fictional country its customs and traditions are drawn from a wide range of real-world African cultures, and in *Black Panther* Wakanda is shown to share borders with the Democratic Republic of Congo, Rwanda, and Uganda, meaning that it is located somewhere around the area known as the Ilemi Triangle (see Roussos 2018, 28).[2]

The MCU's creation of Wakanda joins a tapestry of fictional African nations in American films in recent decades, the majority of which still resort to reductive stereotypes of the continent, its people, and their practices: from Zamunda in *Coming to America* (1988) to the National Republic of Umbutu in *Independence Day: Resurgence* (2016), Nambutu in *Casino Royale* (2006) to Wadiya in *The Dictator* (2012) and Nairomi in *Batman v. Superman: Dawn of Justice*.[3] Mary-Ellen Higgins, in her *Hollywood's Africa After 1994* (2012), explains that these should be regarded "not as a series of detached fantasies that offer pure entertainment, but as projections—entertaining as they may be—that reflect various national and international investments, both material and ideological" (6). How far Wakanda contributes to or contrasts with this assertion became the subject of considerable debate when *Black Panther* was released, as Steve Rose in *The Guardian* asked, "Does the Marvel Epic Solve Hollywood's Africa Problem?" (2016a). Rose goes on to quote the Nigerian author Chimamanda Ngozi Adichie (who, we recall, was asked, "Are there any bookstores in Nigeria?" [see Musila 2018]), who reflected on the potency and the impact of such images which are screened in cinemas and then watched in homes all over the globe, "If all I knew about Africa were from popular images, I too would think that

Africa was a place of beautiful landscapes, beautiful animals and incomprehensible people, fighting senseless wars, dying of poverty and Aids, unable to speak for themselves and waiting to be saved by a kind, white foreigner" (Musila 2018). Higgins asks us to consider these images not just as examples of casual racism but possessing a more pronounced ideological impact on those who are exposed to them in film after film, decade after decade. She wrote, "When we watch Hollywood films set in Africa, do they also participate—consciously or unconsciously—in the winning of hearts and minds, the fostering of resolve to intervene in humanitarian crises in Africa, the building of support for American-enforced security in Africa and elsewhere?" (6).[4] Africa in *Black Panther* is an arresting and exotic backdrop, but it is also one which is explored in more than passing, with its own rich history, populated by dynamic and vividly drawn characters. Wakanda is not just a place where its characters are *from* or *pass through*, or where superheroes visit to rescue beautiful female journalists from evil warlords (see Nairomi in *Batman v. Superman*) or display their prodigious abilities, defeat their enemies, and rescue civilians (see Nigeria in *Captain America: Civil War* or South Africa in *Avengers: Age of Ultron*), but where they live and where the majority of the film's narrative takes place. It is a film that centralizes African culture, traditions, and characters in a way that no large-scale American film about the continent has ever done. Wakanda is a paradoxical construct in many ways: it is fictional but it has real borders and relationships with other actual countries; it is not real, but its culture, architecture, and style is drawn from authentic African nations; and, finally, it is an imaginary creation, but this did not prevent it from possessing a tangible and affective symbolic power when the film was released in February 2018.

This practice of being set in real-world environments has set the MCU apart from its counterpart and sometime rival the DCEU, just as their comic book versions have done since their inception. Thus, the MCU is mostly set in New York rather than the fictional Metropolis of *Man of Steel* or the Gotham of *Batman v. Superman* (and the Nolan trilogy prior to it). One might suggest that this is a key aspect of the MCU's appeal. It does not have to allude to New

York, but rather it revels in its New York setting: in Times Square, where Captain America awakens after forty years asleep at the climax of *Captain America: The First Avenger*; the Chrysler Building, where Thor calls down lightning to help defeat Loki's army in *The Avengers*; Doctor Strange's Santorum at 177a Bleecker Street from *Doctor Strange*; Washington Square Park, where Tony Stark and Spider-Man take on Thanos's children in *Avengers: Infinity War*; or the Staten Island Ferry, which gets ripped in two by the Vulture during *Spider-Man: Homecoming*. Something similar happens when the MCU goes abroad to places like Afghanistan in *Iron Man*, Brazil in *The Incredible Hulk*, India in *The Avengers*, and Hong Kong in *Doctor Strange*, in a process I have previously described as "virtual terror tourism" (McSweeney 2018), a variation of what has been called "trauma tourism" (see Tumarkin 2005; Rothe 2011), the practice of setting scenes in exotic locations (many of which have experienced real-life trauma) and inviting spectators to be thrilled at spectacularly orchestrated scenes of violence that portray American heroes as unambiguously virtuous and responsible. The best example of this without a doubt is the exculpatory globe hopping *Iron Man*, in which the titular hero flies around using hi-tech American weapons unproblematically saving lives in Afghanistan, while the wars there and in Iraq were still ongoing, and headlines appeared about the deaths of soldiers and civilians regularly.

It is worth considering, as we suggested in the introduction, what kind of world an American production like the MCU depicts in the first decades of the new millennium. The films of the MCU emerge as embodiments of a national fantasy and consolidate a range of decidedly American views on the world to the extent that a more comprehensive literalization of American exceptionalism would be hard to find. In the films of the MCU, the United States is at the center of the world, its preeminent economic, military, and moral entity, but at the same time is also shown to be the world's primary victim of acts of violence (see Grieder 2009). It is for this reason, as well as the obvious nature of cultural relevance, that the vast majority of the superheroes within the MCU are American, most obviously so in the case of Steve Rogers/Captain America, who

The Avengers on one of their many extrajudicial incursions around the globe, here in *Age of Ultron* in Sokovia, coded by the film as being reminiscent of Kosovo circa 1991–2001.

Matthew Costello memorably described as "an avatar of American ideology" (2009, 13), but also Tony Stark/Iron Man who Bryn Upton suggested "*is* America after 9/11" (2014, 33, emphasis added). Even the Norse God of Thunder, Thor, who in spite of being from Asgard (one of the nine worlds of Norse mythology), emerges as distinctly American in the way he is constructed, both in the Americanization of his values and Asgard's depiction as a proto-American Empire. This is why Jason Dittmer describes many of the main characters created by Marvel as nationalist superheroes in his book *Captain America and the Nationalist Superhero: Metaphors, Narratives, and Geopolitics* (2012). About the character named in the title of his book, he wrote:

> Significant to this role is Captain America's ability to connect the political projects of American nationalism, internal order, and foreign policy (all formulated at the national or global scale) with the scale of the individual or body. The character of Captain America connects these scales by literally embodying American identity, presenting for readers a hero both of, and for, the nation. (2005, 627)

In film after film in the franchise, the MCU comes to embody the fantasy of how America sees itself on the global stage and directs both American and international audiences to do the same.

II.

It is with Wakanda in *Black Panther* that for the first time in the history of the MCU another nation replaces the United States as its moral center and provides us with a prism through which we are asked to view the events of the film.[5] Black Panther and Wakanda, then, should be understood as just as much of a wish-fulfillment fantasy of the Black diaspora of the second decade of the new millennium as Superman and Captain America were to the US when they first graced the pages of comic books in 1938 and 1941, at the start of World War II. In its original literary form, Wakanda and the Black Panther were created in 1966, more than fifty years before Coogler's film, at a tumultuous time in the history of race relations in the US, the height of the Civil Rights movement, and a similarly turbulent decade in the history of the African continent. For Africa, the decade of the 1960s began with what is widely referred to as the "year of Africa" due to the fact that a remarkable seventeen nations gained their independence from colonial empires in the same year.[6] The years between 2016 and 2018, which saw *Black Panther* move from production to global release, were also considered to be particularly challenging ones for the African American community. The presidency of Donald Trump for many African Americans—although certainly not all, as Trump managed to secure 8 percent of their vote (with Clinton receiving 80 percent)—was defined by his contentious comments concerning Charlottesville, Colin Kaepernick, the emergence of the Black Lives Matter movement, and several high-profile shootings of Black people, that many regarded as being racist (see Tyson and Maniam 2016). Unlike in 1966, the 2018 iteration of Wakanda is primarily and specifically the product of an African American imagination, something that is complicated by the fact that it also emerges from a historically conservative genre and a multinational company frequently accused of perpetuating reactionary politics, one which only ever participates in social movements when it becomes politically expedient and financially profitable to do so.

Geopolitically, the central conceit of the film was outlined very clearly by its co-writer, Joe Robert Cole, who stated that Wakanda "is an African nation that is wholly self-determining and without influence from the outside, without westernizing influence. It's never been conquered or colonized" (quoted in Rock 2018), an idea that should be considered as a diaspora's fantasy and a very deliberate reaction to the stereotypical depictions of Africa perpetuated by American cinema. As Christopher Orr suggests in the epigraph to this chapter, Wakanda is constructed as an African country that could serve as a "beacon of hope," a term very frequently applied to the United States by those who have viewed the country uncritically throughout its history, an America that was, for Ronald Reagan, "the exemplar of freedom and a beacon of hope for those who do not now have freedom" (1981), for George H. W. Bush, "the last beacon of hope and strength around the world" (1992), and for Barack Obama, "the engine of the global economy and a beacon of hope around the world" (2010).[7] There are considerable implications in this position being taken by an *African country* in an *American film*. As Wakanda takes the place of the United States as the moral fulcrum of the MCU, in *Black Panther* it is afforded many of the privileges given to America in the films before it but also in ways habitual to American cinema as a whole. This has historically been the prerogative of national cinemas: to put their own nation at the center of the world, an understandable but inherently ideological process. Thus, in the Chinese blockbusters *Wolf Warrior* (2015) and *Wolf Warrior 2* (2017), the world is seen through the prism of a moral, beneficent China in films that portray the country and those who represent it as the most powerful and humanitarian state on the global stage, which is why both films received substantial financial and material support from the Chinese government and became two of the most financially successful films in the history of the Chinese film industry. These films are widely considered to be examples of propaganda by scholars and commentators in the west, who prove much more reluctant to use the term when discussing American blockbusters, of which the superhero film has become by far the most dominant form.

In the MCU, we might turn to the representation of law and justice in the international community for an example of how this works. Through Phases One and Two of the series, from *Iron Man* in 2008 until *Avengers: Age of Ultron* in 2015, American superheroes had largely gone around the world saving those in need as and when they felt it was necessary, in ways similar to how Americans have traditionally viewed themselves and their country in the cultural imaginary. In *Captain America: Civil War* (2016), the first film in Phase Three of the franchise, the narrative turned its attention to the ramifications of some of these actions and focused on the Sokovia Accords, the international legal responsibilities and requirements of being a superhero, with the proposal that an independent governing body might oversee the superheroes, deciding when, where, and how they might be allowed to act. This emerges as the film's central personal and ideological schism, with Tony Stark on one side and Steve Rogers on the other. In Vienna, in the sequence which culminates in his death in an explosion, T'Chaka rails against the Avengers and their behavior, which he sees as irresponsible and immoral. Standing at the podium, he says, "Our peoples' blood is spilled on foreign soil, not only because of the actions of criminals but by the indifference of those pledged to stop them. Victory at the expense of the innocent is no victory at all!" However, audiences had seen what had happened in Nigeria in the film's prologue and that the superheroes had put themselves in harm's way, as they always do, to save innocents. In the matter of the Sokovia Accords, T'Challa supports his father and Wakanda, but in *Black Panther*, when Wakanda and T'Challa are placed at the center of the story, their attitude about the very same process is fundamentally different, when it is revealed that the Black Panther has been operating all over the world for decades and that Wakanda has spies called War Dogs around the globe, doing exactly what they raised objections to in Vienna. Now secrecy, subterfuge, lack of transparency, and vigilantism, which once seemed unconscionable when done by others, becomes vital, necessary, and morally justifiable when for the Wakandans it is *us* doing it rather than *them*.

These scenes might easily be disregarded, as many are, with the epithet "*it is only a movie*," but we should remember they are part of a dense, compelling tradition of American cultural narratives that have sought to identify and define America's place in the world since the birth of the medium. Furthermore, they are far from merely stories designed to entertain the masses but often receive privileged access and resources in exchange for favorable portrayals of branches of the US military, the cultural implications of which are investigated in detail in works such as David L. Robb's *Operation Hollywood: How the Pentagon Shapes and Censors the Movies* (2004) and Matthew Alford and Tom Secker's *National Security Cinema: The Shocking New Evidence of Government Control in Hollywood* (2017). The examples that the authors consider in detail encompass obviously militaristic films like *The Green Berets* (1968), *Red Dawn* (1984), *Top Gun* (1986), *Air Force One* (1997), and *Black Hawk Down* (2001) among others, but also a huge number of superhero films too, among them *The Rocketeer* (1991), *Batman and Robin* (1997), *Iron Man* (2008), *X-Men: First Class* (2011), and *Captain Marvel* (2019), in which production facilities, expertise, and materiel are provided in exchange for positive representation of characters and events connected to the American military. In each of these examples, one might ask how does the government benefit from favorable representation in such a way that it would seek to participate in their production?

It is ironic that T'Chaka and T'Challa's main criticism of the Avengers is for their intrusion into Lagos, Nigeria in *Captain America: Civil War* which results in the death of numerous civilians including eleven Wakandan relief workers. This event functioned as the catalyst for the journey towards the Sokovia Accords, and the very first mission in *Black Panther* is also an excursion into Nigeria, this time by T'Challa to ask his erstwhile partner Nakia to return to Wakanda with him to participate in the ceremony we explored in the previous chapter. While it is a brief sequence lasting only five minutes, primarily designed to reintroduce us to the film's protagonist and two of the film's other main characters, in doing this it articulates many of the concepts introduced above concerning Wakanda's shifting narrative and ideological status now that it is placed at the center of the film.

Nakia is on a War Dog mission deep in the Sambisa Forest in northeast Nigeria, a place not chosen at random but rather one that

Nakia the War Dog on a mission in Nigeria, actions the likes of which T'Challa and his father had vehemently criticized in *Captain America: Civil War*, but are now endorsed when shown from Wakandan perspectives.

has become widely reported on in recent years for being used as a shelter by Boko Haram (sometimes called the Lord's Resistance Army), widely referred to as a "terrorist" group in the real world. Bodunrin Kayode wrote that "Sambisa is now a key stronghold for Islamic insurgents, and a place of fear" for those living in the region (2014). Rather than calling them Boko Haram, the film and its novelization refer to them as "militants" (2018, 10) even though it quickly becomes very clear that they are the referent for the sequence. Coogler himself confirmed that the scene was "inspired by the kidnapping that is happening in that region" (quoted in Hewitt 2018), about which UNICEF reported that more than one thousand children have been forcibly taken since 2013. The camera follows a convoy of vehicles, some of which are shown containing kidnapped young women wearing hijabs (who the film refers to in the credits as "Nigerian women" and the novelization "Chibok women" [2018, 10]). Among them, and wearing the same clothes, is Nakia, with her importance immediately apparent without a word being spoken, as she is afforded prominence within the frame, the camera lingers on her, and the fact that she is played by Academy Award-winning actress Lupita Nyong'o.

In the jet above, T'Challa insists to Okoye that he will not need her help, but her quizzical facial expression suggests otherwise and hints at the intimacy of their friendship and the trust between the two.

Their palpable chemistry and obvious bond, which will be apparent on numerous occasions throughout the film, is rare in the superhero genre, in which male-female partnerships have tended towards simplistically framed romantic relationships. She tells him "Don't freeze" to which he replies "I *never* freeze."[8] Dropping dramatically from the jet, he hurls small beads at the vehicles below, causing their engines to cut out; we will learn later that they are Kimoye beads and have been designed by his genius sister, Shuri, to have multiple uses, each of which far exceeds any technology in the real world. Engaging with the militants, we are reintroduced to T'Challa's skill and power but for the first time on his own continent. Moving around to the back of the convoy of trucks, he comes face to face with Nakia and does indeed freeze, making it fortunate that Okoye appears to prevent him being shot by one of the militants. Rather than being happy to see her previous partner, Nakia seems both surprised and annoyed, asking, "Why are you here? You've ruined my mission!" She even kicks him in the chest to prevent him from attacking one militant who turns out to be a twelve-year-old boy, telling T'Challa, "*He* got kidnapped as well," offering further connections to Boko Harem as the group has also become infamous for kidnapping male children and brutally indoctrinating them (see Adebeyo 2018). Unlike many female characters partnered with superheroes in the MCU films prior to *Black Panther*, such as Jane Foster, Pepper Potts, or Betty Ross, it is evident that Nakia certainly does not need rescuing and that T'Challa will never be called upon to save her in the film in the way Iron Man does Pepper on numerous occasions throughout the Iron Man trilogy, or Thor does Jane, or Bruce Banner does Betty Ross. In the MCU, even female superheroes are often saved by the men which they are partnered with, as Peter Quill does for Gamora in *Guardians of the Galaxy* (a character who is supposed to be one of the most formidable assassins in the galaxy) and Scott Lang does Hope in *Ant-Man*, despite those films insisting that both women are more than able to take care of themselves.

The scene is a familiar one in the MCU, dramatizing the prowess of a superhero rescuing innocents as Tony Stark once did in Gulmira in *Iron Man*, the Avengers in Sokovia in *Avengers: Age of*

Ultron, and Steve Rogers on the streets of Washington, DC in *Captain America: Winter Soldier*. However, there are some significant differences even in these opening moments that set a precedent for the rest of the film. T'Challa appears much more fallible and human, if only in limited terms, in ways which will come to define his character, despite his superior technology and enhanced athletic prowess. As the MCU has done many times in its history, *Black Panther* offers a mediation on the shifting dimensions of masculinity in the modern era that departs considerably from the muscular heroes of the 1980s like Arnold Schwarzenegger and Sylvester Stallone that Susan Jeffords described as "hard-bodied" heroes in her insightful *Hard Bodies: Hollywood Masculinity in the Reagan Era* (1994). While the contemporary superhero film, for the most part, is an avowedly heteronormative and unashamedly patriarchal space, it offers some of the complexities which define the varied masculinities of the new millennium. Superheroes like T'Challa, Scott Lang, Peter Parker, and Peter Quill are disconnected from the musclebound heroes that defined the 1980s and are to be found regularly discussing their feelings, although reluctantly, almost as often as they dispatch the bad guys they come up against.

Whether Marlene D. Allen's contention that "metatextually, the film also protests the Nigerian government's underwhelming response to Boko Haram's crimes against these young women. It further signifies on the lacklustre global reception to the #BringBackOurGirls campaign and Twitter movement, implicitly making the statement that our world largely ignores the appropriation and consumption of Black female bodies" (2018, 21) is true is up to audiences to decide, but the film was warmly received by Nigerian cinemagoers, who embraced it to the point where it posted record-breaking numbers at the box office (see Chutel 2018) and even was praised by Atiku Abubakar, Nigeria's ex-vice president, who commented that it "contained many lessons for Nigeria" (2018). However, *Black Panther* does not pause to consider the ethics of integrating itself quite explicitly into a real world ongoing African tragedy in ways the MCU has been very reluctant to do with America's own recent cultural traumas. The events of September

11, 2001, have had a significant impact on the superhero film, but are seldom mentioned explicitly in the genre to the extent that it was not entirely clear whether they even happened in the MCU for a number of years, and when they were mentioned for the first time, it was on the lesser televisual strand of the franchise rather than the films.[9] Indeed, recent American cultural traumas seem to be largely off-limits for superhero films produced by the American film industry, while those happening around the globe are eligible to be folded into the genre's narratives often for the sole purpose of making American superheroes appear noble and altruistic. Thus, Coogler and Cole send their main character into the heart of an ongoing tragedy for Nigeria, one with very real victims, offering a wish-fulfillment fantasy of what a superhero might do if he really existed but one which the genre has never dared to do for disturbing events closer to home. While the cinematic Black Panther is able to save all of the Chibok women without a single casualty, in real life the kidnappings continued, and on February 19, 2018, the day after the film's release, more than one hundred schoolgirls were taken in Dapchi, Nigeria, by Boko Haram (see Gopep, Searcey, and Emmanuel Akinwotu 2018).

III.

The Nigeria set sequence also introduces another key element of the film, a vital part of both its world building and desire to define Wakanda as a country with a cohesive sense of place and history, that is the decision as to what language its inhabitants should speak and how extensively they should use it during the film. This has never been an issue for comics featuring the Black Panther, which always simply indicated that Wakandan had been translated, but the cinematic medium provided the creative team with a decision as to whether Wakandans would converse in their *own language* or adopt *accented English*. Furthermore, the choice would be a significant one as, unlike Sokovia and South Africa in *Avengers: Age of Ultron* or Pakistan and China in *Iron Man 3*, the vast majority of the film is set in Wakanda. While this decision might sound trivial, studios have been historically reluctant to extensively use subtitles and foreign languages in American films as studies suggest that mainstream American audiences overwhelmingly prefer films in English and even actively avoid foreign films (see Nochimson 2011). Directors of major releases with a significant portion of their running time devoted to a foreign language, like Kevin Costner's *Dances with Wolves* (1990, Lakota and Pawnee), Mel Gibson's *The Passion of the Christ* (2004, Aramaic, Hebrew and Latin), and *Apocalypto* (2006, Yucatec Maya), each suggested that they had difficulty finding funding for their films because of this one creative decision (see Rosenbaum 2002; Kerry Segrave 2014).

The language spoken throughout *Black Panther* is not an invented one like Klingon, Dothraki, Elvish, or Na'vi, each of which have become familiar to genre fans in recent decades, but rather the very real African language of Xhosa, one of the eleven official languages of South Africa and also spoken widely through Zimbabwe and Lesotho. Xhosa was first heard in *Captain America: Civil War*, spoken by T'Chaka to his son T'Challa at the United Nations in scenes filmed in 2015 before *Black Panther* went into production. This seemed to have been an important factor which prompted Wakandan to be Xhosa in *Black Panther*, as the actor playing T'Chaka, Jon Kani, revealed on the press tour for *Black Panther*:

> I was supposed to say to him, "I miss you, my son, I haven't seen you in a very long time." So I asked the directors, "Why am I speaking English? He's my son, we're from Wakanda." And the directors asked, "What would you say?" I said, "Unqabile nyana, ndikugqibele kudala" (quoted in Mkhabela 2018)

By coincidence, Chadwick Boseman was able to speak some Xhosa after making a film set in South Africa, *Message from the King* (2016), filmed prior to the production of *Captain America: Civil War*. Xhosa is used extensively throughout *Black Panther* and becomes narratively, thematically, and symbolically relevant in key moments, some of which we have already seen: as in the Oakland-set prologue, when the "American" James reveals himself to actually be the Wakandan Zuri, and during the coronation ceremony, most of which is in English but features songs, chants, and some dialogue in Wakandan/Xhosa. As we saw in the previous chapter, these elements emerge as more than just background to the film but key to its construction of a culture and a society that Coogler and his team sought to make feel as real as possible. More than this, the centralization of a real African language is a key part of the film's vision of an empowered African nation free from colonial intervention, a fantasy, of course, but one with dramatic and lingering resonances for those in the real world. Lupita Nyong'o commented in an interview that "so often we watch American movies that have Russian, German and French and all that. . . . But so rarely are people asked to listen to an African language and read the subtitles for it. And the fact that this scene is resonating is proof that our languages resonate just as much as everything else" (quoted in Mkhabela 2018). Atandwa Kanu, another actor in the film, but also a dialect assistant and cultural consultant suggested that he was there "to verify certain rituals, cultures, and things that would and wouldn't be done by members of the Xhosa community . . . [and that the chants signify] strength, unity and a bright future. The Xhosa people are from South Africa which has got a difficult past. What got us through those times was always dreaming of a brighter future. Wakanda doesn't have that same history, but these gestures signify moving forward and always calling back ancestors and realizing we are not alone" (quoted in Wilkins, 20–22).[10] Rather than an afterthought, these choices come to have cultural ramifications, and the decision to centralize African languages was one championed by many, including Google developer Sani Yusuf, who tweeted: "*Black Panther* started with a scene in Nigeria, from an area, I am closely from, where they spoke a language I understood [Yoruba]. A Marvel movie had a language I understood. I felt like flying" (quoted in Hedges-Stocks 2018; see also Kazeem, Chutel, and Dahir 2018).[11]

Its use of Xhosa is not the only way the film binds itself to Africa from a linguistic perspective as its titles and captions are shown in two ways, the one used to represent Wakandan is an adapted form of the Igbo language (present-day Nigeria) called Nsibidi with additional elements of Tifinagh, Ancient South Arabian, and Bamum, constructed by Hannah Beachler and her team. As with many decisions in the film, this one, as she observed, "was a process of trying to pay homage to lost languages but also infusing the idea of Afrofuturism of reclaiming languages lost" (quoted in Desowitz 2018). The script itself is employed in title cards used to introduce locations—including Oakland and Wakanda, which we have already seen, and Busan, South Korea, which we are about to turn our attention to—but it is also densely interwoven into the scenes in Wakanda, found on signs, clothes, shop fronts, and documents. The titles are presented first in this Wakandan script but then make a transition into English, using the font known as "BEYNO," a futuristic sans serif font created by Fabian Korn, who remarked, "I think it's a good fit because the movie itself is revolutionary and a new chapter in movie history. The font is also new, and I hope in the future there will be more like it" (quoted in anon., "The Story of BEYNO" 2018).

While decisions like these might not be noticed by casual members of the audience, it undoubtedly came to mean a great deal for those interested in African culture and society or those from regions connected to the languages chosen. As Chika Okeke-Agulu suggested, "Often, we think of the West as the birthplace of civilized thought and morals. Those untouched by the West are seen as primitive or savage. However, *Black Panther*'s use of this preexisting African script shows us something different. We see a nation that finds hope and strength within its grief, making the *wawa aba* a fitting symbol" (quoted in Karla Clark 2018).

IV.

Sometime later, after the events we have described in the previous chapter and the ritual combat sequence in which T'Challa is crowned king of Wakanda, he and his friend W'Kabi (Daniel Kaluuya) are informed that one of Wakanda's enduring enemies, the

South African arms dealer and terrorist Ulysses Klaue (Andy Serkis), has been located in South Korea, which leads to the film's second excursion abroad. As most superheroes have a primary antagonist, one who is tied to their fate in many films or comic books—Batman and the Joker, Captain America and the Red Skull, Superman and Lex Luthor, and Spider-Man and the Green Goblin—T'Challa has had Klaue since he first appeared in the comics in *Fantastic Four* no. 53 (August 1966). In the MCU, Klaue had been introduced to audiences three years before in *Avengers: Age of Ultron* as an international arms dealer in possession of billions worth of stolen vibranium, but as the prologue of *Black Panther* seems to explain, he got this vibranium with the help of N'Jobu back in 1992. It also becomes clear that the impact of Klaue's robbery was significant; indeed, it was something of a national trauma which has lingered in the years since, proving to many Wakandans that their decision to isolate themselves from the rest of the world was correct. We are led to understand this event as a resonant cultural trauma in the history of Wakanda, as W'Kabi says, "Not a day goes by when I do not think about what Klaue took from us . . . from me," as both of his parents, and many others were killed in the attack. When he learns that he will not be asked to go on the mission to South Korea to apprehend Klaue he asks of T'Challa, "Kill him where he stands or bring him back to us," in what seems like a throwaway line as it is delivered but will be hugely significant moving forward when W'Kabi's allegiance to the king begins to waver. Ryan Coogler even went as far as to compare Klaue to Osama bin Laden in an interview with the British film magazine *Empire*, just as many others who have worked in or written about the superhero genre have turned to the founder of al-Qaeda in the post-9/11 decades (see Hewitt 2018). The co-writer of *Batman Begins*, David Goyer, compared his film's antagonist Ra's Al Ghul (Liam Neeson) to bin Laden, and many did the same for the Christopher Nolan iteration of the Joker played by Heath Ledger (see Briley 2008; Feblowitz 2009), the Mandarin in *Iron Man 3* (see McCarthy 2013), and other antagonists in the genre. The symbolic figure of bin Laden loomed large over popular culture in the period and provides another example of how the superhero

Ulysses Klaue, the South African arms dealer and terrorist, returns to the MCU after his appearance in *Avengers: Age of Ultron.*

film has mined real world anxieties and events and projected them through the prism of its genre.

In *Age of Ultron*, as well as when he appears in *Black Panther*, Klaue's accent as performed by Andy Serkis is self-consciously of South African origin even though it is not explicitly acknowledged in the film (his henchmen later also have South African accents and the script calls him "Afrikaans" [2018, 17] and his men "South African toughs" [2018, 42], one of whom is played by South African actor David S. Lee, credited as "Limbani") in what we might consider as another example of how the MCU and American blockbusters more generally take care to not offend potentially lucrative markets. This South African heritage was a central part of the character in the comic books, where he was a proudly colonial figure from a rich history of colonialists.[12] In an interview, Serkis connected the two media in ways the film is never interested in explicitly acknowledging,

> Well, I mean, certain aspects of the comics. Like his back history. You know, he was a South African, he was a Boer. He was a South African Boer and has always had that attitude towards people of color. There is a kind of racist element to him, for sure. He talks to Killmonger and calls him "boy" in that old South African way. That sense of apartheid that he's grown up with has never left him. (quoted in Kaye 2018)

Klaue does indeed refer to the character played by Michael B. Jordan as "boy," rather than Erik Stevens, as one would assume he knows him as, and also refers to Wakandans as "savages" twice, once at the casino in South Korea to T'Challa and again at the English junkyard just before his death. The connections between a racist South African arms dealer and a secretive African country that has never experienced colonial intrusion are never mentioned, but as with much else in the film, it is left for audiences to consider should they care to.

The film's second (third, if we count the US-set prologue) extrajudicial excursion is to find Klaue in Busan, South Korea, and is introduced with the Wakandan/BEYNO font discussed above. The camera moves over the city at night before settling on the famous Jagalchi Fish Market to the non-diegetic sounds of South Korean popstar Psy's "Hangover" (2014), an artist who a few years earlier had surprising international success with his song "Gangnam Style" (2012). The three characters on the mission in South Korea are the same as those who went to Nigeria: T'Challa, Nakia, and Okoye, but this time they are dressed very differently. T'Challa is not in his Black Panther suit or his ceremonial garb but a stylish and modern western-style black suit; Nakia is not in her tribal costume or the Chibok hijab we first saw her wearing but a dark green dress inscribed with Wakandan script; Okoye is not in her Dora Milaje armor but an elegant red dress interwoven with gold. In an episode of the online series of "Notes on a Scene" produced by *Vanity Fair*, Ryan Coogler suggested that the three characters were deliberately dressed in such a way to underline the film's Pan-African thematic motifs. He suggested, "So when you see T'Challa, Nakia and Okoye in their covert looks you see the colors of the Pan-African flag" (anon., "Notes on a Scene" 2018).

The three of them are visiting a hidden casino behind the Jagalchi market which Nakia gets them access to by posing as a wealthy Kenyan heiress who speaks fluent Korean. The stylistic touchstone for the sequence that follows is undoubtedly the James Bond film franchise (1962–), as many members of the creative team confirmed, including producer Nate Moore, who said, "The Busan casino sequence was our ode to James Bond" (quoted in Wilkins 2018, 91).

Wearing richly symbolic colours Nakia, T'Challa, and Okoye approach the South Korean casino in Busan for the film's second mission abroad.

Indeed, Coogler, when originally pitching his vision for the film, told Marvel that he saw the Black Panther as something of a James Bond figure within the MCU (see Thompson 2018).

In the casino expecting to apprehend Klaue, who is there to sell a stolen Wakandan artifact on the black market, they come across Everett Ross (Martin Freeman), a CIA agent and former Deputy Task Force Commander of the Joint Terrorism Task Force who had been featured briefly in *Captain America: Civil War*. They learn that Ross is Klaue's buyer and is in the process of trying to entrap and take him into American custody. As the scene continues, it becomes clear that even though Ross is a representative of the United States, a country that had been shown as the preeminent power throughout the MCU, T'Challa is not at all intimidated by him or what he represents. Many in the audience might accept their interaction as having a "really fun buddy dynamic," as Nate Moore maintained, but it is another example of the film's striking articulation of Wakanda and the Black experience at the center of its narrative (quoted in Wilkins, 38). In a series of strongly worded exchanges, T'Challa first tells Ross, "Klaue is leaving out that door with me, *you have been warned*" and then, "I'm not here to make a deal." This very deliberate formulation of power relations between the two, an African dictating the terms of an interaction with a representative of the world's most significant global superpower in the real world is a categorical rejection of stereotypical representations of Africans

The relationship and power dynamic between the American CIA agent Everett Ross and T'Challa emerges as a fascinating one that many found problematic.

perpetuated by American films since the birth of the medium. Their relationship will continue to develop but it will not alter from this position; in fact, Ross becomes even further in T'Challa's debt after being seriously injured later and taken back to Wakanda where his life is saved by T'Challa's sister, Shuri, and Wakandan technology. The decision to bring him to Wakanda—and, in so doing, to reveal Wakanda's secrets to not just an outsider but a representative of a foreign government (here the use of the term "foreign" to describe America in an American film is undoubtedly an ironic one)—is questioned by Okoye. But T'Challa disagrees and goes ahead and does it anyway, highlighting how in a monarchy like the one portrayed in *Black Panther*, the future of a country can be dictated by the choices of a single person.

T'Challa might describe Ross as "an old friend," but some were critical of how *Black Panther* frames the relationship between the two and how a CIA agent becomes such a close confidante and ally to an African state. As anyone with even a cursory knowledge of the connections between America and Africa through the twentieth century and into the twenty-first is aware, this relationship is a deeply complicated one. In the real world, African countries that have failed to support American interests on the continent have learned that such decisions can have serious ramifications. The results of this are too numerous to go into detail here but should include noting the overthrow and destabilization of democratically elected regimes and participations in the assassinations of key figures (see Congo in the 1960s with Patrice Lumumba and Ghana with Kwame Nkrumah) and supporting corrupt regimes in others (Hissene Habre in Chad). As Philip Agee wrote in the introduction to *Dirty Work 2: The CIA in Africa* (1980), "Rare is the African country that in recent years could elude intervention by neo-colonialist interests and the retardation of national development that such intervention so often brings" (7–8). In the twenty-first century, in figures that make surprising reading, it was reported that in 2016, 17 percent of American special forces were deployed somewhere in Africa in places like Somalia, the Central African Republic, Libya, and at least thirty-two other African countries, targeting several organizations, one of which, according to a recently declassified account by Donald Bolduc, US Army General of Special Operations Command in Africa (SOCAFRICA), is Boko Harem in Nigeria (see Turse 2017). In another fact that might prove surprising to general audiences, the CIA, like the Pentagon, has played an active role in the American film industry for decades, providing access to materiel, facilities, and advice in exchange for positive representation in films like *The Sum of All Fears* (2002), *Zero Dark Thirty* (2012), and *Argo* (2012), the latter of which won Best Picture at the 2013 Academy Awards and was considered to be "a grand slam" for the agency, in the words of former CIA officer Robert Baer, but was also a film which others suggested "had nothing to do with reality" (quoted in Schou 2016). Numerous authors have outlined this problematic relationship, like Tricia Jenkins in *The CIA in Hollywood: How the Agency Shapes Film and Television* (2012), in ways rarely acknowledged by audiences or the mainstream press. The CIA has featured extensively in the MCU as early as Phase One, in *Iron Man* (2008) and *The Incredible Hulk* (2008), and even before that within the diegetic world, as Nick Fury reveals in *Captain Marvel* (2019), set in 1995, that he was a CIA agent serving in Belfast, Bucharest, Belgrade, and even Bogotá in *Captain America: Winter Soldier.* For some reason, the CIA itself felt compelled to tweet during the 2019 Academy Awards when *Black Panther* was nominated for Best Picture as part of their series #ReelvsRealCIA, in which the agency attempted to show the difference between the real CIA and the one shown in the films. Most of the tweets concerned the difference between real-life technology and that found in Wakanda in *Black Panther* (see "Wakandan Technology Today: A CIA Scientist Explores the Possibilities" 2018).

Those critical of the film's portrayal of a CIA agent and his relationship with an African head of state, like Lynne Stuart Paramore, asked why it is that Ross becomes one of the film's heroes and an African American, who we have yet to explore in detail, who wishes to empower Black people around the globe, is framed as a villain (2018)? Undoubtedly the casting of the mild-mannered and sympathetic Freeman, an actor known for his self-effacing manner in television shows like *The Office* (BBC 2001–2003) and then later in film in Peter Jackson's *The Hobbit* trilogy (2012–14), contributes to this. It is quite understandable, then, that after this very positive portrayal of the organization, some speculated whether the CIA had participated in the film's production, as they have done in many Hollywood films since their creation. Tom Secker at Spyculture. com suggested that the agency denied participating in *Black Panther* (2019), but they might as well have done so given that the film's portrayal of Ross could not be more positive, as he is both admirable and honest; later, after learning of Wakanda's secrets, even though he works for a foreign government, the United States of America, he decides not to reveal them to his own country, an act that might be considered just as far-fetched as some of the remarkable technological advances on display in the film.

When Klaue and the members of his team arrive, unlike the other casino guests they are not asked to relinquish their weapons and a metal detector buzzes loudly, ignored by numerous guards. It is Nakia who sees Klaue first and wants to act but is ordered to stand down by Okoye. It is worth noting that their cover is blown in a very particular way connected to the linguistic element discussed earlier as Okoye's command to Nakia is in Xhosa with the word "Yekla!" and it is this which gets the attention of one of Klaue's South African henchmen who seem to recognize the word being used in South Korea. With this, the action sequence in the casino begins, and like all such sequences in the film, as we have already seen in the Sambisa Forest, they are designed, written, and choreographed to not just fulfill the demands of audiences for spectacular action but also forward both the narrative and develop characters. This is most clear in the striking sixty-three second duration of the long take which the scene features that moves fluidly around the characters and the casino in ways very different to the often jarring and unstable cinematography and editing that have become a hallmark of action films during the last two decades, popularized by the likes of the influential Bourne franchise (2002–), a technique which I have elsewhere called "the quintessential new millennial marker of authenticity" and which the MCU has used extensively since the prologue in Afghanistan in *Iron Man* shot with a frenetic and jagged immediacy self-consciously designed to promote a sense of kinetic realism (McSweeney 2014, 48). While, in technical terms, cinematographer Rachel Morrison's long take in the casino is actually comprised of several different shots, the individual shots are digitally stitched together in ways that audiences might not be able to notice on first viewing, a common technique referred to as an invisible cut (see *Children of Men* [2005] with its longest take of six minutes and eighteen seconds, *Atomic Blonde* [2017], seven minutes, and *Birdman* [2014), a remarkable fifteen minutes) in an era during which one of the definitions of a "good" visual effects shot is that it is *not even discernible as a visual effect* for audiences.[13] Here the stitching is almost seamless as it integrates live action (actors, props, furniture) and CGI (spear, digi doubles, money, and gambling chips) elements (see Eusebio, quoted in Wilkins, 35). Long takes like this are not common in the superhero film, given how difficult, expensive, and time-consuming they often prove to be with so many elements in play within the frame. Prior to *Black Panther*, the most significant in the MCU had been during the climax of *The Avengers* in a shot that swoops between and thereby unifies the once-divided superheroes as they are fighting in the Battle of New York, fulfilling a thematic function as well as being a hugely spectacular thrill for audiences. The shot in *Black Panther* does something similar, providing a sense of unity and cohesion for T'Challa, Okoye, and Nakia. We are able to see T'Challa's skill and determination, Okoye's prowess and even her position as a traditionalist (using a traditional Wakandan weapon and later commenting on her disdain for guns), and Nakia's independence and innovation as she uses any weapon she can lay her hands on (including her high heels). This is not the first time that Coogler has utilized the long take; in his second film, *Creed*, he and his director of photography, Maryse Alberti, shot one of the film's boxing matches in a single shot to achieve the completely opposite effect to the one sought by its use in *Black Panther*. Alberti said, "Ryan very much wanted to stay in the realm of reality and seeing the boxer alone in the ring. Once you're in the ring, you don't have teammates. You are alone. There's no one to lean on. That was kind of the idea" (quoted in Tapley 2015). In *Black Panther*, it is not isolation but rather unity and teamwork that becomes the motif of the sequence as the camera glides between Okoye, Nakia, and T'Challa, concluding with him cornering Klaue and calling him "Umbulali!" or "Murderer!" in Xhosa. Although T'Challa did not lose his family in the 1992 bombing, his best friend, W'Kabi, did, and the wound is still a deep one for Wakanda even many years later. Klaue takes out his weapon, a sonic cannon attached to his missing arm (which was severed by Ultron in *Age of Ultron*), made from vibranium in a nod to the comic book iteration of the character who later becomes an immortal being composed entirely of sound. He discharges the weapon as the long take comes to an end, sending T'Challa flying through the air and using the opportunity to flee into the streets of Busan.

With that the sequence becomes a car chase, moments from which were heavily utilized in the marketing for the film in the lead up to its release. Nakia and Okoye are the ones who react first, leaving T'Challa inside the casino with the remark, "He'll catch up!" in ways we might observe have never happened to Iron Man and Captain America. When he does emerge, he puts on his Black Panther suit, which is now operated through nanotechnology constructed by Shuri, whom he calls to for assistance. In an episode of the *New York Times* series "Anatomy of a Scene," Coogler suggested that the pairings of Shuri/T'Challa and Nakia/Okoye were motivated by the desire to place "an innovator with a traditionalist" (anon. 2018) in ways that emerge as thematically significant, which we will discuss in chapter four. If the scene in Busan is indeed a Bond homage, then

Shuri is Q, with the Kimoyo beads used to disable the vehicles of the Boko Harem in Nigeria now adapted to gain remote access to a car which she drives all the way from Wakanda while her brother is perched on top. In another car, in which Okoye and Nakia are together, the former verbalizes her disdain for the weapons Klaue's men fire at them ("Guns . . . how primitive") and Nakia once again is shown to be resourceful and a match for anything her adversaries throw at her.

The sequence builds to a climax when Klaue's sonic cannon hits a different car that T'Challa is riding on and he gracefully flips as Coogler moves the film into slow motion, footage included in the first trailer released on June 9, 2017, viewed more than 89 million times (see McNary 2017). While the shot itself only lasts a few seconds, the visual effects supervisor responsible for its creation, Kevin Souls, stated that it "was one of the biggest shots we did in the movie" and required two hundred and fourteen versions before it was finished (quoted in Failes 2018). The sequence concludes with T'Challa confronting Klaue, pulling him from his car and asking him, "Did you think we would forget?" Klaue is aware that their interaction is a very public one as a crowd of South Koreans are now watching them and even recording on their phones, and he sarcastically begs for "mercy, king, *mercy!*" resulting in the memorable line mentioned earlier in this book, taken from the comics: "Every breath you take *is mercy from me.*" T'Challa looks to be close to striking him, but Nakia prevents him from doing so telling him in Xhosa, "The world watches!" He then drops the terrorist/arms dealer to the floor.

The whole South Korean sequence has lasted for just twelve minutes, but it was one both praised and criticized by many South Koreans in a similar way to how we have seen the film's portrayal of Africa was received. The popular South Korean website *Ask a Korean* argued that it displayed "little interest in the culture. The real cultural watershed in the US will be when black and white Americans can see Asia as more than an exotic backdrop and Asian Americans can be heroes in American films and not just sidekick or exotic background extra" (2018). While the writer here might be perhaps asking for too much from *Black Panther*, it is certainly true that MCU and the superhero genre as a whole has very rarely had characters from Asian, Hispanic, or Arab backgrounds. While these ethnic groups make up a significant portion of the United States, a combined 37.3 percent according to the 2017 Census, and an even greater proportion of the world at large, it was not until the announcement that Phase Four of the MCU would feature the Chinese martial artist Shang Chi in *Shang-Chi and the Legend of the Ten Rings* (2021) that it had its first.

As is often the case when the MCU travels abroad, Busan in South Korea has no distinctive imagery or South Korean characterizations, but rather provides an exotic backdrop and lucrative tax incentives for the production filming there. As Krzysztof Iwanek observed, it features "western, generalized, and stereotypical 'pan-Asian' imagery" (2018), the likes of which can be found in *Avengers: Age of Ultron*, *Iron Man 3*, and each time the MCU visits Asia. However, the response to the film from Korean audiences was largely positive, evidenced by the $42.8 million it took in at the South Korean box office, where it spent two weeks at number one, as well as in the words of South Korean cinemagoers themselves.[14] Interviewing South Koreans on the street, the popular Asian website *Asianboss. com* found they had some interesting things to say; one remarked, "For most Koreans the main exposure they had to foreigners was through movies, but there weren't many Black people in mainstream cinema, I think that is why Korean people don't have a very good perception of Black people." Another said, "I think they did a great job of getting rid of the stereotype that all heroes are white and all villains are Black." And a third said, "There are lots of movies that portray Blacks as evil. I think through this movie the perception of Black people will improve." Each of which offer testimony to the affectual power of *Black Panther*, not just in America or Africa, but around the world (quoted in anon. "What Korean People Think of *Black Panther*" 2018).

In China, the film also did reasonably well at the box office, earning $105 million during its run. This is not as much as *Avengers: Endgame* ($359 million), released in the same year, as one might expect, but also not as much as *Ant-Man and the Wasp*, also from the same year ($121 million), or *Thor: Ragnarok* ($112 million) and *Spider-Man: Homecoming* ($116 million), released the year before—all films that the box-office take of *Black Panther* comfortably outstripped in most other markets and even *doubled* at the American box office (tripled, in the case of *Ant-Man and the Wasp*). Some considered that this was evidence that China was not quite ready for an American blockbuster featuring a primarily Black cast given the country's often problematic representations of Africa in Chinese film and television. In the same year as *Black Panther*, a film that we have mentioned before in this book, *Wolf Warrior 2*, secured $854 million at the Chinese box office, leading to it becoming the most successful Chinese film ever made.[15] It is set in an unnamed African country ravaged by war and disease, which necessitates its altruistic Chinese military hero, Leng Feng (played by the film's director and co-writer Wu Jing), to save the African civilians caught up in it, who are portrayed in ways just as stereotypical as we have seen perpetuated by American films. Eileen Guo, in an article titled "In China, 'Black Panther' is a Movie about America" that appeared in *The Outline*, interviewed one of several Chinese students who explained that *Black Panther* was received very differently in China, where it was considered to be an embodiment of "the universal values of the United States" with T'Challa and Wakanda behaving "much like how the United States operates in global politics." Guo herself wrote, "So, while American audiences see a celebration of blackness, for some Chinese moviegoers, it's *Black Panther's* American spirit that stands out" (2018).

Returning to the film itself, rather than its reception, after Klaue's capture he is taken to a CIA black site located in South Korea—that is, a secret detention center that operates unacknowledged and enables the circumvention of international law. It is not identified as a black site in the film, but in the script it is (Coogler and Cole 2018, 61). Its use in the film is largely, initially at least, played for laughs as T'Challa and Ross continue their power struggle while Klaue sings Haddaway's 1993 Eurodance hit "What Is Love" in the background. In the real world, however, black sites are a much more serious affair, and in the decade after 9/11 hundreds of suspected enemy combatants, often selected based on flawed intelligence, were flown all over the world and tortured in secret detention centers in places as diverse as Poland, Romania, Egypt, Thailand, South Africa, Somalia, and Kenya (see Mudd 2019). In 2006, the United Nations Committee Against Torture strongly urged that the United States "should take firm measures to eradicate all forms of torture and ill treatment of detainees," but it was a pronouncement not widely reported in the US, and there is considerable evidence that not only do the practices continue but that depiction of them in television and film has had a considerable impact on how they are viewed by the public (see Markert 2011; anon. "Torture on TV Rising and Copied in the Field").

Agent Ross appears to be in charge of the location, further coding it as a black site, but again seems to have no authority over T'Challa, who tells the CIA officer: "After your questioning we'll take him back to Wakanda with us." The Wakandans are reluctant to allow Ross to interrogate Klaue, concerned that he might reveal their true capabilities to the world. T'Challa and Okoye converse in Wakandan about Ross while he is standing right next to them. Ross asks of Okoye, "Does she speak English?" to which the Dora Milaje general replies, "When she wants to," before dismissing him by saying, "*Americans!*"

Connected to that which we have discussed above, there is a brief undercurrent introduced in the scene which is quickly pushed to the side when Klaue informs Ross that he should do business with *him*, rather than the Wakandans, telling him, "I'm much more your speed." But the film—like American cinema in general, with rare exceptions—tends to portray the CIA in positive terms, embodied in heroic figures like Bryan Mills in *Taken* (2008), Roger Ferris in *Body of Lies* (2008), Maya in *Zero Dark Thirty*, and Tony Mendez in *Argo*, several of whom are featured in films the CIA has played an active role in producing.[16] In the real world, the CIA has been happy to contravene international law to further American interests abroad in actions that tend to go uncommented on, and then see themselves glamourized in films that rewrite real-life events to portray their actions as altruistic and heroic. The film offers little more than this one brief sentence, as the MCU has never raised more than the odd ethically problematic moment about American history (see Operation Paperclip in *Captain America: Winter Soldier*). These things are unpalatable for American audiences and are thus elided from its popular culture narratives or even rewritten in the case of *Captain America: The First Avenger* which has African American soldiers fighting alongside their white counterparts in World War II in a film watched by millions of young people around the globe who are likely to think that such a thing happened in real life. Nearly a million African Americans joined the armed forces in World War II in a variety of capacities, but they served entirely separately, had separate training facilities and even had separate blood supplies (see Wynn 2010; Controvich 2015). These unpleasant truths about World War II offer conspicuous challenges to how it has come to be remembered, as an unambiguous war for freedom fought by all Americans as equals and are thus removed from films and television shows about the conflict.

Before Klaue can reveal anything about the Wakandans, a hole is blown through the wall of the building and Ross heroically dives over Nakia, a move which sees him struck in the spine by a bullet and close to death. The South African is rescued by a man wearing an African tribal mask, but what is around the man's neck proves even more surprising for T'Challa: he wears a necklace with a very familiar ring attached to it. It is one that had belonged to T'Challa's grandfather, one of only two in existence. T'Challa has one which was passed onto him by his father, and the other one has long been thought lost, given to his uncle, N'Jobu, who disappeared in 1992. T'Challa had been shown with his ring in the aftermath of his father's death in *Captain America: Civil War*, wearing it at moments in *Black Panther* up until then. He does not know it and neither do audiences watching the film for the first time, but the man is T'Challa's cousin, N'Jadaka/Erik "Killmonger" Stevens, and he is the subject of our next chapter.

CHAPTER 3

"Ungubani?"

N'Jadaka/Erik "Killmonger" Stevens

You know, where I'm from . . . when Black folks started revolutions, they never had the firepower . . . or the resources to fight their oppressors. Where was Wakanda? Yeah, all that ends today. We got spies embedded in every nation on Earth. Already in place. I know how colonizers think. So we're gonna use their own strategy against 'em . . . We're gonna send vibranium weapons out to our War Dogs. They'll arm oppressed people all over the world . . . so they can finally rise up and kill those in power. And their children. And anyone else who takes their side. It's time they know the truth about us!

N'JADAKA/ERIK "KILLMONGER" STEVENS, *Black Panther*

Over the last three decades there have been very little overt representations of the Black experience [in the superhero genre], though there have been several black superheroes, including Spawn and Black Panther, among numerous others. Comics dealing with issues specific to the African American experience, such as racial profiling, discrimination, integration, etc. have been scarce, perhaps because these realities are swept under a rug in order to avoid state responsibility for them.

SHEENA C. HOWARD AND RONALD L. JACKSON II, "Introduction," *Black Comics: Politics of Race and Representation* (2013, 5)

I.

The person who rescues Ulysses Klaue from the CIA black site has not yet been named in the film, but by this time, audiences have seen him twice before: once during the 1992 prologue as a child playing basketball in Oakland, California, and once in a brief sequence in the Museum of Great Britain, explored in detail below. At this point in the film, we have been given no indication that they are the same person and whether audiences would have connected the two on first viewing is hard to discern. Therefore, those with little prior experience of the comic book iteration of Black Panther are placed in a similar position to T'Challa, who also does not know who the man is, only that he is wearing an African tribal mask and his grandfather's ring on a chain around his neck. Until now the character has only been a secondary antagonist to Klaue's charismatic primary figure, but he is one who will soon step into the forefront of the film, in the process becoming not only one of its most interesting figures but also one of the most compelling characters across the whole of the MCU. He, as we have noted, goes by a variety of names throughout *Black Panther*, something very much connected to aspects of his personality, identity, and the communities to which he belongs or from which he is rejected. In the prologue, he is only referred to in passing as "E" by his basketball-playing friends, short for "Erik," which he is called later by the CIA officer Everett Ross, his girlfriend Linda (Nabiyah Be), and Shuri, and the only thing he is called by Klaue is "boy" twice. Erik at times is given the nickname "Killmonger," but he does not answer to this name and rejects it when Shuri refers to him by it later when he finally arrives in Wakanda. At other times, he is referred to and calls himself "N'Jadaka," his Wakandan name, given to him by his father as part of his ancestral heritage. The multiple names presented here are significant for a variety of reasons, not just in the superhero film where they are often carefully chosen to reveal a great deal about a character, whether they are heroes, villains, or somewhere in between, as we will see in the case of how N'Jadaka/Killmonger was received by audiences. Sometimes characters in the genre choose their own name (for example,

Deadpool, Ozymandias, and Magneto), and on other occasions it is given to them (Shazam, Superman, Aquaman), but in every case it becomes connected to what Peter Coogan described as the defining elements of the superhero genre, the "mission, identity, powers" paradigm (see 2006, 30–33). This naming process is especially significant to *Black Panther* given the centrality of issues of identity and naming in the African diaspora (see Martin 1991; Musere and Byakutaga 1998). Many prominent figures in the African American community have rejected their given names, choosing to adopt one more connected to their African roots, a significant act of self-determination and identity reclamation (see the likes of Stokely Carmichael/Kwame Ture, Malcolm Little/Malcolm X, and Cassius Clay/Muhammad Ali et al.). One might observe here that T'Challa has no such variations of his name, as he has had a life of privilege and security with no crisis of identity as N'Jadaka/Erik "Killmonger" Stevens has experienced, and the only other name he adopts is that of the Black Panther, one that has been passed down to him by his forefathers for generations.

Throughout Phases One and Two of the MCU, even though the films were for the most part well received by fans and critics, and tremendously financially successful, the majority of the antagonists were often regarded as being underwhelming. For every mercurial Loki or empathetic Winter Soldier, there had been an Obadiah Stane (*Iron Man*), Emil Blonsky/Abomination (*The Incredible Hulk*), Whiplash (*Iron Man 2*), Red Skull (*Captain America: The First Avenger*), Aldrich Killian (*Iron Man 3*), Malekith (*Thor: The Dark World*), Ronan (*Guardians of the Galaxy*), Ultron (*Avengers: Age of Ultron*), or Darren Cross (*Ant-Man*). Phase Three saw a distinct improvement in this roster of villainy, with the memorable characterizations of Zemo (*Captain America: Civil War*), Ego (*Guardians of the Galaxy: Vol. 2*), Vulture (*Spider-Man: Homecoming*), Hela (*Thor: Ragnarok*), Thanos (*Avengers: Infinity War* and *Avengers: Endgame*), and Mysterio (*Spider-Man: Far From Home*). However, for many viewers it was Michael B. Jordan's character in *Black Panther* who emerged as the most notable of all these, with his performance being almost universally praised. Adam Serwer, in an article called "The

Tragedy of Erik Killmonger," proposed that he should be considered a "profound and complex villain" (2018), an understanding of the character that was frequently returned to, not just due to Jordan's charismatic performance, but also that he is privileged by the narrative and script in ways that MCU antagonists have rarely been afforded, and also that he is *human* both literally and figuratively, with all the things he is shown to have experienced understandably motivating his actions in the present, as problematic as they might be. Many saw even more to him than this, arguing that he should be read as a symbol of conflicts within the Black community at large (Smith 2018). These voices echoed Kelli Weston's contention that N'Jadaka "embodies all the rage and pain of the African diaspora, of a people displaced and cheated out of an inheritance" (2018), regarding him not just an individual but deliberately coded as representative of many of the traumas the African American community have experienced, or as Siddhant Adlakha stated, a symbol of "Black rage incarnate" (Adlakha 2018).

The character originally appeared in the comics less than a decade after the first issue of Black Panther, making his debut in *Jungle Action* no. 6 (September 1973) where he was featured on the front cover brandishing a fierce-looking spiked belt and taunting T'Challa with the line, "Tomorrow's sun will rise on a new king of the Wakandas . . . Me!" His creator, Don McGregor, stated that from the very start he was always considered a contentious one and that he was informed by the editors of the series that the character "could not appear on the covers anymore. People have asked me why they made that demand, and I have often answered, 'You would have to ask the editors,' because I was never told, but I'm pretty sure it was because the comics had never had such a ferocious Black character with such power and intense anger that it made them reluctant to have him so much in the forefront" (2019, loc. 250). Forty-five years later in Ryan Coogler's film, Killmonger—or, rather, N'Jadaka as it seems more correct to refer to him, for the most part—is very much placed at the "forefront" of the narrative, to use McGregor's words. He is the first character in the whole film to speak as the story of Wakanda in the prologue is both requested by and told to him, even though, as we have seen, it might not be entirely clear on first viewing. It is rare that the villain in a modern superhero film is afforded such a privilege, not just in terms of screen time, but also perspective, with many written and played with broad strokes, and little more than superficial character development. In 2019, the year after the release of *Black Panther* Todd Phillips's *Joker*, starring Joaquin Phoenix, took this even further, becoming the first live-action superhero film to centralize its whole narrative around a character who would traditionally have been the antagonist. Several people commented that N'Jadaka's backstory—that is, the tragic loss of both of his parents—was one very familiar to the superhero film, but most often given to protagonists rather than antagonists. It is not too far from how Bruce Wayne loses his parents after a visit to the opera on the streets of Gotham or how Peter Parker is motivated by the death of his surrogate father, his uncle Ben, or how Superman experiences the deaths of both his adopted father and his biological parents, the latter of whom sacrificed themselves so that he could leave Krypton.

Despite the repeated transgressions of the law and moral boundaries that we will see N'Jadaka make in *Black Panther*, for some he emerged as a deeply sympathetic character, with many suggesting that they empathized *more with him* rather than the film's lead and eponymous heroic figure, T'Challa. Indeed, it was Killmonger (with this name written here as it was the one most often used by fans), not T'Challa, who became the primary focus of the internet's interaction with the film. This saw him becoming the subject of numerous memes ("Hey Auntie" and "Is this your king/wifi/paycheck?" [see Kelly 2018]), being printed on T-shirts and articles of clothing with slogans that read "Killmonger was right" and "All hail Killmonger," and featured in editorials and opinion pieces across the globe. Even the title track of the film's soundtrack album by Kendrick Lamar, "Pray for Me" (2018), which went double platinum in the United States (an award given to those which sell more than two million copies) is about Killmonger, not T'Challa, with lyrics about his experiences rather than the entitled life of a king:

I'm always ready for a war again
Go down that road again
It's all the same
I'm always ready to take a life again[1]

Simply put, no other antagonist in the superhero film (with the possible exception of Phoenix's interpretation of Arthur Fleck, aka the Joker) has resonated so profoundly with audiences and generated such discussion concerning real-world issues beyond those usually connected to the genre. The reasons why this might have been and their significance are the subject of this chapter.

II.

Our real introduction to the character as an adult had come in a scene near the start of the film set in the fictional Museum of Great Britain in London, after permission to shoot in the real British Museum had been denied. Coogler commented,

> That museum does not exist, because we couldn't get the British Museum cleared ... I got the idea for that scene here, I was here in the UK for press for *Creed* ... The British Museum is amazing, just being in there and thinking about the character of Killmonger, thinking about Wakanda [...] its relationship with colonization. Being in that museum and seeing these incredible things from all over the world, and just how complicated that is. ... (quoted in Travis 2018)

This idea of it being "complicated" becomes an integral part of a scene that, for much of its length and like the Oakland prologue, is one with no ostensible connections to the superhero genre, but could be taken from another unrelated film representing aspects of the sociocultural experiences of African Americans. In Oakland, until the arrival of a man dressed in a Black Panther suit, we had been witness to an African American family during the 1992 riots, and in London we see an educated young Black man visiting a museum of African history that explores very real ideas intimately connected to issues of Black cultural identity.

After an external establishing shot of the museum, the camera turns to a tall, twenty-something African American male who remains unnamed throughout the scene and is dressed in what the script calls "high-end street wear" (Coogler and Cole 2018, 15), the novelization describes as "very fashionable and very expensive looking" attire (2018, 42) and what Coogler himself referred to in an interview with *Empire* magazine as "Tupac-influenced clothes" (quoted in Hewitt 2018).[2] The man is gazing with considerable interest at a large cabinet full of African artifacts in what is labeled the "West African Exhibit" of the museum when he is approached by a forty-something Caucasian woman radiating an air of self-confidence who seems to be the curator of the museum but remains unnamed (the novelization calls her "Director Manning" [2018, 40], and the credits of the film refer to her as museum director). She possesses a palpable sense of authority as she answers the young man's questions with the confidence that her position brings with it, leaving the implications of having a white middle-class English person being the museum's expert on African artifacts uncommented on.

Erik's pronounced West Coast American accent in the sequence contrasts sharply with the museum director's English RP (received pronunciation), but the scene starts off cordially enough as she informs him in a vaguely patronizing tone about two of the African exhibits: a nineteenth-century mask from the Bono Ashanti tribe (modern-day Ghana) and a sixteenth-century mask from the Edo people of Benin (modern-day Nigeria). As we have seen so often already, geographical and historical elements in *Black Panther* are carefully chosen for their real-world and symbolic resonances, and this scene is no exception. Both the Bono Ashanti and the Edo were the subject of sustained colonial intervention by the British Empire, which they were able to resist for a number of years before finally being overwhelmed in 1900 and 1897, respectively. The residents of the capital of the Edo people, Benin City, saw it burned and looted of much of its wealth and treasures, including artifacts that are now

N'Jadaka/Erik "Killmonger" Stevens remains unnamed in the scene where he is introduced as an adult for the first time in the fictional Museum of Great Britain in London.

referred to as the Benin Bronzes, a series of extraordinary indigenous sculptures and other pieces of art which had been created from the thirteenth century onwards. Several hundred of the Benin Bronzes are now located in the *real* British Museum, one of the things Coogler perhaps had in mind when he referred to the museum as "complicated," and in other museums across the world in New York, Berlin, Oxford, and Vienna, with only a small percentage in the geographical region that they were originally produced (see Dohlvik 2006).

While the scene initially feels inconsequential, it is one very much immersed in the growing dispute concerning the role of museums and their ethical responsibilities in the modern era, a debate manifested in opinion pieces such as, "Colonial Past of Top Art Venues Exposed" (Karim 2018), "The Art World's Shame: Why Britain Must Give its Colonial Booty Back" (Jones 2014), and "Should Colonial Art be Returned Home?" (Thomas 2018). As on so many other occasions, the highly visible platform of *Black Panther* ensured that the film found itself embroiled in public debates germane to these themes, thus articles emerged with titles like "Who Owns History? Museums in the Wake of *Black Panther*" (Coward 2018), "The Claws Are Out: Marvel's *Black Panther* Confronts Museum Authority on Black Heritage" (Gay 2018), and "Why Museum Professionals Need to Talk about *Black Panther*" (Haughlin 2018). The latter of these, appearing in *The Hopkins Exhibitionist*, suggested that "the museum [of Great Britain in the film] is presented as an illegal mechanism of colonialism, and along with that, a space which does not even welcome those whose culture it displays" (Haughlin 2018). Haughlin's description concerns the abrupt change in tone which happens as the scene continues when the young man asks about a third artifact and is told by Director Manning that it is a seventh-century axe from the Fula tribe (also modern-day Benin), only to inform her directly, to her utmost surprise, *that she is wrong*. There is a shocked expression on her face as if she is unaccustomed to being contradicted, especially by *someone like him*, but the young man proceeds to tell her "it *was* taken by British soldiers in Benin, but it's from Wakanda and it's made out of vibranium . . . *Don't trip I'mma take it off your hands for you*," with his West Coast American accent becoming more evident as their interaction continues. Flustered, she quickly informs him, "These items aren't for sale," leading him to reply with the most potent line of dialogue in the scene, "How do you think your ancestors got these? You think they paid a fair price, or did they take it, *like they did everything else?*" It is with this that she tries to shut him down and bring their interaction to an end, but she struggles to complete the sentence. Only then does the young man step into her personal space for the first time and comments that he has noticed the guards "watching me ever since I walked in." He is indeed correct: a museum security guard, sometimes even two, has been at the edges of the shot at various moments throughout their conversation, even from the start when he seemed like a simple American tourist asking innocent questions about the exhibition. The guards had been placed discreetly in the frame by Coogler and director of photography Rachel Morrison, sometimes even out of focus so that they might not have even been noticed, but they are indeed a reflection of the experiences of many African Americans in a process now widely referred to as "shopping while Black," something which fame and wealth prove no protection against, according to comments by prominent African American entertainment billionaires Jay Z and Oprah Winfrey (see Wiltz 2013).

The scene ends by revealing that Erik has arranged for the director to be poisoned, which is followed by the arrival of Klaue, who kills all the security guards, before the two retrieve the vibranium exhibit. Erik is shown drawn to an additional artifact present, one not discussed by the director, a horned mask with a mane similar to those used by the Mgbedike, an Igbo tribe in Nigeria, which he also steals with the only explanation offered being that he is "*feeling it....*" It is this mask that he wears later while rescuing Klaue from the South Korean black site that we described in the previous chapter, and though why he might be "feeling it" is left unsaid, there is a sense that he is drawn to it as a symbol of the heritage denied to him and that it is shaped *exactly* like the Royal Talon jet fighter he had seen in the sky as a boy in Oakland in 1992.

In yet another example of the cultural impact of *Black Panther* and an indication of the wide range of subject areas it found itself discussed in, artifacts from the film's production went on display in a real museum, the National Museum of African American History in Washington, DC, with a selection of its props and costumes shown to members of the public. A statement released by the Smithsonian made claims about the film similar to many we have already heard: "*Black Panther* illustrates the progression of blacks in film, an industry that in the past has overlooked blacks, or regulated them to flat, one-dimensional and marginalized figures.... The film, like the museum, provides a fuller story of black culture and identity" (quoted in Eliahou and Ahmed 2018). The director of the museum, Gus Casely-Hayford, suggested that "Marvel deals in fantasy—fantasy so often heightens and concentrates what we know, but *Black Panther* chose to push the envelope, doing the necessary work to give [the film] a kind of cultural integrity that is some of what we might expect, but that is also so, so much more.... Coogler's rich, confident Africa leaves you questioning what you thought you knew about the continent—and for a continent that is so often misunderstood, or misrepresented, that can only be good" (quoted in Spengler and Sayler 2018).[3]

III.

N'Jadaka/ Erik "Killmonger" Stevens returns to the screen to rescue Klaue in the sequence in South Korea described in chapter two, marking the point where he makes the transition from secondary to primary antagonist. The group (which consists of Erik, Klaue, Linda, and Limbani) go to a junkyard somewhere in England where it seems they are going to separate and arrange to meet and share the profits from their museum robbery later, but Erik turns on Klaue, even killing his own girlfriend Linda when Klaue attempts to take her as a hostage. The cold-blooded murder of Linda is a shocking one, and she is the second woman Erik is shown to have killed in the film after the director of the museum, but it will not be the last. The decision of Coogler and Joe Robert Cole to make the character behave in such a way was criticized, with a number of people suggesting that such choices demonized him and devalued his ideas in a simplistic way that cheapened the otherwise compelling aspects of his characterization (see Rozsa 2018). These acts, and there are many, present a concerted challenge to those who feel a sympathy for N'Jadaka/Erik, for some *too much* of a challenge, but for others it was not enough to compromise his status as an empathetic figure.

Just as shocking, and perhaps even more so, is the death of Klaue at Erik's hands, a character that audiences might have presumed would continue to play a central role in the film given how much he has come to mean to Wakanda and his sustained connection to Black Panther in the history of the comics. It is important to remember at this point in the film that we still do not know who this young African American man is, even though this book has referred to him by his name on several occasions, as he has not been explicitly named as an adult and neither does Klaue know that he is the son of the man he had become a partner with back in 1992, Prince N'Jobu, in order to steal vibranium from Wakanda. Erik informs a dying Klaue that he actually intends to go to Wakanda, an idea the arms dealer derisively laughs at, pointing to the branding on his own neck, "*This* is what they do to people like *us*," but his use of the word "us" is ambiguous. What does it refer to? Foreigners? Arms dealers? Thieves? Terrorists? In any event, Klaue has assumed the man who has killed him *is like him*, and perhaps at this moment we still do. It is then that Erik reveals markings of his own, the scarring that he has done to himself which covers all the skin over both of his forearms, about which he informs Klaue: "Each one is for a kill." But the South African arms dealer remains unimpressed: "You can scar yourself as much as you'd like, to them you'll just be an outsider." It is only when Erik pulls down his lower lip to display his glowing vibranium tattoo—as his father did in the Oakland prologue in 1992, revealing that he is of Wakandan descent—that he surprises Klaue for the first time. Klaue's last words are: "To think I saw you as *some crazy American.* . . ." For viewers watching the film for the first time, it has still not been explicitly stated that he is N'Jobu's son, nor even that the Wakandan prince and brother to T'Chaka, uncle to T'Challa, had a son, but it is at this point in the film that audiences might have suspicions as to who the man really is, suspicions that are confirmed in the following scene.

At this moment, we depart from Killmonger's point of view and return to Wakanda and T'Challa, who is attempting to find out who the man he saw with his grandfather's ring is. It is interesting that the scene in which we learn the truth about N'Jadaka/Erik "Killmonger" Stevens's identity is not actually told from his point of view, but this narrative decision shifts our identification back to T'Challa and enables us to learn of the truth at the same time as he does, even though up until now we have tended to know more than him. The scene in question also comes shortly after we have seen N'Jadaka kill three people, so it goes a long way towards establishing not just *who* he is but also in some ways *why* he behaves the way he does. It is the high shaman of Wakanda, Zuri, who is able to answer T'Challa's questions, even though he is initially reluctant to do so. Zuri's account returns us to the Oakland apartment prologue from 1992 again and a scene which was described by iconic director Francis Ford Coppola, according to Ryan Coogler, who showed him a cut of the film, as "the most important scene in the movie. The scene where everything changed" (quoted in Parker 2018). Zuri does not want to tell T'Challa what has happened, informing him that "some truths are too much to bear," and he had promised king T'Chaka that he would never speak of that day. It is only when T'Challa raises his voice at the elder, a not-insignificant act of rebellion against tradition, and demands it ("*I* am your king now!") that Zuri concedes. His story reveals what we might consider to be the film's foundational traumatic moment, personally and culturally, in a flashback which accounts for what we did not see in the prologue which started the film. Fittingly, from both a narrative and thematic point of view, what we had originally seen in the prologue is what T'Chaka and Zuri had informed everyone had happened, so we too had been placed in the position of being lied to as much as the Wakandans had, if only for an hour of screen time rather than more than twenty-five years. The scene plays out not in the style of the unreliable narration of films like *The Cabinet of Dr. Caligari* (1920) and *Rashomon* (1950), or more recently, *The Usual Suspects* (1995), *Fight Club* (1999), *Memento* (2000), and *Life of Pi* (2012), but with moments that were previously withheld from us now included. Zuri tells T'Challa, "The hardships he saw there radicalised your uncle," and explains, or rather allows N'Jobu to explain, how living among the African American community in Oakland, away from the privileges of his life in Wakanda, changed his perspective on Wakanda's ethical responsibilities, awakened by an awareness, and firsthand experience of the mistreatment of African Americans in the US and Africans around the world. He says:

> I observed for as long as I could, their leaders have been assassinated, their communities flooded with drugs and weapons. They are overly policed and incarcerated. All over the planet our people suffer because they do not have the tools to fight back. With vibranium weapons they could overthrow every country and Wakanda could rule them all, *the right way. . . .*

N'Jobu is, of course, referring to the murders of Malcolm X (1965), Martin Luther King Jr. (1968), Fred Hampton (1969), and, closer to 1992, Huey Newton, the leader of the Black Panthers, in 1989. Sterling K. Brown described his character as "somebody who is eager to be a catalyst for change. T'Chaka is more nationalistic in terms of Wakanda first but N'Jobu's views are much more globalized in terms of all people of African descent having a sense of responsibility. We can't just protect people within our borders without giving some sort of attention to those people who exist outside. I think it feeds from what is going on in our world now" (quoted in Wilkins 2018, 13).

It might be asked, though, why N'Jobu has this realization in Oakland when much closer to his home in Wakanda many Africans were experiencing hardships on their own continent, many of which were the results of colonial interventions. If N'Jobu is in his thirties or early forties in 1992, as he seems to be and as the script describes him as (2018, 3), then he was raised and came of age through the 1960s into the 1980s, and, if Wakandans are given access to information about the world as they seem to be, he would have been very much aware of the tumultuous politics of Africa in those years, the likes of which are too numerous to list here but include South African apartheid (1948–94), the Algerian War for Independence (1954–62), the assassination of Patrice Lumumba in Congo (1961), and the overthrow of Kwame Nkrumah in Ghana (1965), to name just a few, several of which the United States, and in particular the CIA, directly participated in.

After N'Jobu learns he has been betrayed by his friend James/Zuri, as we had seen in the prologue, we are then shown the aftermath that we had not seen before, as N'Jobu pulls a gun and points it towards his erstwhile confidante. Yet the Black Panther, King T'Chaka, quickly strikes, thrusting his claws deeply into his brother's chest and killing him. The moment is over very quickly, perhaps purposefully so on Coogler's part, and it is hard to discern the exact particulars even when returning to it. Certainly, N'Jobu was wrong to pull a gun, but could the king not have resolved the issue without killing his brother? It is fitting, though, that the act is an ambiguous one, but what happens next is not ambiguous at all as the king orders Zuri/James to "speak nothing of this" and decides to leave his dead brother on the floor and his brother's son, the half-American and half-Wakandan N'Jadaka/Erik, behind to an uncertain future. Zuri tells T'Challa it was done "to maintain the lie," but again the phrasing is ambiguous. Is it the lie that N'Jobu is missing and not dead? The lie that the king killed his brother? Or the lie that Wakanda can remain isolated from the world without ramifications? Whatever

Zuri's meaning, it is a lie that carries with it both personal and national consequences in ways rare in the superhero genre, which are primarily about the personal sphere, even though the actions of superheroes often have an influence on many others. Here the act is both a personal one to those in the king's immediate family like his children T'Challa and Shuri, who are told their uncle was never found, but also to the entire country of Wakanda, given T'Chaka and N'Jobu's elevated royal status. Of course, it is to the boy N'Jadaka/ Erik that the cost is the greatest as he is left without either a mother or father and we can only imagine what he went through after that. He had been told by his father, as we had witnessed, about his rich African heritage and his birthright and taught the customs and language of his ancestral home, but all that was taken away from him by a single shocking act of violence, the result of which he is left to see with his own eyes as he returns to the apartment to find his dead father. At this point, we are left to imagine this moment, but later we will see it from N'Jadaka's own perspective as the film shows it to us onscreen in perhaps the most poignant scene in the whole of *Black Panther*.

It is from Ross that we learn what actually happened to N'Jadaka: that he earned a scholarship to university despite his disadvantaged background and then went to graduate school at MIT (Massachusetts Institute of Technology), an institution that Tony Stark graduated from at seventeen *summa cum laude* and was shown returning to in *Captain America: Civil War* to introduce his September Foundation grant, which allowed every student access to funding for their research projects with "no strings attached."[4] He then joined the United States military, serving all over the globe as revealed in an image which highlights his deployments not just in Iraq and Afghanistan but also Mexico, South Africa, Yemen, Pakistan, and Uzbekistan. Ross says Erik joined a JSOC "ghost" unit that "used to work with the CIA to destabilise foreign countries, they would always strike at transitions of power like an election year or the death of a monarch, you get control of government, the military" and that he got "confirmed kills like it was a video game," which is where he earned the nickname Killmonger. Ross tells them, "He's

The places where N'Jadaka/Erik "Killmonger" Stevens has been deployed by the CIA and the US military all over the world.

not a Wakandan, he's one of *ours*," similar to Klaue's use of the term "people like *us*," again with one of the words being ambiguously employed. Does his "*ours*" mean American or CIA? At this point in the film, it seems that Ross himself has become almost entirely disconnected from not just the CIA, but also the United States. The things he tells Shuri and T'Challa that Erik did were perpetrated by the organization and the country he works for, but the film does not dwell on this, and Ross's status as an American and a CIA agent will never be referred to again in the film, not even when he appears for the film's mid-credits scene at the United Nations in Vienna.

What Erik has been through, even though it is placed in the context of *just a superhero film*, offers a rich articulation of a very real phenomenon in African American culture. Erik has had his family torn from him and his connections to the African continent by the loss of his father offering parallels to what was described by W. E. B. Du Bois's as a "double-consciousness," the result of an internal conflict often experienced by oppressed groups in societies where they are marginalized (see *The Souls of Black Folk*, 1903). Du Bois stated that this is the consequence of "a world which yields him no true self-consciousness, but only lets him see himself through the revelation of the other world. It is a peculiar sensation, this double consciousness, this sense of always looking at one's self through the eyes of others" (1969, 45), an analogy that links the process in intriguing ways to cinema and the stereotypes of Africa and African Americans we have considered produced by the American film industry since even prior to D. W Griffith's infamous *The Birth of a Nation* (1915).

Having learned this information about N'Jadaka's past, the audience is placed in a complicated position regarding how to feel about the character, and it is one which will be deepened further when we learn why he is returning to Wakanda and what he hopes to achieve there. Certainly, he is positioned as the film's antagonist, but we are asked, or rather offered the opportunity to empathize with him more than many others placed in similar positions in the genre. Heath Ledger's Joker in *The Dark Knight* is a charismatic presence, but we are not expected to take his side, nor are we for the likes of Hela, Adrian "Vulture" Toomes, Ego, Kaecilus, or Helmut Zemo in the five films before *Black Panther* that made up Phase Two of the MCU. Each of them are, without a doubt, interesting villains with engaging and sometimes understandable motivations, but none prompted audiences to assert that they *agree with them* and what they are doing in the way audiences seemed to react to N'Jadaka/Erik.[5]

IV

The next scene shows N'Jadaka's own "return" to Wakanda in a beautifully framed and lit shot which shows him dragging a heavy object across the ground that he places at the feet of a man who is revealed to be W'Kabi, someone we have seen to have doubts about T'Challa's abilities to guide Wakanda into the future after the king's failure to kill or return Klaue as he had promised. Yet this is exactly what N'Jadaka has done, bringing the body of the South African arms dealer back to Wakanda as a "little gift." For W'Kabi, though, it is much more than that; it is the body of the man who had killed his parents and caused such a trauma for Wakanda back in 1992. Their exchange is in English as W'Kabi naturally presumes this man is an outsider, but on seeing the body he reverts in surprise to Xhosa/Wakandan asking him the most often repeated question in the whole film, "*ungubani?*" or "who are you?" We are not shown N'Jadaka answering the question.

Even though he is the one in handcuffs, N'Jadaka's power in the throne room scene is palpable.

There are a number of key scenes in *Black Panther*, so it is hard to single out one in particular as the most important. We saw Francis Ford Coppola state that Zuri's story about the "moment everything changed" was one and he is right, and Benjamin Dixon said it was T'Challa's first visit to the ancestral plane (2018), but arguably it is the scene in the throne room of T'Challa and N'Jadaka being brought face to face for the first time that is the most significant in terms of the narrative and themes at the heart of *Black Panther*. Even though it is just three and a half minutes long and contains only dialogue and none of the action audiences expect from the genre, it might be the most thrilling sequence in the whole film. It acts as the culmination of several personal narratives up until that moment, and reveals a great deal about N'Jadaka, namely, why he has come to Wakanda, what he desires, and the lengths to which he will go to get it.

N'Jadaka is brought into the throne room by W'Kabi in handcuffs with his hands secured behind his back. He initially seems powerless, as one might expect, but as the scene continues it becomes clear that somehow he is the one with the most power in the room. T'Challa gestures to him and says "T'atta" in Xhosa, which W'Kabi translates for N'Jadaka as "speak." Given a platform in the Wakandan throne room, something we can imagine he has waited decades for, he informs those present in English: "I'm standing in your house, serving justice to a man who stole your vibranium and murdered your people, justice your king couldn't deliver." T'Challa approaches

him, bringing his face closer to the man he now knows is his cousin
and whose father was killed by his own, and asks him what he wants,
but N'Jadaka ignores him, continuing to talk to the council at large,
requiring every moment of their exchange to be a public one, not
private, telling them all: "*I want the throne!*" This prompts laughter
from those present in the throne room, mainly the elders, secure in
the power they possess over an American stranger in handcuffs. It
is then, N'Jadaka gives the reason for his return in a speech reminiscent of the one his father gave to T'Chaka and Zuri in Oakland
in 1992: "Y'all sitting up here comfortable. *Must feel good* . . . There's
about two billion people over the world that *looks like us*. But their
lives are a lot harder, Wakanda has the tools to liberate them all."
N'Jadaka was not in the room back in 1992 when his father appealed
to King T'Chaka with something very similar, but no doubt he had
heard him talk of his desire to liberate oppressed people all over the
world and the responsibilities that Wakanda had turned their back
on. The five sentences he has uttered thus far are hard to disagree
with and can be seen as an unambiguous paean to Pan-Africanism
the likes of which swept through the continent in the second half of
the twentieth century and have gained significant critical currency
in recent decades. Yet it is an idea that has been categorically rejected
by Wakandans who have been content to "hide in plain sight" and
remain isolated, refusing to help those on the African continent and
beyond. In the years since 1992, given that the Wakandans seem to be
aware of everything happening around the world, they would have
known of events like the Rwandan genocide (1994), the Ebola Out-
break (2013–16), and the War in Darfur (2003–), but decided to not
intervene. Accordingly, T'Challa responds, "It is not our way to be
judge, jury, and executioner for people who are *not our own*." It is this
phrase that seems to strike N'Jadaka in particular, "*Not your own?
But didn't life start right here on this continent? So ain't all people
your people?*" T'Challa seems secure in his responses to N'Jadaka,
even though he knows what has brought the man there, as he has yet
to have his ideas comprehensively challenged, certainly not enough
to change his mind and his comments are also very similar to those
he has heard from his own father, just as N'Jadaka's are similar to

N'Jobu's. He informs his cousin, "I am not king of all people, I am king of Wakanda."[6] By now those in the throne room have begun to participate, Ramonda intercedes and suggests the intruder should be thrown out with the command: "Reject his request!" N'Jadaka suggests, "*Ask who I am . . .*" Shuri answers for him, telling everyone that he is "a mercenary named Killmonger," which is both true and not true at the same time, and according to N'Jadaka, "That's not my name, *Princess*," with the line delivery positively loaded, referring to her privileged status and containing more than an element of menace within it. He repeats again, "*Ask me!*" but T'Challa cuts him off, ordering him to be taken away and the scene appears to be coming to an end, indicating that T'Challa too is content for the lie to be maintained during his reign as king as it was during his father's. But as N'Jadaka is being roughly led away, the elder of the River tribe asks above the noise, "Ungubani!?"—the same question asked by W'Kabi in the scene before, which provides him with the opportunity he has been waiting for. He answers not in English, but in Xhosa/Wakandan, with a line which is translated onscreen in subtitles as follows: "I am N'Jadaka, son of Prince N'Jobu!" This is followed by a moment the script describes this way: "A hush falls over the room . . . THIS CHANGES EVERYTHING" (2018, 79; capitalization in original).

The question "who are you?" has already been asked at various moments throughout *Black Panther* and is one central to the superhero genre, as is its answer. It is one asked of Spider-Man in *Spider-Man* (2002), Wolverine in *X-Men 2* (2003), Superman/Clark Kent in *Superman* (1978), and many others. It is the defining question in Iron Man's many appearances in the MCU from 2008 to 2019; in the final moments of *Iron Man*, Tony Stark announces to the world, "I am Iron Man," but it is only in subsequent films that he understands what that really means. After struggling to find a balance between Tony Stark and his metallic alter ego, he returns to the same line in his final appearance and almost his final lines in *Avengers: Endgame* and says once again, "I am Iron Man," with the words the same as they were eleven years before, but the meaning is something very different. In the throne room in Wakanda is the first time that N'Jadaka has spoken in Xhosa, and those inside are stunned to hear it. It is important to recognize that the question here is not just "who are you?" but "ungubani?" which has been asked twice of N'Jadaka in the space of a few minutes. It is a question that African author Blessing Mpofu writes is an important one in African cultures in ways that highlight how *Black Panther* resonated with many as much more than just a superhero film,

> Ungubani is a Xhosa and Zulu word. A question, which translates, "Who are you?" This word-question was also a code of sort. How you answered it located you. It was about one's identity, your lineage and things that would be associated with you. How someone answered this question determined whether they were family or foe. Something we in Africa can identify with, with little effort. Anyone with the same surname or totem as you is immediately treated like family. There are those encounters. The ones where your surname either makes you an instant friend or, enemy. Our names and even tribes we're connected to, locate us. They place us, not in a physical sense, but in our standing with people we encounter. (2018)

This moment might have been a powerful enough reveal to conclude the scene on, a reclamation of identity and lineage as Mpofu discusses above, but it does not end there (see also Mhlambi 2016). Having made his point in Xhosa, N'Jadaka reverts again to English, telling them all, "I found my daddy with panther claws in his chest, *you* [gesturing to T'Challa] ain't the son of a king, you the son of a murderer." This is all too much for those in the room to process, and Ramonda can be heard to shout "lies!" but all he has said until now we have seen for ourselves and is true. N'Jadaka turns to Ramonda and greets her with a smile and says, "Hey, Auntie," a greeting here being used both ironically and literally as Ramonda is in fact his biological aunt, with the term, as Peter Webster describes, used as "an honorific used to address senior women, to show respect and acknowledge relationships" (2015, 50). With this he formally

I am N'Jadaka, son of Prince N'Jobu.

Revealing to those in the throne room the truth in Xhosa/Wakandan with English subtitles.

challenges T'Challa ("I'm exercising my blood rite, to challenge for the mantles of king and of Black Panther"), although the legitimacy of the claim is uncertain. He is a member of the royal family, but whether it is possible to challenge only on the ceremonial day or at any time is not confirmed. T'Challa could, it seems, reject the challenge as some in the room prompt him to do, but he sits on the throne holding his grandfather's ring, of which his cousin has the other, and answers with only two words: "I accept."

The challenge for the throne happens in the scene directly after the one described above and happens at Warrior Falls where we had been taken to at the beginning of the film and saw the fight between T'Challa and M'Baku, but this one is very different for a number of reasons. The first was during the day and this one takes place during sunset; the first was witnessed by what seemed like a huge part of the country and this one only by a few members of the royal family, tribal elders, the Dora Milaje and Nakia. However, the main difference is the attitude of those who are taking part in it: while the stakes are just as high, the throne itself, everything seems much more serious. It is on N'Jadaka's face that much of this is writ large with his expression one of intense concentration and *rage* that brings to mind James Baldwin's frequently quoted observation that "to be a Negro in this country and to be relatively conscious, is to be in a rage almost all the time. So that the first problem is how to control that rage so that it won't destroy you" (quoted in Baldwin, Hentoff et al., 1962, 81). The rage that N'Jadaka feels has fueled him for years, and he tells T'Challa before they begin, "I lived my entire life waiting for this moment . . . I trained, I lied, I killed, *just to get here*. I killed in America, Afghanistan, Iraq. I took life from my own brothers and sisters right here on the continent. And all this death . . . *just so I can kill you*." He is a veteran of American conflicts of the War on Terror era, having participated in the foreign interventions abroad, the wars in Iraq (2003–2011) and Afghanistan (2001–), and, as the image of the globe revealed earlier, in Mexico, South Africa, Yemen, Pakistan, and Uzbekistan. He removes his shirt to reveal his muscular torso, but also a real physical manifestation of this rage, not just the scarification of his arms (which we had seen earlier in the English junk yard) but the rest of his body. He has marked his skin for every life he has taken as a reminder of his past, like the aide-mémoire etched on the skin as tattoos by Leonard Shelby in *Memento* (2001) and Dae-su Oh in *Oldboy* (2003); in N'Jadaka's case this is a bastardization of the traditional tribal scarification process practiced by the Mercy and Boomi tribe, who use the act more to chart lineage, social status, identity, and only rarely to mark their skin for enemies that they have killed (see Vescia 2019).[7]

The small number of people in the crowd do not seem overly worried at first as T'Challa has by now proven himself as a prodigious warrior on numerous occasions. On the surface what is to be decided is a family matter, but at the same time, due to the fact that Wakanda is an absolute monarchy, it will also decide the future of the nation. T'Challa offers N'Jadaka a consolation—"We can handle this *another way*"—but it is too little and too late; the time for this might have been in the throne room, but even then it is hard to imagine that N'Jadaka would agree, given what his ultimate plans are and the fact that the superhero film is defined by resolution only through violent conflict, as Bucky Barnes commented in *Captain America: Civil War*: "It *always* ends in a fight," perhaps because both the genre and the audience that it serves demands it.

Initially T'Challa seems to have the upper hand, striking early blows upon his opponent which are cheered by those watching, but N'Jadaka is a force of nature driven by those years of rage which brought him to Wakanda to face his cousin and all that he represents. Despite his heroism and his abilities, might T'Challa's life of privilege have left him ill-prepared for something like this? A man like N'Jadaka? In the previous fight against M'Baku, at a moment when he wavered, Queen Ramonda had shouted, "Show him who you are!" but it is clear now that N'Jadaka is here to prove the very same thing and as he is about to strike what appears to be a killing blow he yells something similar to what T'Challa had previously: "This is for my father!" This is parried by Zuri, who calls his name, or at least the name Zuri knew him as when he was a boy: "Erik!" Although we spent little time in Oakland in 1992, we recall that N'Jobu described the man he knew as James with the words "I trust him with my life." The implication being that James/Zuri was close to the boy and that his disappearance after N'Jobu's death might also have had a profound effect on him. N'Jadaka's face displays no emotion as he says, "I'll take you both, *Uncle James*," abruptly killing the old man, revealing that he remembers *everything*. We might reflect here that this is another such moment when audience members are compelled to consider their empathy for N'Jadaka, one of many the film has given us, challenged by the cold-blooded murder of an old man. By this time, he has already killed the museum director, Linda, and Klaue to get here and he will kill many more. His final act in the scene is to hurl a wounded T'Challa over the side of the waterfall to what he presumes is his death. Although we know that as the protagonist of the film T'Challa cannot really be dead, these moments always have a brief *frisson* of potency, even if they cannot last, and the characters within the film's diegetic frames do not know what we know. He asks the crowd, "Is this your king?" before answering himself: "Nah . . . *I'm your king*." Seeing T'Challa plummet, the crowd becomes distraught, especially Shuri and Ramonda. It is Nakia who remains levelheaded, and she leads them away as quickly as she can, now aware of what N'Jadaka is capable of. Those remaining offer him a Wakandan salute, even a reluctant Okoye, but although he has achieved what he had desired for decades he shows no sense of satisfaction and the only emotion still visible on his face is rage.

Having deposed the king and ascended to the throne himself, perfectly legally according to Wakanda's laws, customs, and

N'Jadaka's victory seems complete, but it brings him no respite from his rage.

traditions, he is given the same reward as T'Challa, an opportunity to visit the ancestral plane after drinking the heart-shaped herb and being buried in the red sand of the City of the Dead. His experience of the whole process is far removed from his cousin's, which had been a joyous one even before he entered the plane, even though, like T'Challa, he is to be reunited with a father killed in traumatic circumstances. Indeed, the film has deliberately asked us to observe parallels between their lives, offering comparisons and contrasts on numerous occasions. They both lost their fathers, but T'Challa lost a septuagenarian after a lifetime together with other family members there to support and grieve with him, but N'Jadaka was a child who lost his father in traumatic and mysterious circumstances, even finding the body himself, and was left with no one. These moments have led us to empathize with a character who has performed numerous immoral actions, by emphasizing his humanity in ways that other villains in the genre are rarely provided with.

Like T'Challa's journey to the ancestral plain N'Jadaka's begins with sepia footage, a return to his foundational trauma that we had heard about but not yet seen from his perspective. For T'Challa and his father, the ancestral plane had been a rich and luxurious landscape, full of acacia trees with his proud descendants taking the form of panthers on their branches, but N'Jadaka's is very different. We return to the Oakland apartment where the film began for the third and final time. Through its windows, we can see purple skies rather than those of Oakland, showing us it is the ancestral plane but one in which N'Jobu has been disconnected from his homeland in the afterlife just as he was while he was alive. He has been denied a return to his ancestors, his brother, and even his own father. Initially it is an adult N'Jadaka who walks through the empty apartment, with the television showing only static rather than the Rodney King riots as it had previously. He makes his way over to the hidden portion of the room where N'Jobu and "James" had hidden their "straps," and, once again, Huey Newton's iconic photo and the Public Enemy poster can be seen briefly on the wall, on opposite edges of the frame. Inside he retrieves his father's journal and the ring/necklace we have seen a number of times, the one that had sparked so many questions for T'Challa. We see inside the diary very briefly, some of it written in Wakandan script and some in English, and catch a glimpse of the coordinates to Wakanda (2 39'30.19 S; 29 0'29.36 E), which explains both how he was able to find his way "home" and how he knows so much about their customs even though he has never had contact with the place. The diary is only seen for a few moments, too quickly for us to read it while watching the film theatrically, but pausing the image allows us to see exactly what it contains. It reads with text central to many of the questions we have explored in this book.

> Ungubani? Who are you? I asked this question of myself many times. Often times, I do not know. But I do know I am no longer the man my country knew. Maybe love? My son? It has all changed me. T'Chaka must see what we can do, how we can change the course of time for the people who struggle so much in this land. Strangers to me, but my brothers and sisters still. How can I look at them, with the same skin as me, stolen from the same place I came from and not reach out to them? How can I sit idly by and watch in pain and return to Wakanda as if there was nothing to see at all? Who am I? A war dog who will not leave the lost tribe behind again. Who are you, my son? You will ask this one day and know the answer: N'Jadaka, son of N'Jobu.

In a heartfelt few lines written with a sincerity often absent in the superhero film, N'Jobu reflects on his own identity and obligation to those with the same skin color as himself all around the world, those which he understands Wakanda has turned their back on. It begins with the question we have returned to often and ends with the exact lines N'Jadaka told everyone in the throne room just a few minutes of screen time before. It is only then that N'Jobu himself appears in front of his son, gently chastising him for going through his things. N'Jadaka then is seen as a child with the film proceeding to alternate shots between the adult and child versions of himself as he interacts with his father. N'Jobu sits opposite his son, and there is a sadness and a distance in their exchange very different from the one between T'Challa and T'Chaka when they met in the ancestral plane, a meeting that was overwhelmingly joyous and saw them embracing and T'Challa falling to his knees before his beloved father. T'Challa is never shown as a child in the ancestral plane in *Black Panther*, and only once in a brief flash lasting less than a second in the whole film, symptomatic of his fully formed personality perhaps and a sharp contrast to N'Jadaka whose life and personality changed drastically in 1992 after the trauma he experienced. Their exchange is a brief one, out of narrative necessity perhaps, as conventional superhero films do not spend so much time on their antagonist's backstory and character development, every moment of which takes us away from the hero's own journey. Yet every line is loaded with meaning as delivered by Sterling K. Brown, whose presence lingers far beyond the few minutes of screen time he is given in the film. He asks the boy, "What did you find?" but it is not clear whether he means in the book or elsewhere in his journey to Wakanda as an adult as the boy answers, "Your home." N'Jobu says, "I gave you a key hoping you might see it someday [indicating the vibranium inner lip tattoo] . . . The sunsets there are the most beautiful in the world. But I fear you still may not be welcome." N'Jadaka asks "why?" (as he had once done in the film's prologue), and N'Jobu answers, "They will say you are lost." N'Jobu sadly asks, "No tears for me?" in four

The trauma that N'Jadaka has experienced and the depth of his suffering as an adult and child is shown on the ancestral plane.

words that are perhaps the only indication that he is aware that he is in fact dead and on the ancestral plane himself, to which the child N'Jadaka replies, "Everybody dies, *it's just life around here*." It is only then that the adult N'Jadaka is shown to have a single tear running down his cheek, and his younger version has too. N'Jobu concludes the scene expressing a concern as to what impact his decisions will have had on his son: "Well, look at what I've done. I should have taken you back long ago. Instead we are both abandoned here." N'Jadaka replies, "Well maybe *your home is the one that's lost*," as the scene comes to an end. It is hard to recall another film from the genre prior to *Black Panther* that has offered the antagonist such time and sensitivity, the result of which is a complicated relationship between N'Jadaka and audiences who empathized with him, despite his many questionable actions.

The scene has lasted only two and a half minutes, but like much of the film, it is an evocative one, much more than what it appears to be on the surface. What N'Jobu is shown to have experienced is a disconnection from his cultural heritage because of his desire to liberate African Americans, albeit through methods many deem to be deeply problematic, which has meant he loses his connection to his homeland in the afterlife in the same way his son has experienced in the film's real world. In this way it might be considered that the film offers a very clear judgement on those who identify as "Black radicals" or "militants," with both N'Jobu and N'Jadaka possessing voices or ideas that we are allowed by the film to empathize with but at the same time understand as very much the incorrect direction for the African American community. Thus, the film indicates that what N'Jobu has done is wrong, so wrong that he is denied connection to his ancestral homeland in the afterlife for eternity.[8] Once again we see how the film uses its characters as representative of broader debates, in this case one central to the civil rights movement for decades: the ethics of using violence as a means of emancipation. In the popular imagination, this has become simplistically categorized as the difference between the beliefs of Malcolm X and those of Martin Luther King Jr. The reality, of course, is much more complicated than this as it always is when complex real-world figures are condensed to a single idea in the cultural imaginary. Given this, it was only to be expected then that some would view the film through the prism of these two defining African American figures of the mid-twentieth century. In a genre that revels in violent altercations—indeed, one founded with violence as righteous and just—not only is *Black Panther* unable to endorse violence as emancipation for oppressed people all over the globe but it portrays the two men who would advocate it as villains, showing one to be in league with a terrorist like Klaue and the other a sociopath that targets women on numerous occasions and will later advocate killing children (see Sanghi 2018). Thus, as Dikeledi A. Mokoena argues, "Moving back to the concept of unacceptable Black people, the demonization of Erik, evident with him being named Killmonger, is also reminiscent of how Black revolutionaries are portrayed. . . . The construct of the

On numerous occasions, *Black Panther* asks audiences to draw parallels between N'Jadaka and T'Challa, one of many devices which prompt identification with the film's antagonist.

moderate Black person is upheld while the death of the Black radical is symbolic of dictating what kind of political and economic route we should follow as Black people" (2018). The idea here is that Black nationalism has been demonized in popular culture, even in films, television shows, and literature produced by members of the African American community, and that N'Jadaka/Erik is merely the latest in a long line of figures to be portrayed in the same way. This emerges as even more complicated because of the huge cultural reach of a film like *Black Panther* and the fact that many regarded it as a progressive film in many ways, which indeed it is.

The parallels and juxtapositions between T'Challa and N'Jadaka continue throughout the brief scene and indeed the film as a whole. It is no coincidence that we have seen both fathers in the ancestral realm reflect on how they might have failed their sons but in very different ways: T'Chaka reflects that he might not have prepared T'Challa for his death ("A man who has not prepared his children for his own death has failed as a father"), and N'Jobu reflects that his son was raised in an environment that would lead him to say, "Everybody dies, it's just life around here." On the connections between the two cousins, Michael B. Jordan expressed the idea that "one was raised in comfort and one was raised on the streets and had to figure out things on his own. They both deal with loss. Erik's dad died and he had to go into foster care. T'Challa's dad died and he became king. He got a castle and a throne. So I think there's jealousy and resentment there. T'Challa got the life Erik could have had" (quoted in Wilkins 2018, 54).

When he returns from the ancestral plane, N'Jadaka is as consumed with rage as he has ever been and has found no peace there; it is obvious from his facial expressions and his aggressive pose when he wakes, as if he is ready to fight. It is very different from T'Challa's reunion with his father, which he returned from with a sense of harmony. Nothing has been resolved for N'Jadaka; in fact, he is ready to put the next stage of his plan into operation. This begins with the decision to burn all the remaining heart-shaped herb plants so that there will be no kings after him; at the same time, he commits yet another act of violence against a woman, lifting the spiritual elder against the wall by the throat when she questions his actions.

N'Jadaka enters the throne room as the new king of Wakanda and the Black Panther, a room that just a few days before he was led into in handcuffs. To mark and even provide a commentary on this sense of discombobulation, the camera rotates 360 degrees on its X axis, embodying our own feelings and those of the Wakandans who have witnessed millennia of tradition overthrown in a matter of hours. As Patrick Keating observed, such dynamic camera movement can "mimic a character's subjective states" or "might contribute to an overriding goal—evoking feelings" (2019, 3). Previously N'Jadaka had revealed only in vague terms what he wanted, implying rather than directly informing us of his desires, but now he tells all those in the room exactly what his plans are: "You know where I'm from when Black folks started revolutions they never had the firepower or the

"Burn it all!": N'Jadaka and the myopism of the colonizer.

resources to fight their oppressors. *Where was Wakanda?*" N'Jadaka might be referring to the unsuccessful slave rebellions in the United States by the likes of Gabriel (August 1800), Denmark Vesey (June 1822), and Nat Turner (August 1831), the latter of which was turned into the film *The Birth of a Nation* (2016), written and directed by, and starring, Nate Parker. He informs them that "I know how colonizers think so I'm gonna use their own strategy against them," because he has worked among "them" for much of his career in the military.

N'Jadaka continues his speech, delivering his most problematic line of dialogue for some—yet another challenge for those who continue to empathize with him. He states that during his reign as king, Wakandans will "arm oppressed people all over the world, they can finally rise up and kill those in power *and their children and anyone else who takes their side.*" Ross had observed earlier that "his unit used to work with the CIA to destabilize foreign countries. They would always strike at transitions of power like an election year or death of a monarch," an exciting line in the context of a superhero film or a thriller, but it is what the CIA has done in the real world on numerous occasions (see Valentine 2016; Blum 2014). N'Jadaka knows how colonizers think *because he is one*, and if there is any doubt the next line confirms it as the scene comes to an end: "The world's gonna start over and this time we're on top, the sun will never set on the Wakandan Empire," a phrase widely used in descriptions of the British Empire. Throughout the twentieth century, as the British Empire declined and was replaced in prominence

N'Jadaka assumes the throne of Wakanda, he is now king and Black Panther: a state introduced in a discombobulating 360-degree rotation of the camera.

by the United States, it was just as regularly applied to the US. As early as 1897, articles with titles like "The Greatest Nation on Earth" were suggesting that "the sun never sets on Uncle Sam" (see Jordan). In more recent years, the phrase has been used more critically of American geopolitical aspirations, as in Joseph Gerson and Bruce Birchard's *The Sun Never Sets . . . : Confronting the Network of Foreign U.S. Military Bases* (1999). Since then, and despite claims to the contrary, the US has aggressively pursued this in the interests of national security which has resulted in it having around eight hundred military bases around the globe in the year of the film's release, 2018 (see Slater 2018).

V.

This chapter has sought to provide an exploration of the film's antagonist, whether we choose to call him N'Jadaka, Erik Stevens, or Killmonger, offering an insight into why he might have resonated with audiences in the way that he did as well as why his characterization was criticized by many. Whatever one's perspective, it is hard to deny that he is one of the most compelling figures the superhero film has offered in recent years. An important question we are left with might be: "How do Coogler and Cole wish us to understand him?" We have learned of his difficult childhood and even seen with our own eyes the trauma he experienced on the night of his father's death. We know of the considerable impact this must have had on him and also the knowledge that he is half-Wakandan, even a prince just as much as T'Challa is, from a mystical place with a rich history that he was promised by his father he would one day see. But all this has been denied to him in circumstances that have understandably provoked the rage that is a central aspect of Michael B. Jordan's memorable performance. At exactly the same time, we have seen numerous examples of his inhumanity and sociopathic behavior, as by this moment in the film he has killed two women and assaulted another, murdered Klaue, even apparently the film's protagonist, and hundreds, if not thousands, more, if we are to believe his assertion about the scarification on his skin. He has claimed that his desire is to liberate oppressed people all over the world, but this will be achieved through violent means also resulting in the deaths of many innocents. We have been afforded an intimacy with him offered to no other antagonist throughout the MCU, with the exception of adopted Asgardian prince Loki, a process which cannot help but suture us to the character in some ways. However, there are many differences between Loki and N'Jadaka, as it is hard to imagine that even the most ardent admirers of the character or the actor who portrayed him, Tom Hiddlestone, really believed that what Loki was doing was correct (taking over the Earth, killing his brother, killing his father, etc.) even if they cheered on his undeniably entertaining antics while they were happening. Yet this seems to be *exactly* what transpired for many of those who came to empathize with N'Jadaka, who frequently detailed how they were able to forgive him for his actions and embrace him in the way that Cole and Coogler seem to *suggest that we should not*. This is something that was confirmed by producer Nate Moore:

> I think that Killmonger thinks he's a good guy, which is the best kind of villain—a villain who actually believes in what they are doing. . . . I think his methods are what make him villainous in that he is willing to cross lines that a hero like T'Challa wouldn't cross in order to get what he thinks is

right. But what's interesting is that I think you'll see the audience is going to agree with a lot of Killmonger's ideas, and they're going to be ideas that T'Challa is going to have to take in and actually figure out if he believes in them. So there's a real conversation there that we think is interesting rather than a villain who just wants to take over the world, which is sometimes where we think superhero movies go wrong. (quoted in Roussos 2018, 256).

Thus, we find many audience members, writers, and academics emphasizing the same thing: that even though N'Jadaka is the film's antagonist and villain, it is *he they were compelled to support and identify with.* As Hamid Dabashi articulated clearly:

I was T'Challa. I was Black Panther—until N'Jadaka, Erik "Killmonger" appeared. Then I was Killmonger. The movie wanted me to take a side: you are either Black Panther or Killmonger. It would not allow you to be both. I took a side. I stayed with my defiant brother N'Jadaka to the bitter end. The movie failed to change my heart and politics.

Dabashi suggests that "the movie wanted me to take a side," but arguably this is not the case at all. As Moore indicated, and in comments made by both Coogler and Cole, as much as the character of N'Jadaka is written and performed for us to sympathize with, there is nothing that our close reading of the film has found that suggests that he is to be considered an appropriate choice over T'Challa. Thus, the *preferred* reading of the film, to use the term originally employed by Stuart Hall in his "Encoding/Decoding" (1980), is one in which we identify with and root for T'Challa, even if we empathize with N'Jadaka. Those who favor N'Jadaka, and there were many of them, might be suggested as having an *oppositional* reading of the film, that is favoring its antagonist despite the fact he commits many incontrovertibly unethical acts onscreen and off. These viewers saw T'Challa in a much more critical light than he is ostensibly presented in the film, not as simply a hero but a man born into privilege, a man who never suffered a day in his life until he lost his father, a man who showed no concern for the outside world even when he saw it for himself in Nigeria or was told about it by his former partner, Nakia. On the other hand, N'Jadaka is someone who has suffered considerably, with a past that we are encouraged to view sympathetically even though he is a violent and unpredictable man who "cannot see beyond his own rage" (Serwer 2018). Audience members who continue to identify with him despite these factors are those who chose to ignore or reconcile themselves with them, focusing on N'Jadaka's humanity and his desire to overthrow oppressors all around the globe instead. Malik suggests that "this conflict is the moral core of the film. It's not that Killmonger's desire to wage war, or his view of all whites as colonizers, is commendable. It is, rather, that the pain and fury he expresses, and the moral tensions he embodies, mirror that of so many Black people, from Ferguson, Missouri, to Johannesburg. The meaning of identity, of Blackness, of resistance, even of humanitarian intervention—all tumble out of his conflict with T'Challa. Yet the film barely explores any of this. Killmonger becomes little more than a straightforward baddie whom T'Challa has to overcome" (2018).

To use a colloquialism, the cards are very much stacked against N'Jadaka from this perspective even though he is given a privileged position compared to most "villains" in the genre. The film almost revels in his repeated violence against women, has him voice that powerful and disturbing line about *killing children*, and also, by the time of the film's end, reveals him to be a hypocrite concerning his superficially altruistic motivations. But, as Tom Secker says, the film becomes defined by what it does not show as much as what it does: "*Black Panther* never shows the racism that Killmonger is responding to with his calls for violent revolution. It is referred to in dialogue but we never actually see it" (2019). Yet, despite all of this, many, like Hamad Dabashi above, saw *themselves* in N'Jadaka, and Steven Thrasher asked "Does the film ask us to root for the wrong character?" Yet Thrasher concludes: "I could not bring myself to root against Killmonger's desire to help the Black diaspora any more than I could begrudge him wanting to take the throne of the child of the man who'd killed his father" (2018). The reasons why audiences might have been able to overlook the less savory aspects of the character are interesting in themselves. As Délice Williams wrote,

> Killmonger understands Blackness in terms of shared suffering and mutual obligation, and his understanding of Blackness has far more in common with the conceptions of Blackness that American audiences would recognize. This historical consciousness, this awareness of the imagined community of the Black diaspora, is what Wakanda needs from him in order to expand its ethical vision. And it is also why Black audiences need Killmonger to help us lay claim to Wakanda. Because Wakandans cannot be Black without someone to articulate the claim that they are part of a larger community. Killmonger, in his monstrosity and tragedy, both assert claims of blackness on Wakanda and embodies the need for the fantasy world to confront the results of this history of violence and injustice. Wakanda is a fortress that defends against history. Killmonger breaks in on that fortress to assert his claim— Black people's claim—to kinship. (2018, 28)

It should not be surprising that audience members might feel empathy for N'Jadaka when a character inside the film's diegetic world does, namely, W'Kabi. Some even supported the character using language that might make casual viewers of the film slightly uncomfortable. For example, Andrews says, "The undeniable truth at the heart of *Black Panther*, is that Killmonger is right. He's right to be angry, and could not possibly be any more right about the need to fight back against the oppression facing Black people across the globe. Unfortunately, the movie makes him into a terrorist rather than a radical. One of the deepest fears of Whiteness is that one day we will get the upper hand and be just as savage to our oppressors" (Andrews, n.d.s.).

Therefore, the culmination of this idea—even more than Thrasher's and Dabishi's suggestion that they chose Killmonger instead of T'Challa—is the assertion that the character might actually be *the true hero of the film*, which was argued by a number of people including Slavoj Žižek, who wrote, "In *Black Panther*, Erik Killmonger is the real hero. He follows even the steps of the hero's journey as Campbell recognizes it." All of this testifies to N'Jadaka's status as much more than a one-dimensional villain in a comic book movie, the likes of which have frequently defined the superhero film. By contrast, N'Jadaka is a character who moves beyond even the genre's tendency in recent years to explore the antagonist's motivation more explicitly than before (see Thanos, Adrian Toomes, Hela, Mysterio, etc.). The characterization of N'Jadaka embodies several strains of critical discourse pertaining to the African American community and the relationship between Africa and African Americans. In *Black Panther*, he is a literal manifestation of Wakanda's failure—that is, the failure of its systems and its isolationist geopolitical outlook— and, as Andre Domise wrote, "In a sense, Killmonger's story is an allegory for a certain generation of Black men, born into communities where fathers were all too often absent, incarcerated, or dead. Each of us knows a boy like N'Jadaka who grew into their own Killmonger, scarred in body, if not psyche, unable to love in healthy ways because they'd either long forgotten or never learned" (2018).

N'Jadaka's burden is, of course, his own tragic personal circumstances, but it's also, as framed by Coogler and Cole, a cultural and symbolic one. This collective and socio-psychological trauma was one characterized by Jörn Rüsen, in *Historical Memory in Africa: Dealing with the Past, Reaching for the Future in an Intercultural Context* (2010), as a "fateful generation chain [which] has a mental dimension effective in traditions, prejudices, resentments, threats, hopes, value systems, basic convictions and—to not forget—the forces of subconscious attitudes and instincts guided by repressive forces.... The burden of the past, pressing human identity into the responsibility for things that happened without their participation" (168). This is an articulation of a collective and very real transgenerational trauma, the likes of which Marianne Hirsch characterized as "postmemory" originally in "The Generation of Postmemory" (2008), a process that "describes the relationship of the second generation to powerful, often traumatic, experiences that preceded their births but that were nevertheless transmitted to them so deeply as to seem to constitute memories in their own right . . . that descendants of survivors (of victims as well as of perpetrators) of massive traumatic events connect so deeply to the previous generation's remembrances of the past that they need to call that connection memory and thus that, in certain extreme circumstances, memory can be transmitted to those who were not actually there to live an event." (105). Hirsch's work primarily explored the concept through the prism of the Holocaust (1941–45), but others have applied it to the holocaust that was the Atlantic Slave Trade, which contemporary estimates suggest took the lives of around twelve million human beings (see Eyerman 2001; DeGruy 2005).

The result of this is an understanding of the character N'Jadaka not as a simple villain but a living symbol of the enduring cultural trauma of colonialism on Africans and African Americans. This is indeed a complicated debate, and whether its intricacies are apparent to the majority of the film's audiences is doubtful, but many of these aspects raised by the characterization of N'Jadaka are intimately connected to contemporary critical discourse concerning identity and, particularly, the legacy of slavery and the subject of reparations in the US. A year after the film's release this matter was again brought into public debate when US Senator Mitch McConnell remarked:

> I don't think reparations for something that happened 150 years ago for whom none of us currently living are responsible is a good idea . . . We've tried to deal with our original sin of slavery by fighting a civil war, by passing landmark civil rights legislation. We elected an African American president. . . .

It is an argument that, on the surface appears, logical: why should someone be held responsible for something that they did not have a direct role in perpetuating? But this was countered by Ta-Nehisi Coates, whose comic book iteration of *Black Panther* had a significant impact on aspects of Coogler's vision, who said the following:

> This rebuttal proffers a strange theory of governance, that American accounts are somehow bound by the lifetime of its generations. But well into this century, the United States was

still paying out pensions to the heirs of Civil War soldiers. We honor treaties that date back some 200 years, despite no one being alive who signed those treaties. Many of us would love to be taxed for the things we are solely and individually responsible for. But we are American citizens, and thus bound to a collective enterprise that extends beyond our individual and personal reach. It would seem ridiculous to dispute invocations of the Founders, or the Greatest Generation, on the basis of a lack of membership in either group. We recognize our lineage as a generational trust, as inheritance, and the real dilemma posed by reparations is just that: a dilemma of inheritance. It is impossible to imagine America without the inheritance of slavery.

As Coates proposes, these years are not as far removed from our own as they first appear: indeed, in the case of *Black Panther*, the unnamed elder of the mining tribe played by Connie Chiume was born in 1953, a year before the US Supreme Court ruled in the case *Brown v. Board of Education* that racial segregation in schools was unconstitutional and two years before the Rosa Parks bus boycott. And the unnamed elder of the merchant tribe, played by Dorothy Steel, was born on February 23, 1926, three years after the infamous Rosewood massacre of 1923 (a series of racially motivated murders and the destruction of a Black town in Levy County, Florida) and the year before the 30,000-strong KKK march on Washington in 1925, an era when African Americans were still being lynched in the US. When Dorothy Steel was born not only were former slaves still alive in the United States, but the last survivors of those Africans caught, captured, and brought to America on the slave vessel *Clotilda* in 1860 were too. The practice still continued even though importing slaves had been made illegal more than half a century before, in 1807, and in 1860, the *Clotilda*'s last voyage was to transport more than one hundred slaves from Benin, a place mentioned numerous times in *Black Panther*, to Mobile, Alabama. The ship never reached its final destination and was thought lost forever, but its wreck was recovered in 2019 (see Bourne Jr. 2019).

CHAPTER 4

"It's hard for a good man to be king"

T'Challa's Journey from Prince to King and Black Panther

You were wrong . . . all of you were wrong . . . to turn your backs on the rest of the world! We let the fear of discovery stop us from doing what is right. No more! I cannot stay here with you. I cannot rest while he sits on the throne! He is a monster of our own making! I must take the mantle back. I must! I must right these wrongs!

T'CHALLA, *Black Panther*

History, as nearly no one seems to know, is not merely something to be read. And it does not refer merely, or even principally, to the past. On the contrary, the great force of history comes from the fact that we carry it within us, are unconsciously controlled by it in many ways, and history is literally present in all that we do. It could scarcely be otherwise, since it is to history that we owe our frames of reference, our identities, and our aspirations.

JAMES BALDWIN, "The White Man's Guilt," *Ebony*, August 1965

I.

Prior to Killmonger's arrival and his defeat of T'Challa at the top of Warrior Falls, events described in the previous chapter, the film had explored some of the difficulties faced by T'Challa as the new king of Wakanda following the death of his father. The challenge that the film places at the center of its narrative, becoming key to T'Challa's development, is whether to continue the path taken by generations of rulers before him, keeping Wakanda isolated and hidden from the world, or to step out of the shadows and engage with other countries by informing them of Wakanda's extraordinary technological and economic prowess. It is a dilemma introduced as early as the film's prologue with the young N'Jadaka's question of "why?" and has involved perpetuating the lie that Wakanda is "one of the poorest countries in the world," as a BBC newsreader reports, known primarily for its "shepherds, textiles, cool outfits," according to Everett Ross. The case for both sides of this argument are offered in *Black Panther*, rather than a one-sided debate as we might expect, with most of the film's main characters providing their own point of view. Our previous chapter demonstrated N'Jadaka's position on the matter and his belief that, by refusing to intervene in the liberation of Black people all over the world, Wakandans had failed in their moral responsibility to those who share their ethnic background. His position, as we have seen, is a persuasive one, although how he proposed to act on it emerges as much more problematic. It is clear that his beliefs are also undoubtedly compromised by his sociopathic behavior, which saw audience members divided in their reactions to him: some argued that his plans for violent insurrection were morally reprehensible, some remained bound to his cause despite this, and others supported him wholeheartedly. It might be regarded as ironic that two of the most persuasive cases for Wakanda turning its back on tradition come from N'Jobu and N'Jadaka, two men we are asked to empathize with but see as morally compromised due to their actions in the film. Their reasons for advocating for Wakanda's intervention into world affairs are compelling, but how they envisage doing so proved to be a contentious issue for audiences.

Those who argue for the opposite in the film, that Wakanda should remain isolated, do so for numerous reasons, and they too are sincere in their beliefs. Their opinions are informed first and foremost by a respect for Wakandan traditions that reach back generations and the idea that Wakandan needs should come *before* others, in this case the global Black diaspora, and by the fear of what it might do to Wakandan society and culture if such a decision were made. As T'Challa told N'Jadaka in the throne room while his cousin was in handcuffs, "I am not king of all people, I am king of Wakanda!" This position has been handed down to him by his father and his ancestors, so to challenge this idea initially seems incomprehensible for the young king who has idealized everything about his father since he was a child. It should be remembered that T'Challa's ancestors are not distant, relegated to memory and fading photographs, but in accordance to African traditions, they continue to be venerated; in fact, T'Challa *even met them* when he visited the ancestral plane near the start of the film. It is for these reasons that he is understandably reluctant to deviate from millennia of tradition, as he informs Nakia: "We are not like these other countries . . . if the world found out what we truly are, what we possess, *we could lose our way of life*." In one of the film's deleted scenes included on the Blu-ray release, "Voices from the Past," which is set on the day of the events in Oakland in 1992, a young T'Chaka (Atandwa Kani) is shown returning to Wakanda and interacting with T'Challa as a boy in the City of the Dead. T'Chaka tells him, "I was forced to make a difficult choice today," referring either to the decision to kill his brother or to leave N'Jadaka in Oakland but one that T'Challa will only learn the truth about many years later. To this, T'Chaka's young son responds, "I'm sure you did what was right for Wakanda, *you always do*." In another deleted scene, "T'Challa Remembers his Father," T'Challa talks of T'Chaka as if he were a superhero, which he quite literally is, as he recalls to Zuri "My whole life I would watch him wearing the suit. He could pick up a grown man with one hand, run as fast as a zebra." T'Chaka's own death in the explosion in Vienna shown in *Captain America: Civil War* is also used as a justification for Wakanda continuing to follow its traditions, as evidence of what happens when they do choose to interact with the wider world directly. It is something that remains unsaid and is only implied in the film, but in the novelization T'Challa states it

While T'Chaka is dead before *Black Panther* begins, he casts a looming shadow over the film's narrative as fathers in the superhero genre often do.

explicitly: "Look what happened when my father extended his hand to the outside world. It cost him his life" (2018, 52).

More contemporary voices are shown to agree that Wakanda should continue its historical practice of remaining separate from the world, among them T'Challa's friend, bodyguard, and general Okoye, who is so deferential to Wakandan traditions that she does not oppose N'Jadaka's ascension to the throne at first because, according to Wakandan law, his challenge was a legal one. At the new king's first council meeting she argues against N'Jadaka's desire to intervene in global affairs by stating that "Wakanda has survived so long by fighting when it is only *absolutely necessary*. . . ." In this, she echoes an idea that T'Challa had suggested earlier that "waging war on other countries has *never* been our way." Her partner, W'Kabi, is also shown to be something of a traditionalist at the beginning of the film, but for a very different reason, when he tells T'Challa: "You let the refugees in, they bring their problems with them and then Wakanda is like everywhere else." During the same conversation, he had also remarked, "Now, if you said you wanted me and my men to go out there and clean up the world, *then* I would be all for it." It is this desire, alongside T'Challa's failure to bring back or kill Klaue, that motivates him to shift his allegiance from his childhood friend to N'Jadaka. He tells T'Chaka, "For thirty years your father was in power and he did nothing. With you, I thought it'd be different. But it's more of the same," and in the throne room emphasized his desire for a new way forward by concurring with N'Jadaka's decision to intervene with force around the world with the line: "Wakanda survived this way in the past yes, *but the world is changing....*"

On the other side of this debate, those arguing that Wakanda should turn its back on millennia of tradition and reveal itself to the world, also have a number of reasons for doing so, with each character arguing for a different form of intervention. First among them is Nakia, who has spent a good part of her life outside of Wakanda as a War Dog. She argues, "I've seen too many in need just to turn a blind eye. I can't be happy here knowing that there's people out there who have nothing." Her reasons are largely altruistic, understanding that Wakanda could do significant good in the world for those who need help and she even has a plan as to how this would work: "Share what we have, we could provide aid and access to technology to those who need it. Other countries do it, *we could do it better.*" She informs T'Challa of this during a stroll through the marketplace of Birnin Zana after his coronation as king. Yet, at that moment of his development, he cannot accept what she is saying as he has yet to have his view of Wakanda's place in the world challenged by the existence of N'Jadaka and the revelation about his father's actions in the past. Princess Shuri also advocates for a deviation from tradition in ways less explicit. She is the one, alongside Nakia, who appears most familiar and engaged with the outside world and is eager to refine, update, and develop rather than remain satisfied with all that had come before in the name of tradition. This is articulated in her very first appearance in the film when her brother returns in the Royal Talon Fighter from Nigeria with Nakia and Okoye. She tells him: "Just because something works doesn't mean that it cannot be improved!" She advocates a similar position all through the film, chafing at the traditional bone corset she is required to wear at the coronation, gleefully participating in the mission in South Korea, and then showing Ross around her laboratory after having saved his life using vibranium technology the CIA officer finds hard to believe exists.

T'Challa's journey between these two opposite positions might be seen to have begun even before the film had started, when he had agreed to provide shelter to Bucky Barnes at the conclusion

T'Challa receives advice from many concerning Wakanda's future: here the progressive Nakia argues for intervention in the wider world.

of *Captain America: Civil War* and allowed Steve Rogers to visit Wakanda in scenes included in the middle of the credits of the film. T'Challa's second moment of change is also prompted by an interaction with the wider world and an injured white American male in a sequence we have already observed in *Black Panther*: he decides to take a seriously wounded Everett Ross back to Wakanda in order to save his life. It is a decision challenged by the traditionalist Okoye ("This man is a foreign intelligence operative. How do we justify bringing him into our borders? . . . It is his duty to report back to his country") and supported by Nakia, the agent for change, who asks, "So now are we just supposed to let him die?" Okoye is right to comment on Ross's status and responsibilities as a CIA agent, but even though it appears that Wakandans have knowledge of the outside world in its diegetic frames, they do not seem to be wary of allowing an American governmental operative into their country, as they seem to exist in a world where the CIA has not intervened on the African continent on numerous occasions, often with disastrous consequences, throughout the twentieth century and into the twenty-first. Ultimately this decision, in the terms of the film's narrative, is revealed to be the correct one as Ross provides T'Challa with vital information about the man the CIA agent knows as Erik Stevens and later plays a key role in saving Wakanda in the climactic battle on Mount Bashenga at the conclusion of the film. Furthermore, Ross somewhat incredulously appears to keep Wakanda's secrets from his own government as T'Challa's announcement at the UN at the end of the film suggests.[1] Of all the film's speculative fictions, this one rooted in the real world might be considered as its most challenging, suggesting that the CIA and the country it represents, would not seek to profit from the information that Ross becomes party to. This narrative strain seems so disconnected from the real world that it is entirely logical to speculate about whether the CIA participated in the production of the film, even though multiple sources denied it (see Secker 2018).

Of course, it is when T'Challa learns about the truth of what happened on that day in Oakland 1992 that his long-held beliefs about his father and Wakanda are most tested. The very existence of N'Jadaka is a challenge to T'Challa's idealization of his father and his assumption that the traditional practices of Wakanda were both moral and geopolitically expedient. Up to that point, he had heard both sides of the argument from people he had trusted, but with this secret revealed his understanding of the world and Wakanda's place in it is fundamentally altered. Thus, N'Jadaka is a literal and metaphorical problem for what Wakanda has stood for and what it has come to represent for its citizens. This is why T'Challa tells Nakia, "My uncle N'Jobu betrayed us but my father, *he may have created something even worse*," with his description evoking the phenomenon Chalmers Johnson described as "blowback" in his *Blowback, the Costs and Consequences of Empire*, an idea that came to define many people's critical attitude to American foreign policy in the post-9/11 era, with the term meaning the unintended long-term consequences for past policy decisions. In this way, N'Jadaka/Erik Stevens is once again more than a character but also a symbol, a physical manifestation of blowback in a variety of ways: of T'Chaka's killing of N'Jobu, of his choice to leave the child alone in America, and of his decision to lie about it all in order to not compromise Wakanda's centuries-long political beliefs that he has spent his whole life protecting and advocating.

As it is clear to see and as was very frequently pointed out by audiences and writers, T'Challa's debate about the future of

Wakanda is one with very real associations to the world beyond its fictional frames and indeed was one being discussed in many countries around the globe, not just the United States, with a particular vibrancy in the second decade of the new millennium while the film was in pre-production, through production, and into release. In the case of America, this debate is one with a rich history but was brought into startling focus throughout 2016 during the presidential election campaign when it emerged as one of its central issues. One of the reasons that Donald Trump resonated with voters was because he advocated for an "America First" policy supported by the assertion that America had become a laughingstock in geopolitical affairs under the Obama administration, taken advantage of all over the globe by ally and enemy alike, and that if he were to become president, this would come to an end, a series of ideas manifested in the defining slogan of the election and Trump's subsequent administration, "Make America Great Again," shortened by many to "MAGA" (see Herbert, McCrisken, and Wroe 2019). It was for these reasons that some saw aspects of what would come to be referred to as the "Trump doctrine" in *Black Panther*, an idea which we will return to later in the book.

II.

Having had his worldview so thoroughly challenged by the existence of N'Jadaka and having been defeated by him in the ceremonial ritual combat as we saw in the previous chapter, T'Challa is thought dead by both those who love and hate him. However, the film reveals that he miraculously survived being thrown from the top of Warrior Falls and was rescued by members of the Jabari tribe, who then shelter him. T'Challa's mother, sister, Nakia, and Ross are unaware of this when they visit the Jabari in order to ask M'Baku for assistance against N'Jadaka, with Nakia even offering him the sole remaining heart-shaped herb, which would have enabled the Jabari chief to achieve that which he was shown to desire near the film's beginning, the throne of Wakanda. Yet M'Baku refuses, having come to respect T'Challa (whom he had once described as "just a boy not fit to lead"). M'Baku points out to Ramonda and Shuri that what happened to T'Challa "was less a murder than a defeat" as N'Jadaka's challenge was a legitimate one, the second person to do so after Okoye reluctantly observed the same, remarking, "I am loyal to the throne *no matter who sits upon it*." Yet the film cannot bring itself to criticize such an archaic and disingenuous political practice, nor does it suggest explicitly that Wakanda is anything less than a utopia at any time in the film.

Instead of taking them up on their offer, M'Baku leads them to a seriously wounded T'Challa, who they give the heart-shaped herb to, leading him to return once again to the ancestral plane for a final time and a very different interaction with his father and his ancestors to the one at the start of the film. This time T'Challa is not shown emerging from the red earth, as earlier, nor does he kneel respectfully at his father's feet; instead, he is shown standing straight away and facing the great acacia tree he had previously seen his ancestors in. He slowly turns to face his father, and behind T'Chaka one can see many of his ancestors all wearing clothes from the different tribes of Wakanda. It appears they are there to welcome T'Challa into the afterlife forever as his father says, "The time has come for you to come home and be reunited with me." T'Challa does not greet T'Chaka, but instead begins with a single question in Xhosa/Wakandan, the same one a young N'Jadaka asked in the film's prologue: "Why?" The expression on his father's face changes as T'Challa passionately questions him, saying, "Why didn't you bring the boy home? Why, Baba?" T'Chaka responds only by saying, "He was the truth I chose to omit," which is very close to Zuri's assertion that "we had to maintain the lie." T'Challa continues his challenge of his father in ways he had never done while the revered patriarch was alive: "You were *wrong* to abandon him." T'Chaka attempts to defend his choice by explaining, "I chose my people, I chose Wakanda. Our future depended . . ." but he is interrupted by T'Challa with Chadwick Boseman's most emotional line reading of the entire film and a significant turning point for his character: "You were wrong . . . *all of you were*

"You were wrong! All of you were wrong!": T'Challa and his final visit to the ancestral plane.

wrong!" To raise one's voice at elders in African traditional culture is a great taboo, but he does it here, even shaking with intensity as a single tear is shown dripping down his face in a similar way we had seen N'Jadaka cry when he met his father in the ancestral plane. T'Challa continues:

> All of you were wrong . . . to turn your backs on the rest of the world! We let the fear of discovery stop us from doing what is right. No more! I cannot stay here with you. I cannot rest while he sits on the throne! He is a *monster of our own making*!

The phrase "monster of our own making" is an interesting, malleable, and potent one, used in a variety of contexts over the years, but is worth highlighting as relevant to the discourse surrounding *Black Panther* in two of its variations. Its most frequent use is in a post-colonial context and is similar to the term "blowback," as suggested by Chalmers Johnson earlier in this chapter. It was also frequently applied to Donald Trump during the 2016 presidential election campaign, which was ongoing as *Black Panther* was in production. In this use of the phrase, the "our" tended to be applied to the excessive media coverage that was provided to Trump at the expense of those who ran against him, whether his Republican opponents in the primaries or ultimately Hillary Clinton, the Democratic nominee (see Chuang 2016; Kendzior 2016).[2]

III.

The stage is then set for the film's extended climax, which, as the genre has historically demanded, consists of an extended fight scene between those on the side of the protagonist and those on the side of the antagonist. As much as *Black Panther* has deviated in some compelling ways from the codes and conventions of the superhero film, in this way it does not. The sequence is designed to provide that which audiences have come to demand from contemporary iterations of the genre—spectacularly orchestrated action—and at the same time it brings the film's thematic motifs together in ways in which the superhero film has rarely been able to do. The battle between T'Challa and N'Jadaka is not only to see who is the strongest, but is also informed by their personal histories and rival ideologies, only comparable perhaps to the fight between Captain America and Tony Stark at the end of *Captain America: Civil War*, where the stakes were similarly personal. However, in the case of *Black Panther*, the two combatants are not only fighting to kill each other but also to decide the future of Wakanda.

It is at this moment that the film now has two people who might correctly be considered as the Black Panther, both T'Challa and N'Jadaka, with the former having lost his privileged position but retained his suit, and the latter now sitting on the throne of Wakanda possessing a new suit of his own. N'Jadaka's directive to W'Kabi has been to send vibranium weapons to his War Dogs in order to facilitate an uprising by arming "oppressed people all over the world"— initially, we are told, in London, New York, and Hong Kong.[3] Fittingly the climax of the film takes place on and later inside Mount Bashenga, where the meteor had struck Wakanda millions of years before, the place where vibranium is mined and where Shuri has her laboratory deep underground. N'Jadaka appears to be a legitimate king to those around him, as they and he believe that T'Challa was killed during the ceremony, but when he appears on the horizon, demanding that the challenge is not yet over, N'Jadaka refuses with the line: "All that challenge shit is over with!" N'Jadaka brushes tradition aside as he was only interested in the rules when they suited him, something we might also say about T'Challa himself and his family, whether that might be T'Chaka's signing of the Sokovia Accords while his son was performing secret missions as the Black Panther all over the world, or Shuri and Ramonda seeking to dethrone N'Jadaka after T'Challa was lawfully defeated in ritual combat. W'Kabi also knows that the challenge is not yet over, but he ignores this too as he has cast his lot in with N'Jadaka against his childhood friend and also his partner, Okoye.

While *Black Panther* has asked us on numerous occasions to compare T'Challa and N'Jadaka, it has also asked us to consider how their behavior and actions are different, and there can be no doubt that the film *expects us* to side with T'Challa. In this scene, they both are shown wearing Black Panther suits, but their sartorial choices become reflective of their own character. T'Challa's suit is the one we have seen him in before, a balance between tradition and innovation, very similar to the one his father has worn for decades, but with more modern elements added by his sister, who retrieved the suit and handed it back to him in M'Baku's throne room. N'Jadaka's is flashier and brighter with gold a prominent part of its design (it is referred to in the script as "gaudier" [2018, 36]) and it is the one that T'Challa had declined to use much earlier in the film with the remark, "Tempting, but the idea is to *not* be noticed." Perhaps for the very same reason N'Jadaka has chosen it himself, as, unlike T'Chaka, he wants to be seen, recognized, and most importantly, acknowledged.

It is N'Jadaka's refusal of T'Challa's legitimate claim that prompts Okoye to finally turn against him. By refusing to go along with it, he has broken Wakandan law and now is not a legitimate king but instead a usurper, and she rallies the Dora Milaje who instantly form around her, but her partner's men, those of the Border tribe, follow W'Kabi and fight against both the Dora Milaje and T'Challa himself. Okoye confronts N'Jadaka, telling him, "Your heart is so full of *hatred*, you are not fit to be king," as he takes on several of the Dora Milaje, fighting against women in what we have seen as a pattern in his behavior until now. He even kills one by cutting her throat,

The climax of *Black Panther* on Mount Bashenga: N'Jadaka is ready for war.

his face revealing a real sense of pleasure, to which Okoye cries out simultaneously in an expression of rage and grief.

It is then that the film separates into three parallel contemporaneous actions:

a. On the surface of the mountain, the battle continues between W'Kabi's men (assisted later by their giant war rhinoceroses) against the Dora Milaje and the Jabari who arrive to join even though M'Baku had indicated he would not participate, with their chief exclaiming, "Witness the might of the Jabari firsthand!"

b. Underneath the mountain, Shuri has tasked Ross with using a remote-controlled jet to target the three Wakandan aircrafts, known as Dragonflyers, taking the vibranium weapons abroad to London, New York, and Hong Kong. She tells him, "I've made it American style for you.... We can't let those weapons get beyond Wakanda." Ross here is instrumental in securing the future of Wakanda and even the world, in a sequence that situates him quite clearly as a drone pilot. The scene plays out as a thrilling one with the clock ticking against Ross as he tries to complete his mission, but has problematic associations, given the real-world context of the devastation American drone technology has wrought in the last decade in Africa and the Middle East, something that is rarely discussed in the western media. In an article in the *Institute of Security Studies*, "Drone Strikes a Growing Threat to African Civilians," Zachary Donnenfeld argued that the escalation of drone use on the continent and in war zones in the Middle East during the period between January 2004 and July 2019 resulted in a policy that "violates human rights and other international norms" (2019), and according to the Bureau of Investigative Journalism, a minimum of 6,786 American drone strikes killed anywhere between 8,459 and 12,105 people, a thousand of which were confirmed to be civilians, between 253 and 397 children, in operations in Somalia, Yemen, Afghanistan, and Pakistan.[4] As Ross's personal battle continues, he risks his life even further when his control pod is targeted directly by one of N'Jadaka's other aircraft, but instead of leaving he chooses to potentially sacrifice himself by remaining in his seat.

c. Finally, in the film's most important narrative strain, T'Challa and N'Jadaka come face to face in a battle inside the mountain. They find themselves on the magnetic railway tracks that can be turned on and off to ensure vibranium is safe as it is unstable at high speeds in its unrefined form.

As one might expect, the film ends its final battle with those on the side of the protagonist victorious: Okoye, M'Baku, and the Dora Milaje defeat the Border tribe, with its final moment coming when W'Kabi tries to kill M'Baku by riding his giant rhinoceros into him only to see it abruptly stop when Okoye steps in the way. W'Kabi asks his partner, "Would you kill me, my love?" to which she replies, "For Wakanda, *without question*," leading him to drop his weapon on the floor. Ross also completes his mission, destroying the three rogue aircraft moments before his own control pod is blown up, but he escapes safely. Inside the mountain it is the fight between the two cousins that provides the film with its dramatic and emotional climax. N'Jadaka's rage is still present throughout the scene as he finally reveals what has been driving him in the twenty-five years since the murder of his father in Oakland, something that we

The clash between T'Challa and N'Jadaka is more than a physical one; it is also one of contrasting ideologies.

have suspected but never heard him openly articulate: "The world took everything away from me, everything I ever loved! But I'mma make sure *we're* even." This personal note projects everything he has experienced onto T'Challa, with his cousin's life of privilege, security, and belonging representative of all that could have been N'Jadaka's but was taken away from him without explanation in 1992. He has indicated that he sought a revolution and liberation for those around the world, but this is revealed to be secondary to his desire for revenge over those he feels have done him wrong. While the action is initially dominated by the two figures being rendered in CGI as was often the case in Phase One of the Marvel Cinematic Universe, Coogler and Cole wisely have the magnetic railway strip them of parts of their vibranium suits, including their masks, allowing the audience to see the human beings inside. In most films in the genre, the final battle between protagonist and antagonist tends to be a simple one, with audiences asked to unambiguously cheer for the former over the latter. Who would support the Vulture instead of Spider-Man at the end of *Spider-Man: Far from Home*, or Orm Marius (Ocean Master) instead of Arthur Curry (Aquaman) at the end of *Aquaman*? Yet, as we have seen, many felt so much sympathy for N'Jadaka that they wanted to see him prevail against his cousin, the film's ostensible, eponymous heroic protagonist.

Just as the genre demands that the film ends in an extended violent battle, it also requires that the protagonist, the person who the film is named after, emerges victorious, as T'Challa ultimately does. Although T'Challa had been defeated by N'Jadaka a few days before when the stakes were just as high, this time he seems to have a greater awareness of his position in the world and uses his cousin's anger against him in ways he was not able to do before. At the climax of their fight, he plunges a vibranium spear into N'Jadaka's chest in a way not too far removed from how his father had killed N'Jobu back in 1992. It is only in the moments after, as N'Jadaka knows that he has lost and is dying, that he lets his guard down for perhaps only the second time in the film (the first comes during his brief visit to the ancestral plane and the solitary tear shed during his conversation with his father). Jordan plays N'Jadaka as suddenly cognizant of everything around him, as if recognizing where he is and what he has done for the first time. He tells T'Challa, "My pops said Wakanda was the most beautiful thing he had ever seen," but it is a place he had failed to appreciate or even see in any meaningful way until now, overwhelmed as he had been by his rage and his decades long quest for revenge. He recalls that his father "promised me that he was going to show it to me one day. . . . You believe that? A kid from Oakland running around believing in fairy tales." N'Jadaka's pain, as conveyed by Jordan's performance in this scene, is shown as being not only from the wound in his chest, which will ultimately kill him, but also an emotional one. In response T'Challa carries his dying cousin to the surface of the mountain, offering a sense of conciliation as he has often been shown to do, revealing to him the Wakandan sunset N'Jobu once talked of. At this moment, the two cousins are able to find a moment of connection that the film had not allowed them to have before, as it is a genre which rarely embraces the complexities of human emotions, even though *Black Panther* has sought to do more than most in this way.

T'Challa then offers to use Wakandan technology to save him as it saved another American, Everett Ross, but N'Jadaka refuses with the film's most resonant line of dialogue: "Just bury me in the ocean with my ancestors that jumped from the ships, 'cause they knew death was better than bondage." It was this line that became the film's most-discussed, with Matthew Teutsch calling it one that "essentially sums up the entire traumatic and violent history of the

The final thing N'Jadaka sees before his death is the Wakandan sunset his father spoke of.

slave trade in one line" (2018), and Jayson Dawkins saying, "That's a line you expect from *Roots* [ABC, 1977] or *12 Years a Slave* [2013], not Marvel" (2018). It is a line that certainly connects the present and the past, the real world and the fictional, in the same striking way that *Black Panther* has emphatically done throughout the course of its narrative.

The sunset is also significant as N'Jobu promised his son that "the sunsets there are the most beautiful in the world." Here it is the last thing N'Jadaka will ever see, and all he can say is "*It's beautiful,*" with Jordan's line reading playing as if he is agreeing with his long dead father. The soundtrack at this moment returns to the Baba Maal song that was heard playing over the sunrise two hours of screen time earlier when T'Challa, Nakia, and Okoye returned to Wakanda. When it was first played it was thematically connected to the death of king T'Chaka, but here N'Jadaka is provided with the same privilege although whether he is king or what name it would be right to call him by at this moment is hard to discern. One might also ask: Where will N'Jadaka's place in the ancestral realm be? Will he go back to his father and remain confined in the claustrophobic Oakland tenement with purple skies seen only through the windows? Or might his father now be reunited with his own ancestors? However, it is hard to imagine N'Jadaka, after all the film has asked him to do, on the veldt with his uncle T'Chaka, although maybe in the afterlife the three of them might be able to find a sense of forgiveness and reconciliation they were unable to while they were alive.[5]

In later scenes which we will return to in the conclusion to this book, we will hear that T'Challa has changed his mind about the direction Wakanda will take in the future and that he will seek to engage with the world in ways very different to that which his father and his ancestors had done. We have seen how he has heard from many of those around him expressing their opinion of how Wakanda should behave, but it is clear that none of them have had as much of an influence on him as N'Jadaka has. Which antagonist in the superhero genre has ever had such an impact on a protagonist and his worldview? Was Batman and his worldview ever changed in such a way by the Joker, Bane, or Ra's Al Ghul? Superman by Lex Luthor, Zod, or Doomsday? Tony Stark by the Mandarin, Obadiah Stane, or Ultron? If anything, the opposite tends to be true, with the superhero's ideology *reinforced* by the actions of the antagonists they find themselves pitted against. N'Jadaka's very existence, his experiences, his argument, and his actions, as flawed as they are, prompt T'Challa to reconsider how Wakanda will deal with the world during his reign as king and Black Panther.

CHAPTER 5

The Women of *Black Panther*

Transcending the Disappointments of the MCU

Words can't even describe what this movie has meant to me and other black people . . . and I know this is for you Chadwick [Boseman], but I wanted to take a second to thank the black women [in the film] too, because they were so strong on their own terms and answered to no one but themselves. . . . I think that is so important. they weren't strong because they were angry, they weren't strong because they were hurt, they were strong because they were strong and that meant the world to me, so thank you . . . Wakanda forever!

UNNAMED WOMAN FEATURED ON *THE TONIGHT SHOW STARRING JIMMY FALLON* **(NBC,** 2014–), February 28, 2018 (episode no. 823)

Despite many cultural advances over the last fifty years, Black women in the media, especially within the superhero genre, are still constructed as exotic sexual spectacles, as erotic racial "Others." In contrast to the dominant model of male heroes, and in distinction to non-ethnically identified female characters in the comics, Black superheroines are often presented as hypersexual and metaphorically bestial. Moreover, popular Black superheroines like Storm, Vixen, Pantha, and the Black Panther are explicitly associated with exoticized notions of Africa, nature, noble savagery and a variety of Dark Continent themes, including voodoo, mysticism, and animal totemism.

JEFFREY A. BROWN, "Panthers and Vixens: Black Superheroines, Sexuality, and Stereotypes in Contemporary Comic Books" (2013, 134)

I.

Much of the reception of *Black Panther* and the debates that it inspired were understandably connected to its groundbreaking representation of ethnicity, both inside the superhero genre and in mainstream Hollywood film as a whole. As this book has explored over the last four chapters, it was the first superhero film to feature a Black protagonist in the MCU specifically and the first in the genre more generally since *Hancock*, almost exactly ten years before. What was not considered anywhere as frequently was the film's representation of gender. The year after the release of *Black Panther*, *Captain Marvel*, the MCU's twenty-first film, was another important landmark for the series, the first to have a lead female protagonist with her name in the title and a female (co-) director, Anna Boden. Prior to this there had been a number of female superheroes (Gamora, Scarlett Witch, Black Widow, etc.), but they were all undoubtedly secondary characters by quite some margin and were commonly defined by their vulnerability, whether that is physically, psychologically, or emotionally, in ways that male characters very rarely, if ever, are. So the comic book incarnation of Gamora might have been referred to as "the deadliest woman in the galaxy," but she is saved by Peter Quill at various points throughout *Guardians of the Galaxy* and *Guardians of the Galaxy: Vol. 2*, and the film is, without a doubt, his story and not hers. The same is true for Black Widow and Scarlett Witch, both compelling characters but neither deemed worthy of their own story until *Black Widow* (2021), the twenty-fourth film in the franchise, and *WandaVision* (Disney+, 2021–), one of the early MCU television shows featured on Disney's streaming service known as Disney+, . The previous appearances of Black Widow and Scarlett Witch had been criticized for how they had been pushed to the margins of the narrative, lacked agency, and had powers characterized as specifically "female" that are even encoded into their names (see Ginn 2017). In *Age of Ultron*, Scarlett Witch, who might well have been the most powerful of all the Avengers until the arrival of Captain Marvel, experiences something of an emotional breakdown during the Battle of Sokovia, prompting Hawkeye, a man whose greatest skill is to fire arrows accurately (at that time the franchise's only superhero identified as a parent), to respond "I can't do my job *and* babysit!" Until 2021, despite a layered performance by Scarlett Johansson throughout the series, Black Widow was never afforded the priority given to the likes of Captain America and Iron Man, or even Thor or the Incredible Hulk, each of whom were given their own film (or films) as early as Phase One of the franchise (2008–2012).

Outside of superheroes, female characters like Jane Foster, Betty Ross, Christine Palmer, and Pepper Potts found themselves marginalized even further. They are all given what seem to be important professions (astrophysicist, cellular biologist, emergency surgeon, and CEO), but they tend to function only for what they can offer the man who is at the center of the narrative and whose name is, more often than not, also the title of the film. As in most mainstream blockbusters, the women featured in superhero films are either victims to be saved or rewards for the heroism of their men, most often at the very same time. When both Jane Foster and Pepper Potts are accidentally given powers in the course of *Thor: The Dark World* and *Iron Man 3*, respectively, the idea is something seemingly so inappropriate that they are depicted as having to be removed almost immediately *in order to save them* by the film's hero. In this way, we can observe that the MCU promotes a superficial level of female empowerment at the same time as it participates in their marginalization and objectification, thus functioning as a reification of heteronormative patriarchal culture and its values.

What is being observed here is not anecdotal, even if it seems to be, but rather empirical, as many studies conducted by individuals and organizations have observed, the most prominent of which are those undertaken by the Media, Diversity, and Social Change Initiative at USC Annenberg (School for Communication and Journalism), the Geena Davis Institute on Gender in Media, and the Center for the Study of Women in Television and Film. In 2018, the USC Annenberg study covering the period between 2007–2017 reported that only 31.7 percent of speaking characters

The complicated "girl power" shot in *Avengers: Endgame*: inspirational or patronizing?

across the top 1,100 films were women (2014 was the worst year at 28.1 percent), with 70.7 percent of all characters featured being white, 12.1 percent black, and 6.2 percent Asian. At the same time only 7.3 percent of the same films were directed by women, 10.1 percent written by women, and 21.7 percent produced by women. Furthermore, Dr. Smith commented that "women of color are nearly invisible in film production—whether as directors, producers, or in below-the-line crew positions."

With this disconcerting context provided we are free to explore the women of *Black Panther*, primarily those in front of the camera, but also "behind" it as well, that is those involved in its production, like Hannah Beachler, the film's production designer who had worked with Coogler on both his previous films *Fruitvale Station* and *Creed*, but also on *Moonlight, Miles Ahead* and Beyoncé's iconic music video for the song "Lemonade" (2016). We have noted her contribution to the creation of the world of Wakanda on numerous occasions even though we might not have always used her name and *Black Panther* saw her become the first African American to win an Academy Award for Production Design. She also collected similar accolades from the Art Directors Guild, the Saturn Awards, the Black Reel Awards, and a variety of other organizations. The same can be said for the film's costume designer, Ruth E. Carter, who also won an Academy Award for her work on *Black Panther* and the prestigious Costume Designers Guild Award. The person responsible for putting the remarkable designs created by Beachler and Carter on film was also a woman, director of photography Rachel Morrison, one of only a few to be working on projects of such scale in the contemporary American film industry. Morrison also worked on *Fruitvale Station* and was nominated for an Academy Award for her work on Dee Rees's *Mudbound* in the previous year, the first time a woman had ever been nominated in the category since its inaugural ceremony in 1927–28. Morrison was the first female director of photography across the MCU and one of only four percent of female DoPs in the top-grossing films of the year in 2018.

Moving in front of the camera, *Black Panther* has several female characters of note that we have touched on in the course of this book, each of which are worth returning to in more detail: Shuri, T'Challa's sister and Wakanda's tech genius, described by the Russo brothers as "the smartest person in the Marvel Universe" in a video interview with *Wired* in August 2018; Nakia, T'Challa's former lover but never defined by the film only as that, a strong and formidable spy and individual in her own right; Okoye, commander of the Dora Milaje, general, the king's bodyguard, and close friend to T'Challa since childhood; and the wise matriarchal figure of Ramonda, the queen of Wakanda, wife of T'Chaka, and mother of T'Challa and Shuri. These are four of the film's main characters, each of whom are all female, and between them, they occupy a significant amount of screen time, but *Black Panther* has several other women that play less prominent roles who each have lines of dialogue, among them Ayo (Florence Kasumba), another Dora Milaje guard present in many of the film's key scenes (and had also appeared in *Captain America: Civil War*), the unnamed elder of the mining tribe (Connie Chiume), and the unnamed elder of the merchant tribe (Dorothy Steel) who has a few memorable lines in the film, one being in the throne room before T'Challa goes to apprehend Klaue in South Korea when she tells him, "Wakanda does not need a warrior right now, we need a king!" Additionally, there are N'Jadaka's girlfriend, Linda (Nabiyah

Be), who is shot by him in a junkyard somewhere in England and the high shaman (Sope Aluko) in charge of the cultivation of the heart-shaped herb who is assaulted by N'Jadaka and ordered to "burn 'em all" by her new king.[1] All of these characters are not simply women but Black women, a group that has found itself rarely portrayed in the MCU and in mainstream American cinema more generally.

In case having these nine female speaking roles, four of which could be categorized as main characters, does not seem of any particular significance, a comparison to a few other films from the MCU should be offered by way of context. We might ask of them the seemingly innocuous question, "How many women characters do they feature, what do they do in the film, and how often do they speak?" However, the answers are as surprising as they are disappointing. In *Thor* only six women speak: Jane, Darcy, Sif, Frigga, and two unnamed nurses; in *Iron Man* eight women speak and only five of these are named Pepper, Christine Everheart, Ramirez (the soldier in the Humvee at the start), and two television news-readers, real-life Zoriana Kit and fictional Amira Ahmed (the three others are two stewardesses and a mother in Gulmira); and in *Captain America: The First Avenger* there are only two women who are even named onscreen, Agent Peggy Carter and Mandy, a girl at the World of Tomorrow exhibition who does not speak a single line of dialogue. Across the 112-minute running time of *The Incredible Hulk* only five female characters speak and just three of those are named in the credits: Betty Ross, Martina, Major Kathleen Sparr, an unnamed woman selling clothes in the market, and an unnamed newsreader. Of these five characters only one, Betty Ross, has anything meaningful to do in the film and even she is an example of the girlfriend/damsel in distress stereotype we observed earlier in this chapter.

These examples detailed above are not carefully selected but very much the norm for films of the genre and of mainstream Hollywood blockbusters in general, even though we live in an age that is widely understood as one in which diversity is to be found onscreen more than ever. Thus, the achievements of *Black Panther* are considerable for these reasons as well as the others we have previously considered.

The prominent roles afforded to females in the film also resonate with contemporary cultural discourse pertaining to issues of identity and representation of Black women, both in film and out of it, such as what has become referred to as "Black Girl Magic," a term originated by CaShawn Thompson in 2013 in order to "to celebrate the beauty, power, and resilience of Black women" (Wilson 2016; see also Thomas 2015), or challenging reductive stereotypes of African American and African women perpetuated in American popular culture (see Salami 2019; Allen 2019).

Yet it is not just the *frequency* that is important here, but also how these characters are portrayed in the context of the scenes in which they feature and how they were understood and received by audiences. Prior to *Black Panther* there had been only a few female Black characters of note in the MCU and not a single one in any of the films mentioned above. In Phase Three, this situation improved, if only slightly, with the appearances of the compelling figure of Valkyrie (Tessa Thompson) in *Thor: Ragnarok* and MJ (Zendaya) in *Spider-Man: Homecoming*.[2] In the epigraph to this chapter, Jeffrey Brown's assertion is a powerful one that primarily refers to comic book representations of Black women, but is just as applicable to how they have been portrayed in the superhero film since *Superman* (1978), where even if they did appear it was often as an erotic racial Other or a character on the fringes of the narrative, sometimes both at the same time (see Storm or Angel Salvadore in the *X-Men* franchise). While Nakia, Okoye, and Shuri are not the protagonists of *Black Panther* in the way that T'Challa is, they are rare examples of women in the genre that are

a. not exclusively defined by their relationships with the men around them
b. not characterized by their physical or emotional vulnerability
c. not passive figures rescued by the male superheroes
d. not overtly sexualized by their costumes and actions

Indeed, they are, at least in the cases of Nakia, Okoye, and Shuri, arguably important characters who propel the narrative of *Black*

Panther forward in several key moments in ways seldom offered to women and certainly not Black females in American cinema.

II.

The character of Nakia, played by Academy Award-winning actress Lupita Nyong'o, a Mexican-born performer of Kenyan parentage, is introduced to us within the first ten minutes of the film in Nigeria where she has been on a mission to, it seems, infiltrate or confront the group the film codes as Boko Harem but refers to only as militants. When T'Challa arrives and attacks the men, Nakia informs him rather brusquely, "You've ruined my mission!" It is clear that this is not Nakia's first time in the field; rather, she is an accomplished War Dog with a history of many assignments, implied or alluded to in a number of ways, from her fluency in Korean revealed in Busan to a mention of a "*disagreement* with some ivory traders" and her assertion to T'Challa, while strolling through the streets of Birnin Zana, that "I've found my calling out there. I've seen too many in need just to turn a blind eye." It is clear from this opening sequence that she is far removed from the damsel-in-distress stereotype or even the modern variations of it offered by the MCU in Phases One and Two of the Infinity Saga like Pepper Potts, Jane Foster, Betty Ross, and Christine Palmer, characters who are provided with a superficial veneer of independence and agency but have no real life outside of the relationships with the male superheroes with whom they are partnered. In fact, she is much closer to a superhero in her own right than the stereotypical girlfriends that the MCU and the superhero genre as a whole has been historically populated with. She is also coded from the start as being more progressive than T'Challa, the film's protagonist, as Marlene D. Allen writes: "From the moment we first see her, Nakia is working not only in the interests of Wakanda, but of the African diaspora as a whole" (2018, 21), an approach that T'Challa will eventually come around to himself after two hours of screen time, but one which she articulates quite clearly in the above scene in Birnin Zana and can even be seen to

Nakia and T'Challa in the casino in Busan, South Korea.

embody from her first appearance in Nigeria. She provides T'Challa with wise counsel on numerous occasions, and while it seems like N'Jadaka has the biggest influence on his final decision to depart from centuries of isolationism, it is clear that she plays a substantial role in this too, even though the film does not acknowledge this as emphatically as it might have done.[3]

When T'Challa arrives in Nigeria, rather than be delighted to see her former partner she is irritated with him and even strikes him in the chest with a powerful kick, telling him that not only has he compromised the mission but that the "militant" he was about to hit is "just a boy," challenging the actions and judgement of the film's hero in ways love interests infrequently do in the genre. We might compare her to Gamora in *Guardians of the Galaxy*, who also challenges the film's hero, Peter Quill, on numerous occasions about his habits and attitudes, but unlike Gamora, Nakia is not rescued on a single occasion by T'Challa; in actual fact, she rescues him (and his family) more than once. She performs several acts of narrative importance in *Black Panther* which arguably secure the future stability of Wakanda: she saves Ramonda and Shuri after N'Jadaka wins the ceremonial fight at the waterfall by leading them away quickly, she is the one who infiltrates the City of the Dead and retrieves what might be the last heart-shaped herb before N'Jadaka orders them all to be burned (which she also refuses to take herself when offered by Ramonda), she fights bravely at the film's climax on Mount Bashenga, and is tasked by T'Challa as having a central role in T'Challa's new vision for the future of Wakanda in a scene which we will consider in the conclusion of this book.

She is initially seen wearing a hijab in the traditional clothes of the Nigerian Chibok women, then later in her River tribe ceremonial costume at Warrior Falls, before changing her clothes regularly throughout the film, but she is never shown wearing revealing or what might be considered as overtly sexualized clothes, nor is she presented as a sex object for display in the way Black Widow was introduced in *Iron Man 2*, being ogled at by Tony Stark in her underwear followed by a scene of her changing her clothes, or the skimpily dressed flight attendants dancing around poles on Tony Stark's private plane in *Iron Man*. Nakia's own sartorial choices, in outfits designed by Ruth E. Carter, are always interesting and very often reflective of her character or the film's themes, like the elegant green dress she wears in South Korea inscribed with traditional Wakandan symbols (which when combined with T'Challa's black suit and Okoye's red dress formed the colors of the Pan-African flag) or at the film's climax on Mount Bashenga, when Shuri tells her to put on the armor of the Dora Milaje, but she is reluctant to do so. In what might be a throwaway moment, Coogler alludes to a life outside of the screen and choices we have not seen or been party to.

Nakia is T'Challa's love interest in *Black Panther*, and they share a kiss at the film's end, but she is not a conventional one the likes of which the genre has traditionally put on the screen. What is not clear is whether this is evidence of Coogler and Cole's own interests and perspectives, or them reacting quite consciously to contemporary developments in the real world and an awareness that perhaps audiences by 2018 were demanding more from female characters than they had in 2008, the year the MCU released *Iron Man* and *The Incredible Hulk*. By 2018, the superhero film featured female characters as leads or co-leads in *Incredibles 2* and *Ant-Man and the Wasp*, plus dynamic female superheroes in Spider-Gwen in *Spider-Man: Into the Spider-Verse* and Meera in *Aquaman*. There is an awareness of this in the script, as in when T'Challa tells Nakia, "If you were not so stubborn you would make a good queen," to which she replies, "I would make a great queen *because* I am so stubborn. . . . If that is what I wanted." Nowhere is this more evident than in the extended fight sequence and chase scene in Busan, South Korea, which affords the women almost equal prominence to the film's eponymous protagonist. What other superhero film has a fight sequence with three characters, two of which are women, that leaves the male hero momentarily incapacitated as the women proceed with their mission together, one of them (Okoye) remarking, "He'll catch up!"? The Busan sequence is certainly Coogler's homage to James Bond, and as we saw, he envisioned T'Challa as a Bondian figure, but Nakia fills this role in just as many ways, especially considering that of the two she is the one who is *actually* a spy. The film's producer, Nate Moore, even remarked, "She really is their James Bond to some degree" (quoted in Roussos 2018, 172), as did Coogler himself when he said, "We saw Nakia as being a spy, being craftier and grittier and grimier, kind of like Daniel Craig's James Bond" (quoted in Pearson 2018). Those involved with films often make remarks like this about their female characters, which frequently have no real substance to them. Take, for example, those included in the director's commentary for *Thor: The Dark World*, on which director Alan Taylor mistakenly suggests about Jane Foster, "Natalie's character brings something fresh to a female heroine in the picture" or Simon Kinberg's egregious categorization of *Dark Phoenix* as "a feminist movie" and "a reflection of the shift we are experiencing all around us, [the film] is a celebration of that" (quoted in Nikolov 2019). Yet, in the case of Nakia and *Black Panther*, many of them, including those of Moore and Coogler reproduced above, have merit.[4] However, whether it is true that, as Evette Dionne argued, it was not T'Challa who should be considered as the hero of *Black Panther*, but actually Nakia who "is the real revolutionary" (2018), is up to audiences to decide.

One might suggest it could be the fact that Lupita Nyong'o's profile as an Academy Award-winning actress (for her performance as Patsey in Steve McQueen's *12 Years a Slave* [2013]) prompted the screenwriters to give her a character worth her time, but this has not always been the case (see Natalie Portman's role as Jane Foster and Gwyneth Paltrow's as Pepper Potts, both of whom have won an Academy Award, for *Black Swan* [2010] and *Shakespeare in Love* [1998], respectively). Steven Thrasher maintained that it was "wonderful to see Lupita Nyong'o as Nakia not in bondage as she was in *12 Years a Slave*, nor hidden inside of the CGI character Maz Kanata in the recent Star Wars films [2015–2019]. Instead, we are treated to Nyong'o in her full beauty as a mighty, intelligent warrior and, so terribly rare for a dark-skinned woman in a Hollywood film, as the love interest of the title character" (2018). Thrasher's comments about the rarity of such a characterization in the superhero film are entirely correct as Nakia manages to transcend the genre's history of offering women limited roles defined only by their relationships to men and instead in *Black Panther* playing a dynamic, engaging, and progressive figure who emerges as more compelling than the film's titular hero in a variety of ways.

III.

The second most prominent female character in the film is Okoye, played by Danai Gurira, an American actress of Zimbabwean descent who made her name in a similarly action-oriented role as Michonne in *The Walking Dead* (AMC, 2012–). Okoye also makes an important contribution to *Black Panther*, afforded just as much screen time as Nakia in another characterization rare in the genre for a number of reasons. She is shown to be intelligent and to occupy a position of power and respect in Wakandan society as both a general and a warrior; in fact, she is Wakanda's "greatest warrior" according to Nakia. It is not just this which is notable, but also her closeness to T'Challa and their relationship, which involves an intimacy not born of sexual or romantic attraction but a friendship between a man and woman that is infrequent in the superhero genre and even mainstream American film as a whole. For his part, T'Challa often turns to Okoye for advice, even though he does not always act on it, and on more than one occasion, it is Okoye who is proven to be correct, not the king. This closeness remains unremarked upon in the film, but is instead communicated through performance and

The powerful and independent Okoye, a character the likes of which has never been seen before in the superhero film.

gesture. It is clear as early as the first five minutes of *Black Panther*, inside the Royal Talon Fighter as they are flying over Nigeria, when T'Challa informs Okoye that he will take on the mission to retrieve Nakia unaccompanied, "No need Okoye, I can handle this alone," to which she only responds with a noise, "*hmmm*," and a revealing facial expression, the first of many, communicating a great deal about their relationship without a word being spoken. It is she that reminds him "don't freeze," only for T'Challa to reply, "I never freeze"—but freeze he does when he comes face to face with Nakia on the ground. Also, it is Okoye who appears at that moment, having disobeyed her (about to be) king and prevents the militant from hitting them. A few moments later, as the scene concludes, she orders the freed Nigerian women sternly to "speak nothing of this day" in order to keep Wakandan secrets hidden, but at the end of the line she adds a slight smile to which they all respond with gratitude.

As we suggested of T'Challa—that his character possesses multiple dimensions in the film: son, friend, warrior, king, etc.— something similar is afforded to Okoye, even though she is not the film's protagonist. In addition to being T'Challa's friend, confidante, and bodyguard, she is also the head of the all-female warriors the Dora Milaje, a group described as "similar to the U.S. Navy SEALs" (Roussos 2018, 164). The fact that the Dora Milaje are all women is never referred to in *Black Panther*, as while it might be unusual and significant for us in the audience, for Wakandans it is so much a part of the fabric of their culture it would have been strange to mention it. Gurira's athleticism is a central part of the character, combining a gracefulness with power in ways rarely seen in American genre cinema, especially in roles taken by African American women. While in combat, her moves are fluid and expressive, born of a lifetime of training and military service: in the casino she wields the traditional vibranium spear with skill and authority, then in the car chase through the streets of Busan, she uses it to anchor herself on top of the speeding car driven by Nakia. When the vehicle is struck by Klaue's powerful sonic weapon (which is also constructed with vibranium from Wakanda), the car explodes and she is thrown through the air . . . yet still manages to grab the spear and land elegantly on her feet in one of the film's most crowd-pleasing moments.

As important as her narrative prominence and her physical ability is the fact that like Nakia she is never overtly sexualized through her costumes or her behavior, and she is far from one of the characters that Jeffrey Brown describes in the epigraph to this chapter as "exotic sexual spectacles" (2013, 134), although she quite easily could have been in the hands of a different director, writer, and cinematographer. She is shown mainly wearing a variation of the Dora Milaje armor, although the one belonging to her has more gold plating compared to others, signifying her advanced rank, but also in a red dress in the South Korean sequence described above (which we observed was highly symbolic when placed alongside T'Challa in black and Nakia in green). It is in this scene that she is shown to chafe against the fashions of those outside Wakanda, in particular the wig she is wearing in order to allow her to "blend in" in Busan. She calls the wig "a disgrace!" as the Dora Milaje all have their heads shaved, displaying their tattoos (a mark of status in Wakandan culture). This brief moment in the film, which takes a few seconds of screen time and is expressed in a single line of dialogue, became discussed widely as we have seen several moments in the film appropriated in a similar way. In this case, a range of writers regarded the scene as a direct challenge to the habitual process of de-Africanizing African American women in western media, by having Black actresses wear western hairstyles rather than their natural hair. Danai Gurira was aware of these dimensions, and in an interview commented, "I don't think we've seen that idea of turning the concept of femininity on its head before. I do believe that she is deeply feminine. I totally see she has an absolute sway in her hips and a confident, easy, feminine energy. She didn't forgo that to be a woman of combat" (quoted in Wilkins 2018, 36). Okoye's hair, and also that of Nakia, Shuri, and Ramonda, were the subject of discussion both online and in print in further examples of how *Black Panther* became a hugely significant popular culture artifact in multiple dimensions through 2018, many of which were concerned with its women as well as its men (see Byrd and Tharp 2002).

IV.

The character of Shuri, played by Guyana-born and British-raised Letitia Wright, is present in many, though not all of the scenes described above, often sharing the screen with Nakia, Okoye, and her brother, T'Challa. She is first seen after the mission in Nigeria, where the affection and intimacy between the two is clear from the start. Their sibling relationship is one also infrequent in the genre (the only other notable example in the MCU is Wanda and Pietro Maximoff, aka Scarlett Witch and Quicksilver). On his arrival she affectionately chides him for his old-fashioned ways, referring to the Kimoye beads that he had used to disable the vehicles of the Nigerian militants, one of many inventions that the film shows her as having been responsible for creating. Despite just being a teenager she seems to be in charge of a large part of Wakanda's entire technological development, a fact which led to the Russo brothers comment from *Wired* referred to earlier in this chapter that the smartest person in the MCU is not Tony Stark, Bruce Banner, or Stephen Strange, but a young woman from Wakanda who was not yet nineteen years old. As we noted earlier, females have very often been pushed to the sidelines of the MCU, with roles for Black women even more scarce, so the significance of a young African woman being described in such a way is considerable. It would

The teenage genius and "smartest person in the MCU," Shuri in her Afrofuturist lab with her brother.

have been possible for T'Challa to be the film's genius, a role that is more greatly emphasized in the comics, but it is Shuri who is shown as inventing not just the Kimoye beads, but also variations of the Black Panther suit, curing Agent Ross's seemingly fatal wound and also designing the magnetic railway which runs underneath Mount Bashenga transporting vibranium safely, among many other creations. The laboratory she works in becomes an extension of her own character, decorated as it is with vibrant Afro-futurist graffiti, indicating that she is the film's futurist (just as Tony Stark was often considered during his time in the MCU).

Like the characters of Nakia and Okoye, Shuri is afforded much more screen time than she might have been and is played with a charismatic, youthful exuberance by Wright. It is undoubtedly her youth and her modernity that resonates, and even though her age is not explicitly mentioned in the film itself, the script states that she is eighteen (2018, 13) as does the novelization of the film. Her portrayal has much in common with the MCU's iteration of Peter Parker, played by Tom Holland, the first teenage actor to play the character rather than one in his twenties (Tobey Maguire) or even thirties (Andrew Garfield). Like Peter, she is shown referencing "old" films from the 1980s—in her case, "the old American movie Baba used to watch," referring to *Back to the Future* (1985), in the same way Peter Parker refers to *The Empire Strikes Back* (1980) in *Captain America: Civil War* as well as *Aliens* (1986) in *Avengers: Infinity War*. Shuri also becomes the source of much of the humor of *Black Panther*, often derived from the juxtaposition of her royal role and her youthful informality, as in her raised middle finger to her brother followed by "Sorry, mother!" as well as her joke during the ceremony on Warrior Falls about the uncomfortable bone corset, the scene in which she tricks T'Challa into striking the Black Panther suit and causes him to be thrown across the room, and her line to Ross: "Don't scare me like that, colonizer!" This last line comes after the CIA agent wakes up in her lab, having been healed from a wound that would have killed or paralyzed him in America, a fact about which he is incredulous since he has never been exposed to vibranium technology firsthand before. Just as we observed that the relationship between T'Challa and Ross was an interesting reversal of power relations, this is even more the case in the one between an American CIA officer, a character type at the center of many American genre films, and a teenage African girl, who has, initially at least, power over the man whose life she has just saved.

The fact that Marvel had been purchased almost ten years before by Disney for $4.24 billion in 2009 led several writers to argue that Shuri should be regarded as not just a member of the Wakandan royal family, but a Disney Princess, with all the cultural baggage that comes with such a title. If so, she certainly is the most impressive figure to have been referred to in such a way, as Disney Princesses have historically been defined by their lack of agency, even though more recent additions to the canon like Mulan, Merida, and Moana have been self-conscious attempts to redress this. Shuri is also the one who appeared, at the time of writing, in the most financially successful film, with *Black Panther* earning more money than any other to feature either an official or unofficial Disney Princess. She is also the only one we might identify as a genius as well as being a rare nonwhite addition to the roster. Letitia Wright seemed to recognize this when asked about her status as a Disney Princess, with the enthusiasm palpable in her responses in ways that suggested her own personality was not too far removed from the characters she plays on the screen. She said, "I'm so honored, seriously. I grew up on Disney movies and grew up with the Disney Princesses and they didn't really look like me. But now, you can go buy action figures and say this is a Disney Princess . . . right on!" (quoted in Haring 2018).

V.

In my 2018 book *Avengers Assemble: Critical Perspectives on the Marvel Cinematic Universe*, I lamented the lack of mature female characters across the MCU, observing that there were many aging yet still active and virile patriarchal figures such as Nick Fury, played by Samuel L. Jackson, who was sixty when *Iron Man* was released and in his seventies by the time of *Captain Marvel*; Anthony Hopkins, who was seventy-five at the time of *Thor*; William Hurt, who was fifty-eight for *The Incredible Hulk*; Jeff Bridges, who was fifty-nine at the time of *Iron Man*; Stellan Skarsgård, who was sixty during *Thor*; and Michael Douglas, who was seventy at the release of *Ant-Man*. Yet their female equivalents were too few and far between, with certainly no comparable agency. What aging and similarly dynamic matriarchal figures does the MCU offer in Phases One and Two with comparative screen time and influence? Only the likes of Rene Russo, who played Frigga in *Thor* at the age of fifty-six, Jenny Agutter, who was sixty in *The Avengers* in 2012, or Glenn Close, who was fifty-eight at the time she played Irani Rael in *Guardians of the Galaxy*. None of these characters have anywhere near the narrative centrality of the likes of Nick Fury, Odin, Thaddeus Ross, Obadiah Stane, Erik Selvig, or Hank Pym, each of which are very often key characters in the films in which they are featured. In Phase Three, the situation improved somewhat, although not by as much as it should have, with Tilda Swinton being fifty-five when she played the Ancient One in *Doctor Strange*, Marisa Tomei fifty-one at the time of *Captain America: Civil War*, Michelle Pfeiffer at sixty when she played Janet van Dyne in *Ant-Man and the Wasp*, and finally Annette Benning the same age when she played Mar-Vel in *Captain Marvel*.

Angela Bassett joins these women with her character of Ramonda, performing the role while in her late fifties after a career featuring many notable films in the 1990s, including some of those previously mentioned in this book, among them Spike Lee's *Malcolm X* and John Singleton's directorial debut *Boyz n the Hood*, before her Academy Award-nominated performance as Tina Turner in *What's Love Got to Do With It?* (1993). In recent years, Bassett had made the transition to playing a variety of powerful women, including CIA director Sloane in *Mission Impossible: Fallout* (2018), US ambassador to the United Kingdom Crane in *Survivor* (2015), and Secret Service Director Lynne Jacobs in the Gerald Butler action films *Olympus has Fallen* (2013) and *London has Fallen* (2016).

Playing the mother of a superhero in a film has traditionally been a thankless task, with most offered very little to do or even seeing themselves killed in order to justify the superhero's worldview and actions. As many have observed, the relationship between fathers and sons is central to the superhero genre, far more than mothers and sons (see Coventry 2015). The MCU and even the genre as a whole is littered with mothers who do not survive either the hero's childhood or even the first act of the film they are featured in, when at exactly the same time the father is shown to play an instrumental role in the superhero's emotional and psychological development. The examples of this are almost too numerous to mention, but in the MCU both Howard and Maria Stark die on the same day, but it is his relationship with Howard that is shown to be the most important one in *Iron Man 2* and it is his father whom he is reconciled with when he goes back in time during *Avengers: Endgame*, with hardly a thought given to Maria. In the same way, it is Hank Pym who plays a central role in *Ant-Man* and *Ant-Man and the Wasp*, with Michelle Pfeiffer's character Janet van Dyne, aka Hope the Wasp's mother, only appearing very briefly in the latter as the object of the film's rescue mission. Thor's defining relationship is not with his mother, Frigga, who is killed off in *Thor: The Dark World*, but with his father, Odin, who plays a very important role across the whole of the Thor trilogy and whose love and respect Thor and his brother Loki compete for.

Black Panther does little to remedy this, as much of T'Challa's character arc is driven by his relationship with his father, even though he died before the action of the film formally begins. Yet Bassett's Ramonda is provided with a greater screen presence than many mothers in the genre and certainly more than many mature women in the superhero film. She fulfills the primary requirements demanded of matriarchal figures in the genre—that is, to be dignified, loving, and stately—but she is invested by the script and

Queen Ramonda flanked by her daughter Shuri and their bodyguard Ayo.

Bassett's performance with layers not present perhaps in other royal queens like Frigga in the MCU and Queen Hippolyta in the DCEU. Her scenes with her children allow her to pass on wisdom, but the film never asks why she might not be the monarch of Wakanda after her husband's death rather than her son. At least she is not a mother who is threatened, disappears, or kidnapped (see Martha Kent in *Man of Steel* and *Batman v. Superman* or Janet Van Dyne in *Ant-Man and the Wasp*) or killed-off as motivation for the protagonist's revenge (see Frigga in *Thor: The Dark World*, Meredith Quill in *Guardians of the Galaxy: Vol. 2*, or Martha Wayne in *Batman v. Superman*). It is Ramonda who inspires T'Challa during the ritual combat between him and M'Baku ("Show him who you are!"), she goes on the journey to the Jabari territory to persuade M'Baku to join in what we might consider the Wakandan civil war orchestrated by N'Jadaka, and she is always included in scenes in the throne room when decisions are being made, sometimes offering her own advice.

Three of the four characters discussed above would be of note in any superhero film if they appeared *on their own*. As we have seen, the genre has been ordered overwhelmingly around the experiences of men, but the fact that all three of them appear in a single film, and not only that, that they are Black women, is even more remarkable. While they are not the lead character of *Black Panther*, they do occupy the film's privileged spaces and are arguably dynamic in a range of ways. Aisha Harris, in a *Slate* article titled "Black Panther Is the Most Feminist Superhero Movie Yet" wrote,

"Just as Wakanda is a utopian symbol for black people in its depiction of a nation relatively untouched by colonialism, so does it now represent an ideal world in which men and women coexist respectfully, on an equal playing field." But this understanding of the film and its female characters was challenged by Minna Salami: "*Black Panther* deserves an Oscar—but is it a feminist film? No way." It is easy to agree with Salami's initial argument: "The most obvious reason [that *Black Panther* is not a feminist film] is that Wakanda, the fictional African country where *Black Panther* takes place, is a patriarchy. In other words, it is a country where men hold power and where society is organised along male lineage. Feminism, last time I checked, seeks to end patriarchy—yet the women of Wakanda seem mostly happy to support it." However, her second assertion, which is central to her argument, is one that is debatable. She states, "But the most important reason *Black Panther* is not a feminist film is because the female characters are denied complexity. The women of Wakanda are literally picture-perfect. They are goddesses, divas; powerful, sexy, fearless women, always prepared to give therapeutic, balsamic words of wisdom to their king, who in turn goes through a complex range of emotions." Salami's point here is a valuable one with element of truth to it, but just as many welcomed the film's portrayal of strong, independent women, the likes of which had never been seen in the genre before, and it was for this reason, as well as the many others we have explored in the book, that the film resonated so profoundly with audiences in 2018.

Beyond the Frames of the Screen

"In times of crisis the wise build bridges . . ."

The superhero genre deals directly with issues of power and its responsible use. Superheroes change the world and never doubt their capacity to make a difference. This political drama unfolds in bright primary colors, often lacking the nuances necessary to foster real-world change, but such fantasies provoke debates about possible alternatives to the status quo. . . . In numerous ways, superhero blockbusters offer resources for social movements: because they are ordinary; because they can be appropriated and transformed so freely; because they constitute a realm where we might imagine alternatives to current social conditions; because they foster shared desires that may help sustain struggles for social justice; because they speak about feelings that might not be expressed in any other way; and because they may bridge cultural divides.

HENRY JENKINS, "What *Black Panther* Can Teach Us About the Civic Imagination," *21st Century Global Dynamics*, May 22, 2018, volume 11, no. 27

With all due respect King T'Challa, what can a nation of farmers offer to the rest of the world?

FRENCH AMBASSADOR TO THE UNITED NATIONS IN *BLACK PANTHER*

I.

This book has attempted to explore *Black Panther* with the scrutiny that it deserves as one of the most financially successful and culturally impactful films of the last decade. Rarely is space given to interrogate a single film in such a way, certainly not from a genre that remains critically, if not culturally, marginalized. The result is, as I have attempted to reveal, a text that is certainly worthy of such close consideration and one that is, without a doubt, an important moment in the history of the American film industry for a number of reasons. A small indication of this can be found in the diverse awards for which it was nominated and very often won, including a nomination for the Humanitas Prize, an American Music Award for Best Soundtrack, a BET (Black Entertainment Television) Award for Best Movie, being placed in the list of top ten films of the year by the National Board of Review, and receiving four wins out of fourteen nominations in the Saturn Awards. The culmination of this undoubtedly was its nomination for an Academy Award for Best Picture, the first ever film from the superhero genre to have received such an accolade, although it ultimately lost to *Green Book* (2019).[1]

The sheer variety of ways with which the film was engaged with by audiences and the debates it inspired should also be considered as further evidence of this broad cultural reach. We can see this in a cursory glance at the number of magazines, websites, and journals it saw itself featured in: from the likes of *Architectural Digest* ("The Real-life Possibilities of Wakanda," February 2018) to *Black Hair* ("Lupita Nyong'o. The Big Screen's Leading Naturalista," March 2018), *The Economist* ("Wakandanomics," March 31, 2018) to the *American Alliance of Museums* ("Museums Should Take Notes from Black Panther and Beyoncé," February 2019), *Time* ("A Hero Rises," February 2018), and even *The Scientific American* ("The Shuri Effect: A Generation of Black Scientists?" February 2018).[2]

In February 2018, the Brooklyn Academy of Music hosted a film series called "Fight the Power: Black Superheroes on Film," inspired by *Black Panther* and featuring films with Black heroes, although given the relative paucity of African American superheroes onscreen its films contained not always those of the "super" variety. Some were well known, like *Blade* and *Spawn*, and others less so, like *Abar: The First Black Superman* (1977), the first feature film to star a Black superhero, and the remarkable yet little seen *The Spook Who Sat by the Door* (1973). In the field of fashion, several designers participating in New York Fashion Week that same month created custom pieces inspired by *Black Panther*, with one, Rodney Cutler, echoing one of the central aspects of our project with his comments, "There's not really a separation, it's like music, movies, social inspirations, fashion, and beauty all tied into one" (quoted in Maloney 2018). During the 2018 French Open, tennis champion Serena Williams wore an all-black body suit, to the consternation of match officials, that she described as a "Wakanda-inspired catsuit" (quoted in Dicker 2018). As if to accentuate the connections between the fictional and real-world versions of the Black Panther, Michael B. Jordan dressed as a member of the Black Panther Party for the March 2018 cover of *GQ Magazine*, where he was clear about what he saw as the film's potential to have a very real impact on African American lives, stating, "We're giving black people power" (quoted in Powell 2018). Indeed, the former leader of the real-life Black Panthers, Sekou Odinga, used the cultural impact of the film to highlight the fact that many civil rights-era activists remain incarcerated even after all these years. Odinga said, "This is an opportunity to remind people of the real heroes of the Black Panthers and the conditions they live in today" (quoted in Sam Levin 2018).

Additionally, the film seeped into other aspects of popular culture with a frequency and longevity the likes of which has been rare. While box-office successes usually find themselves fodder for late-night television hosts, *Black Panther* became a topic for months before and after its release: Conan O'Brian joked that the 2020 Olympics were going to be held in Wakanda (February 26, 2018), a parody of the film at the MTV Movie Awards (June 18, 2018) featured Tiffany Haddish as the Black Unicorn replacing M'Baku to challenge T'Challa at the Warrior Falls, joking, "Oh my god! I just shanked Chadwick Boseman, aka James Brown, aka Jackie Robinson!"[3] At the Academy Awards on February 25, 2019,

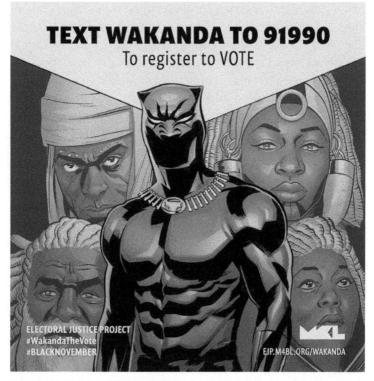

The Electoral Justice Project campaign used *Black Panther* in an attempt to inspire members of the African American community to get out and vote in 2018.

more than a year after the release of the film, host Jimmy Kimmel returned to *Black Panther* on a number of occasions, once pointing into the audience and saying, "There's Chadwick Boseman, the king of Wakanda! Imagine that! A country with a Black leader. Wouldn't that be swell?" once again connecting *Black Panther* to the contemporary political sphere, if only in humorous form. Later in the same ceremony, the South African comedian Trevor Noah, who played the voice of the artificial intelligence Griot in the film, mounted the stage and introduced the Best Picture nominee with what he said was "a great Xhosa phrase . . . Abelungu abazi' uba ndiyaxoka," which meant, according to him, "In times like these, we are stronger when we fight together than when we try to fight apart." What he did not say was that for anyone who speaks Xhosa its meaning was very different and actually translates to "White people don't know I'm lying" (quoted in Loughrey 2019).[4]

Moving into the realm of the real-world American political process, members of the Electoral Justice Project set up voting registration booths outside of cinemas screening *Black Panther* with the intention of getting more Black people to vote than had participated in the 2016 presidential election, which had seen a decline for the first time in two decades to 59.6 percent after a record high of 66.6 percent in 2012, the year which saw Barack Obama secure his second term in office (see Krogstad and Lopez 2017). Kayla Reed, Jessica Byrd, and Rukia Lumumba, the founders of the project, stated that they wanted to meet "communities where they are, whether that's in the streets, at the city council meeting, or in the movie theater" (quoted in Anapol 2018).[5]

For some the film and its geopolitical environments came to be regarded as an aspirational heterotopic space that the real world should turn to as a model for the future, not only figuratively, but in some cases literally. Writer Sean lxg Mitchell, in his *How Do We Build a Real Wakanda?* (2018), suggested that it should be used "as a metaphor in regards to the emergence of a new Africa-centered paradigm" (7), asserting that it could be embraced as an exemplar by the Black community moving into the twenty-first century in an effort to reconcile their collective past with the present. The successful African American singer known as Akon had a similar idea, but one that moved beyond metaphor into the realms of reality when he expressed his desire to build "a real-life Wakanda" not too far away from Dakar, the capital of Senegal, to be financed by the singer's own crypto-currency, Akoin (quoted in Robinson 2018). The literal and figurative were blended by historian Nathan Connolly who wrote,

> Yes, let us dream of a land high-tech without a history of environmental degradation. Let's, all of us, be "black" without the crucible of colonialism. And let's, if only for a time, be the richest nation on Earth, without the existential pain of cultural genocide or the elevation of white aesthetics to the exclusion

of all else. Then, buoyed by dreams of Wakanda, let's return
home and face the world that actually needs remaking. (2018)

Connolly's sentiments were echoed by many others, both in Africa,
like Stellah Wairimu Bosire, CEO of the Kenya Medical Association,
who remarked, "It's [Wakanda is] a reflection of what we would want
our societies and countries to look like [in Africa]" (quoted in Lu
2018), and in the United States, such as Larry Madowo, who said,
"Wakanda looks like a place I want to be a citizen of, because it looks
like such a beautiful, egalitarian society, where the women wear
their hair natural and they are powerful warriors. It is beautiful in
that sense, as a utopia of sorts. . . . And if you just think, if you build
a model for the perfect African country, Wakanda is that" (2018).

These responses to the film are characteristic of the way it was
broadly engaged with in popular culture through 2018 and into 2019
and prove to be a fascinating testimony to its status as an aspirational wish-fulfillment fantasy. However, in doing so they choose
to disregard some of the film's more problematic elements, much
as the ideological dimensions of the MCU have been rarely considered in any depth by audiences or scholars since 2008. Con-
nelly, Bosire, and Madowo overlook, consciously or not, Wakanda's
patrilineal, absolute monarchy and the fact that democracy *does
not exist* in the country, but still consider it a "utopia" or "perfect."
It is only by ignoring these elements that one is able to make such
statements, by disregarding the fact that ascension to the throne is
determined by ritual combat to the death or that its extrajudicial
incursions around the globe, exactly of the type that both T'Chaka
and T'Challa criticized others for doing, are similar to the way the
United States has operated throughout the twentieth century in
places like Iran (1953), Guatemala (1954), Cuba (1959), Dominican
Republic (1961), Vietnam (1965), and Chile (1970), to name but a few.
In this way, Wakanda is very far from a "paradigm" for the future
as contended by Sean Ixg Mitchell, but rather follows the template
established by other films in the MCU, which have portrayed such
actions as entirely moral, necessary, *and* effective from its opening
film, *Iron Man*, and Tony Stark's missions in Afghanistan. In their

International Politics and Film: Space, Vision and Power (2014), Sean Carter and Klaus Dodds correctly point out that this unsanctioned behavior is portrayed as entirely essential: "in order to secure justice or otherwise, the superhero is required because s/he is able to operate beyond the law and this is made possible, in part, because they are tolerated, even encouraged, by grateful city authorities and/or national governments" (2014, 55–56). What is remarkable about *Black Panther* is that it is an African country now afforded the sense of primacy and legitimacy that has historically been given only to the United States of America in films made by an American industry that has been reluctant to offer positive images of Africa on the cinema screen. What we are left with, then, are a range of reactions to the film that seem only able to focus on the progressive aspects of its representation, which are indeed considerable, unable to recognize the more contentious aspects of its ideology that it contains at the very same time, something which may very well be the film's most affecting paradox.

Interestingly, these aspects which are embraced uncategorically in the film had been interrogated very effectively during Ta-Nehisi Coates's recent tenure with the character in the comic books that began in *Black Panther* no. 1 (April 2016), "A Nation Under Our Feet." In the comic book narrative, rivals to T'Challa and the Wakandan monarchy emerge after the events of the series known as "Secret Wars," which saw Princess Shuri killed and the Wakandan population profoundly dissatisfied with the social and political situation in the country. This storyline was also connected to the tumultuous times in which it was written by scholars and writers on comic book literature in the same way as we have observed the film was, in articles with titles like "A Powerful Symbol for the Black Lives Matter Generation" (Williams 2017). In the comic, protests against the monarchy are marshaled by a rebel called Tetu, the leader of a group who call themselves The People, but none of these complexities make their way into a single frame of Coogler's *Black Panther*, which valorizes Wakanda's political and social structures entirely uncritically in a film we should remember was widely regarded as "radical" (Powell 2018) and even "revolutionary" (Jamil Smith 2018).

In the real world, only three African sovereign states still have hereditary monarchies on the order of Wakanda: Lesotho, Morocco, and Eswatini (formerly Swaziland), and none of them are held up as being examples to be imitated in Africa or outside of it. In fact, each state has been criticized for human rights violations by Amnesty International going back decades.[6] In the latter, King Mswati III is a monarch with sweeping powers over the population, and in April 2018 decided to change the name of the country to Eswatini. He was able to do this as he has the same authority as T'Challa has over Wakanda and, one should observe, as N'Jadaka briefly had. The reign of Mswati III has been marked by domestic and international protests, and in 2017 Action for Southern Africa (ACTSA) produced a report which described the country as a "deeply patriarchal society" with the king himself "unwilling to make any change" and, furthermore, that "parties pressing for a transition to greater parliamentary democracy have been severely repressed, with grassroots leaders beaten and imprisoned and groups banned from participating in civil society" (quoted in anon. "Your 'Rabidly Intolerant Regime Is a Dismal Failure,' Swazi's King Mswati III Told" 2017).

There were some critical of the film's valorization of Wakanda's patrilineal hereditary monarchy and the way it was embraced by audiences, but most were drowned out in the waves of admiration directed at it. Patrick Gathara, in an article titled "'Black Panther' offers a regressive, neocolonial vision of Africa" (2018), suggested that "this is a vision of Africa that could only spring from the neocolonial mind. It is really telling how close a "Black redemptive counter-mythology sails to the colonial vision of a childish people needing a strong guiding hand to lead them" (2018). Gathara's point is a valid one, but his final line is a criticism that should not only be directed at *Black Panther* but rather the genre as a whole as the superhero film is a profoundly undemocratic narrative form, one which places at its center conflicts that are only ever resolved by violence and most often by superpowered individuals with little thought or screen time for "childish people needing a strong guiding hand to lead them," whether that hand belongs to T'Challa, Tony

Stark, or Steve Rogers, within the MCU, or Bruce Wayne, Superman, or Aquaman outside of it.

We have seen the film's politics described as "radical" (Powell 2018) and even "revolutionary" (Jamil Smith 2018), but how radical and revolutionary can a mainstream blockbuster actually be if it's part of the Disney multinational conglomeration—especially one self-consciously designed to sell tickets, toys, and branded lunch-boxes all around the globe? This is what Gene Demby of NPR called the film's "corporate apparatus" (2018), arguing that it had a considerable impact on how it was constructed. Thus, for every voice suggesting how *empowering* the film's diversity is, which is certainly true, there are others more critical of, for example, how the film forces audiences to choose between "two radical imaginings in front of them: an immensely rich and flourishing advanced African nation that is sealed off from white colonialism and supremacy; and a few black Wakandans with a vision of global black solidarity who are determined to use Wakanda's privilege to emancipate all black people" (LeBron 2018), which are not reconciled and results in a "shocking devaluation of black American men" (LeBron 2018). Benjamin Dixon describes Wakanda not in the glowing terms we have seen most frequently in this book but as "a xenophobic, iso-lationist nation led by an elitist monarch focused on maintaining their own ethnostate" (2018). Might this "corporate apparatus" be why the film is unable to portray Black radicalism in anything but derogatory terms, first in the form of N'Jobu, who is killed because of his desire to liberate Africans all over the globe, and then in his son, N'Jadaka/ Erik "Killmonger" Stevens? It is entirely understand-able that Marvel, a subsidiary of Disney, will, in producing a family film, be wary of associating itself with radical Black politics when its primary motivation is to make money for its shareholders.

It is difficult to disagree with aspects of the argument posited by LeBron and Dixon, but at the same time other writers we have seen like Carvell Wallace, as well as those who called the film a "watershed" (see Pitts Jr. 2018; Robbins 2018; Turner 2018) or a "mile-stone" (see Jamil Smith 2018; Mock 2018), seem equally genuine in their appraisal of the film's relevance and efficacy. Furthermore, we cannot help but remember the unnamed woman who appeared on Jimmy Fallon's show ("Words can't even describe what this movie has meant to me . . .") and Ilona Williams, interviewed by Philadelphia television channel 6ABC Action News ("I can hand down this to my grandchildren . . ."), or Kayla Sutton's son who inspired the phenomenon that became #whatblackpanthermeanstome ("He's Black like me . . ."). What is clear is that the film has meant profoundly different things to different people, even if they share the same ethnic background, a tendency of a mainstream cinema that has deliberately sought to create malleable enough narratives for many to see their own perspectives projected within it. Whether this capacity is a strength or a weakness has been widely discussed: is it evidence of intellectual vacuity, or profound relevance, that a text resonates with many? It was in this context that Slavoj Žižek discussed *Black Panther* in his review of the film in the *Los Angeles Review of Books*.[7] He suggests:

> The first sign of ambiguity is the fact that the movie was enthusiastically received all across the political spectrum: from partisans of black emancipation who see in it the first big Hollywood assertion of black power, through liberals who sympathize with its reasonable solution—education and help, not struggle—up to some representatives of the alt-right, who recognize in the film's "Wakanda forever" another version of Trump's "America first" (incidentally, this is why Mugabe, before he lost power, also said some kind words about Trump). When all sides recognize themselves in the same product, we can be sure that the product in question is ideology at its purest—a kind of empty vessel containing antagonistic elements.

Žižek correctly identifies three ways in which the film was received, although there are more as we have seen, asserting that this malleability results in something of an "empty vessel." Yet some of the most potent films of twentieth-century American cinema have produced contrasting, if not paradoxical, interpretations. If we recall the unlikely company *Black Panther* found itself in on Rotten Tomatoes,

Black Panther strikes Donald Trump in a vivid approximation of how some considered the film as an act of resistance (reprinted with permission from original artist Guile Sharp).

those with which it shared a 97 percent "fresh" rating: *La Grande Illusion* (1937), *Psycho* (1960), *Alien* (1979), and *Boyhood* (2014). All have led to a body of writings that offer very different explanations of how they should be read. Rather than evidence of limitation, in the case of *Black Panther*, this might in fact be a part of its efficacy and even explain why it resonated with global audiences; its international box-office revenues generated $646 million of its $1.3 billion gross.[8]

Therefore, reviews from all around the globe should be also regarded as testimony to its affectual power. In France, Monique El-Faizy wrote, "In the racially charged America of the Donald Trump era, even a superhero movie can become a flashpoint" (2018), and in an article entitled "El superhéroe negro contra el 'supervillano' Donald Trump," or "The Black Superhero against the 'Supervillain' Donald Trump" in the Spanish newspaper *El País*, Jan Martínez Ahrens argued that the film should be considered not just as a super-hero film but something more: "A country so in need of finding itself that a film starring a black superhero has become a political

Mr. Joe · a year ago · edited

There is no black "conversation" to be had folks. It's always been a doomed race that will forever be unable to assimilate to the logic of citizenship and American culture and decent moral values. This is also revealed worldwide and particularly in Africa. End of story. Cut - Print.

4 ∧ ∨ · Reply · Share ›

Dlink · a year ago

I actually hate this review of the movie. And I completely disagree that black actors or actresses are marginalized in Hollywood. Actually, nowadays it is the complete opposite.

4 ∧ ∨ · Reply · Share ›

SteamRollEverything · a year ago

Not seeing it. No way this is what JN says. Most of these guys could not spot Leftist propaganda if it bit them in the rear. Wonder Woman and Guardians of the Galaxy 2 went full SJW, DONE with Marvel and DC movies, period.

3 ∧ ∨ · Reply · Share ›

95Theses · a year ago

I don't know about Rotten Tomatoes, but *Black Panther* will probably end up garnering a Rotten Watermelon score of 99%. :/

1 ∧ ∨ · Reply · Share ›

Black Panther became embroiled in a cultural battle for meaning and significance online in the forums of conservative sites like breitbart.com, shown here.

phenomenon able to mobilize the African-American community.... Seen in a cinema, it is an act of vindication: the superman who jumps over Trump. That is what it represents at least for thousands of Americans who have expressed it on Twitter, YouTube and Instagram, and on Friday night they flocked to its premiere, picking up the torch of the African-American collective" (2018).⁹

Returning to Žižek's review, the film did quite surprisingly find itself viewed from the perspective he overly simplistically calls "representatives of the alt-right, who recognize in the film's 'Wakanda forever' another version of Trump's 'America First.'" More correctly, others on the right side of the political spectrum who might not all identify themselves as alt-right did indeed see Trump reflected in *Black Panther*, even to the extent that John Nolte, writing at *Breitbart*, asserted that T'Challa should be seen as a Trump-like figure in his review, "The Movie's Hero is Trump, the Villain is Black Lives Matter." He wrote, "T'Challa is big on border security, believes Wakanda and Wakandans should come first, and fiercely protects his country's culture from outsiders, including refugees. If this is all starting to sound familiar, it should" (2018). Others, like Brandon Morse, accused the film of "casual racism" directed towards white people (2018), and Aaron Gleason argued that the film's villain Erik "Killmonger" Stevens (Michael B. Jordan) "has drunk deeply of Obama's anti-colonial well and decided it's time for vengeance upon the white world" (2018).

Seemingly antithetical to this is Žižek's other group, those he calls "partisans of black emancipation who see in it the first big Hollywood assertion of black power." One certainly does not have to fit this description to recognize how significant *Black Panther* is for the American film industry in terms of representation and its cultural and commercial impact. However, one might be wary about using the kind of hyperbolic language some have to describe the film, while at the same time understanding why they might have employed it, such as Van Jones, who said, "This film is a godsend that will lift the self-esteem of black children in the US and around the world for a long time" (2018). What is clear is that *Black Panther* came to mean fundamentally paradoxical things to different individuals and groups, which, for some, might be regarded as evidence of its vacancy, but for others, of its fecundity. None of these perceptions should be regarded as incorrect or inappropriate, even if they appear so far removed from each other they are seemingly impossible to reconcile. Žižek's final group, those who he describes as "liberals who sympathize with its reasonable solution—education and help, not struggle," is a direct reference to the film's concluding scene, which we will explore below.

II.

After his cousin's death, there are two brief scenes in Wakanda before the film moves abroad for its closing sequence. Firstly, T'Challa is shown entering into the throne room that is his once more, with the cinematography deliberately employed to contrast with N'Jadaka's memorable entrance earlier. The discombobulating 360-degree rotation that had marked that scene is now replaced with a smooth gliding motion encompassing within it the understanding that stability and harmony has returned to Wakanda. On his first visit to the ancestral plane, T'Challa had asked his father how he could best protect Wakanda, and T'Chaka had replied, "You need to surround yourself with people you trust." It seems he has now done this as the tribal elders are present, as are his mother, sister, and even M'Baku after the Jabari tribe had spent so many years in antagonistic isolation in the mountains. This is followed by a sequence of shots of Birnin Zana showing the people of Wakanda going about their daily business, which again seems to emphasize stability, with a number of children shown within the frame, thereby metaphorically connecting itself to the film's central theme about the future of Wakanda. It concludes with a conversation between T'Challa and Nakia in which he thanks her for not just saving him but the whole of the country. After they kiss, he says to her, "I think I know a way you can still fulfill your calling," referring to her previously stated desire that Wakanda has a moral responsibility to help those outside of its borders. A crane shot slowly moves above the streets of Birnin Zana before a slow cross-dissolve transports the film 10,000 miles across the Atlantic Ocean to Oakland in a shot that is held for longer than it might have been were it not so symbolically significant. We are returned to the basketball court at the foot of the apartment block where N'Jadaka/Erik once played more than twenty-five years before, to another group of young African American boys, not too different from those who were shown doing the same in 1992. Their clothes are more modern, they play on a real hoop rather than a milk crate one, and the music on the film's soundtrack is now "Sleep Walkin" (2017) by Mozzy (aka, Timothy Paterson) rather than Too Short, but the camera follows them in almost exactly the same way as it did in the prologue. The scene offers deliberate parallels to that sequence while also implying a sense of progression in ways more than chronological. It is now day rather than night, and instead of hiding as it once did, the Royal Talon Fighter appears in plain sight when T'Challa presses one of his Kimoyo beads, revealing itself to the basketball playing teenagers. They are, as are all the inhabitants of the MCU since *The Avengers* in 2012, aware that superheroes and aliens exist in their world, but only now are they about to learn the secrets of the mysterious country of Wakanda.

T'Challa tells Shuri, who is there with him, that he has purchased several of the apartment blocks in the area, including the one where "our father killed our uncle" and that they will be the first sites of what he calls Wakanda International Outreach Centers. T'Challa has undergone a significant transition in attitudes about how Wakanda must engage with the world, one which sees him depart from the millennia-old tradition of his ancestors passed down to him by his father. Of course, he is not the only character to change his mind about something important in the MCU: there is Captain America's evolution from blindly following orders in *Captain America: The First Avenger* to questioning the government's right to dictate when, where, and how superheroes should act in *Captain America: Civil War*, before deciding to retire for good in *Avengers: Endgame*; or Peter Parker's journey from being desperate to become an Avenger in *Spider-Man: Homecoming*, only to desire to hold onto his teenage years while he still can, then in *Spider-Man: Far From Home* where he attempts to reconcile himself to a world without his mentor Tony Stark at the same time as it seems to turn to him as a potential replacement for the world's most famous Avenger. T'Challa's personal arc is not too dissimilar to these two characters, but his growth is not only one with personal ramifications owing to the fact that he is a king and his decisions about the future shape those of a nation.

T'Challa has another burden on his shoulders, one not shared by figures like Captain America and Spider-Man. It's also a burden that moves beyond the diegetic frames of the screen and is connected to the weight of cultural representation that superheroes who are not from certain groups never have to contend with. Thus, films in the genre featuring either Black, Asian, or female superheroes as their protagonists are charged with representing not just themselves but the group they are taken by many to epitomize. As Alex

Simmons remarked, "The Panther legacy must also represent—as seen by some—an entire race of people. It represents their individualism, cultural values, history, and their worth in society. No one individual or creation should carry such weight" (2019, loc. 387). T'Challa's decisions, which of course are orchestrated by Ryan Coogler, Joe Robert Cole, and Kevin Feige, are noteworthy for the Wakandans featured in the film, but they also became important for many African Americans or Africans for whom he has become a significant figure. While some might regard this symbolic potency as ephemeral or even somewhat perverse given his fictional status as "just" a character in a superhero film, one must observe that fictionality has never been a barrier to real-world resonance. We should be wary of dismissing fictional creations and their very tangible connections to the configurations of national identity which formed them even though they are *imaginary* like Uncle Sam in the United States, John Bull in England, Barat Mata in India, Zé Povinho in Portugal, and Marianne in France, to name just a few. Superman has often been read as an articulation of quintessential American values from the moment he first graced the pages of a comic book in 1938 through the years of World War II and beyond.[10] In similar ways, contemporary iterations of these characters like T'Challa, Batman, and Wonder Woman are also richly symbolic creations even if they seem on the surface to be simplistic and superficial characters in comic book movies.

Some wondered whether outreach centers might be the best answer to the problems that the film had introduced as very real ones through the characters of Nakia and N'Jadaka, or whether they would have the impact on systemic inequality not just in the United States but also all around the globe, as *Black Panther* seems to imply they will. Osha Neumann asked (and answered) as follows:

> What does the Black Panther do (or rather what is he allowed to do by the script writers and script doctors and directors and producers and funders of this movie)? He comes to Oakland and rehabs a decaying high-rise into a community center. He does not empty the prisons; he does not open the vaults of the

banks and distribute to the wretched of the earth the wealth stored there by the 1%; he does not storm Wall Street and send all the stock brokers off for rehabilitation; he does not send all the nuclear weapons into space to travel harmlessly beyond the galaxy; he does not take back the White House and paint it the colors of Kenti cloth. No, what the poor kids of Oakland with their shitty schools, and rat infested housing get is a better place to play basketball. (2018)

While this might be too much to ask of the film's hero, the criticisms raised, given the film's status as "revolutionary" by many, are certainly relevant. As we have seen, the genre itself is a fundamentally reactionary one in ways seemingly embedded in its codes and conventions. James Wilt argued that outreach centers are evidence of the film's conservatism and what he calls its "fundamentally reactionary understanding of black liberation that blatantly advocates bourgeois respectability over revolution, sterilizes the history of real-life anti-colonial struggles in Africa and elsewhere, and allows white folks such as myself to feel extremely comfortable watching it—which, given Marvel's sole purpose, is almost certainly the bottom line" (2018).

As we have seen so many times throughout the course of this book, many of the film's elements took on extra-textual significance in ways it would have been hard for its creators to anticipate. Connected to T'Challa's desire to create outreach centers first in Oakland and then in other locations was Walt Disney Company chairman and chief executive officer Bob Iger's donation of $1 million to the Boys and Girls Club of America (BGCA) to expand its STEM (Science, Technology, Engineering, and Math) programs, with one center in particular a new STEM Center of Innovation to be located in Oakland itself (see Bui 2018).

All but one of the teenagers crowd around the Wakandan Royal Talon Fighter, instead walking slowly towards T'Challa, now standing alone at the edge of the basketball court with the abandoned apartment block still visible behind him. The boy—played by Alex R. Hibbert, who had starred as Little in *Moonlight* (2016)—looks very much like "E" did back in the film's 1992 prologue, something

Black Panther returns to Oakland where the narrative had begun, but this time to inspire a new generation of young African Americans in scenes which mirror how the film functioned beyond its diegetic frames.

the film's editor later confirmed was a deliberate choice on the part of Coogler (see Sharf 2019). T'Challa never knew his cousin at that age, but we, as audience members, did, and one wonders if he is considering that now. Is the film suggesting that this boy could be a Killmonger of the future, but T'Challa is there to provide him with an example in almost the same way we have seen many contend that the Black Panther character functions in real life? This was something expressed by Siddhant Adlakha, writing in the *Village Voice*:

> Killmonger was born under a makeshift hoop, gazing up at a Wakandan airship that left him behind, slipping away in the dead of night as his father was killed. That same royal airship returns to this spot decades later, this time in full view of the Oakland youth, bringing with it the promise of a better

future, the kind of promise young Erik Stevens was never afforded. The film's final moments involve a similar young boy under that very same hoop, his future hanging in the balance. But rather than violence and abandonment, he's offered the promise of Wakanda—what the fictional fantasy of Wakanda represents, and, by proxy, what America ought to represent at its best: hope, innovation, opportunity, aspiration for Black youth upon seeing Blackness excel. (2018)

The boy asks, "This yours?" pointing to the jet and then poses a question we have seen asked many times in the film in Xhosa as "Ungubani?" and in English as "Who are you?" T'Challa does not reply as he does not need to; the film has answered this question for us in the audience and for himself. He has shown that he is his own man, one not beholden to the past, one that cares for the people of Wakanda, but also recognizes the responsibility he has for others too given his privileged position. The camera moves slowly towards T'Challa's face for a slight beat with his expression an ambiguous one before cutting abruptly to black and the end credits.[11]

The credits themselves are accompanied by key moments from the film, recreated in ways very similar to the opening story of Wakanda which appeared to be rendered in granular vibranium as Kendrick Lamar's jubilant "All the Stars" plays. Thus, as the "directed by" credit appears in BEYNO with Ryan Coogler's name, there is an image of a single statue of the panther god Bast, which then becomes two as the credit shifts to "written by" for both Ryan Coogler and Joe Robert Cole. This is followed by an image of the Wakandan throne for the "produced by" credit and Kevin Feige's name, representative of Feige's status as the metaphorical king of the Marvel Cinematic Universe. Shortly after, when names of the cast appear, each is combined with an image illustrative of their character: Chadwick Boseman is shown as both Black Panther and T'Challa at the same time, and Michael B. Jordan appears first wearing the horned mask which slowly disappears as if blown away by the vibranium sand to simply reveal his face. These are followed by Danai Gurira shown in one of Okoye's formidable spear wielding poses, Daniel Kaluuya's

W'Kabi riding a fierce-looking rhinoceros, and Letitia Wright not as her character, Shuri, but symbolized by the vibranium powered gloves she invents, just as Winston Duke's M'Baku is by the gorilla mask he once wore near the start of the film.

The final shot of T'Challa and the ending described above would have been a fitting one for *Black Panther*, but in the years since *Iron Man* (2008), the MCU has conditioned audiences to expect more and even to the idea that Marvel films never *really* end but instead offer connective tissues to those that will follow in the franchise. These mid- and post-credits scenes have become such a part of the MCU experience that audiences have, as Matthias Stork proclaimed, become "almost Pavlovian trained" (2014, 84) to expect them. By the end of Phase One, they tended to follow an established pattern whereby the mid-credits scene offered a short sequence that was usually connected to the film's narrative, either adding to it, introducing new characters who would appear in later films, or foreshadowing future events (for example, the introduction of Thanos in *The Avengers*; Quicksilver, Scarlett Witch, and the Sceptre in *Captain America: The Winter Soldier*; or Scott Lang becoming trapped in the quantum realm in *Ant-Man and the Wasp*). Then, after the credits, an additional short scene, usually not narratively connected to what had gone before, was often more lighthearted in tone or was considered something of a treat to the most devoted of MCU fans willing to wait in their seats for so long (for example, the Shawarma scene in *The Avengers*; the Howard the Duck scene in *Guardians of the Galaxy*; or Aunt May discovering Peter is Spider-Man in *Spider-Man: Homecoming*). [12]

In the case of *Black Panther*, there is both a mid-credits and a post-credits scene that adheres to the pattern outlined above. The mid-credits scene returns us to the United Nations building in Vienna, Austria, which T'Challa enters alongside Okoye, Nakia, and Ayo. [13] Standing at the podium in the same building where his father had died not too long before, he addresses the dignitaries present with several lines of dialogue that many regarded as the film's most explicit gesture towards contemporary real-world politics in the month of February 2018, when the film was released. T'Challa states,

The end credits of *Black Panther* provide a commentary on the action contained in the film and sometimes even the status of those who created it.

Wakanda will no longer watch from the shadows. We cannot. We must not. We will work to be an example of how we, as brothers and sisters on this earth, should treat each other. Now, more than ever, the illusions of division threaten our very existence. We all know the truth: more connects us than separates us. But in times of crisis the wise build bridges, while the foolish build barriers. We must find a way to look after one another, as if we were one single tribe. [14]

Some considered the brief eighty-eight word speech, reproduced above in its entirety, as Coogler and Cole's deliberate rebuke to what had emerged by then as some of the essential tenets of the Trump presidency: categorizing it as either a "direct message for President Donald Trump" (Cox 2018) or an "attack against Trump and his defining campaign promise" (Goldberg 2018). [15] For Spanish writer Gabriela Nava it was a moment "que los mexicanos aplaudan de pie" or in English one "that the Mexicans would give a standing ovation" (2018). It is clear to see how T'Challa's speech might be interpreted in such a way, but those responsible for the film repeatedly denied the connections were deliberate. When Chadwick Boseman was asked about the speech he demurred with a noncommittal, "I guess it is. I don't know. I would say it's certainly ironic that you can point to it" (quoted in Gilbey 2018). [16] Ryan Coogler himself stated that the expression was taken from an existing source and that the line was written some time before Trump had even demonstrated himself to be a viable presidential candidate. He stated,

That's an African proverb that my wife found while we were working on it. We wrote that stuff when Obama was president. Oh man, I wish that dude was really around!—because the world looks like the real place—Oh, I wish there was an Iron Man that could jump in a suit and do cool stuff and say cool stuff at press conferences. For us, I found myself looking up to [T'Challa] and aspiring to that. (quoted in Vallaverde 2018)

Coogler's phrasing here is ambiguous, with his "I really wish that dude was around" initially referring to either Barack Obama or to T'Challa. As the sentence continues, it becomes clear he is referring to T'Challa, expressing the desire that the character might be able to step from fiction into the real world the way many have fantasized about superheroes through the history of the genre since the appearance of Superman in 1938. Given the elevated cultural currency of the superhero film since the turn of the millennium, it should come as no surprise that many have used the superhero as a potent metaphorical figure through which to encapsulate and comment on those prominent in the real world. Donald Trump's supporters certainly envisioned him as something of a superhero when he turned from entrepreneur and reality television star to aspiring presidential candidate in 2016. About this tendency, Andrea Schneiker wrote, "Just like Superman, Spiderman or James Bond, the superhero that is marketed by Donald Trump is an ordinary citizen that, in case of an emergency, uses his superpowers to save others, that is, his country. He sees a problem, knows what has to be done in order to solve it, has the ability to fix the situation and does so" (2018, 217). It was a role that Trump was not only happy to see himself cast as, but one he actively sought out, comparing himself more than once to Batman (see Salinger 2015) and in March 2016, after being told by one journalist, "We don't have Superman presidents," replied, "No . . . but we will if you have Trump" (quoted in Bradner 2015).[17]

Later in 2018, Donald Trump stood in front of the real United Nations General Assembly (in New York rather than Vienna) and gave a thirty-four-minute speech covering topics as diverse as the US's withdrawal from the UN Human Rights Council, the International Criminal Court (ICC), and the Global Compact on Migration. Trump, who in 2014 had taunted Obama by saying, "We need a president who isn't a laughing stock to the entire world" (Tweet, August 9, 2014, 12:30 a.m.), began the speech in a way that was recorded by the White House's official transcript as: "In less than two years, my administration has accomplished more than almost any administration in the history of our country. America's—so true. [Laughter.]

Didn't expect that reaction, but that's okay. [Laughter and applause]."
The speech that followed was vastly different in content and tone
to T'Challa's, with some of its most memorable lines nevertheless
very much connected to the themes we have seen at the heart of
Black Panther. He repudiated globalism ("America is governed by
Americans. We reject the ideology of globalism, and we embrace
the doctrine of patriotism"), returned to the topic of borders and
walls on seven occasions ("We've started the construction of a major
border wall, and we have greatly strengthened border security"), and
announced that America under the Trump administration would be
reconsidering its role in the world ("America will always act in our
national interest . . . we are committed to maintaining our independence from the encroachment of expansionist foreign powers. . . .
As for Americans, we know what kind of future we want for ourselves. We know what kind of a nation America must always be").
The speech, in ways many of Trump's routinely are, was called by
some a display of "commanding leadership" (Murdock 2018), but by
others one full of "outright lies" (Timmons 2018).

   Given all this it is entirely understandable why those writing
about the United Nations scene in *Black Panther* saw it through
the prism of the Trump presidency during which the film was
released, and these interpretations are relevant in understanding
how and why the film resonated in 2018. However, as Coogler and
Cole repeatedly pointed out, the film was conceived and written
during the Obama presidency and thus should be considered as
an example of what many referred to as "Obama Cinema" (see Izo
2014; Hoberman 2012). This process saw films as diverse as *The
Help* (2011), *Lincoln* (2012), *Django Unchained* (2012), *The Avengers*
(2012), *The Hunger Games* (2012), *Beasts of the Southern Wild* (2012),
The Bourne Legacy (2012), and *12 Years a Slave* (2013), among many
others, read as an engagement with the "Obama era" in American
political and social history. As reluctant as Ryan Coogler appeared
to even mention Donald Trump's name in the veritable avalanche of
interviews he conducted in 2018, he returned to the topic of Barack
Obama numerous times quite happily. In one interview, he discussed
Obama's influence on the evolution of the script in the following

way: "It was one of those things, man. Obama was President at the time, and we talked about Obama a lot in terms of, Man, it's gotta be crazy difficult to be the political leader of this place, and there's gotta be conflict there" (quoted in Pearson 2018). Similarly, the actor who played T'Challa, Chadwick Boseman, commented, "And then, of course, there was Obama. When the idea for a Black Panther movie was first hatched, a black man was president of the United States," adding that he modeled his performance of aspects of Obama's character and even mannerisms of a "leader who's not going to respond to criticism—the type of person who can hold his tongue and hold his ground" (quoted in Eeles 2018). Boseman does not mention him by name here but it is quite clear that he is referring to Obama's successor Donald Trump as he is when he concluded the interview above with a question and also an answer: "Who would you want to get the call at three in the morning? I'd rather it be someone like [Obama] or T'Challa than…somebody else" (quoted in Eeles 2018).

As we have seen, *Black Panther* is indisputably a product of the times during which it was made, but its relationship to those times is a complicated one that should be approached with more caution than many have adopted while writing about it. Marvel had considered bringing the character to the screen as early as 1992, and some years later, Kevin Feige officially announced that a Black Panther film was "on our development slate right now" during the production of *Iron Man* in February 2007 (quoted in Radford). In January 2015, actor Chadwick Boseman said the film was in a "brainstorming phase" (quoted in Huver 2015), and Ryan Coogler was confirmed as director in January 2016 with the script being written by Coogler and Joe Robert Cole during the course of that year. Principal photography began in January 2017, and the film premiered almost exactly a year later: January 29, 2018. There is a temptation that lingers for writers to make bold pronouncements about the direct relationship between cinema and society, however, as Geoff King warns:

Exactly how we understand these relationships is an important, often neglected issue. We might view films, variously,

as *products of* a situation (very strong linkage); as not products of but as being *shaped by* particular real-world contexts
in some respects, even if they might have appeared otherwise; or as having *resonances with* something such as the dis-
courses and practices associated with the "War on Terror,"
without necessarily arguing for the existence of any direct
form of determination. (2016, 52)

King is undoubtedly correct, and in the case of the connections
between the post-9/11 era and what has come to be referred to as
post-9/11 American cinema that he refers to, the relationship is a
complicated and multidimensional one requiring a nuanced analysis of a range of political, industrial, social, and ideological factors.
Despite this it is clear to see that many American films in the two
decades after 9/11 were fueled by the shifting coordinates of the
fears and anxieties of their times and as a result provide a remarkable testimony to the "War on Terror" era, whether we consider the
horror genre (*The Mist* [2007], *Land of the Dead* [2005], and *Hostel*
[2005]), science fiction films (*Cloverfield* [2008], *Children of Men*
[2006], and *War of the Worlds* [2006]), or the genre at the heart of
this book, the superhero film (*Iron Man* [2008], *The Dark Knight*
[2008], and *Captain America: The Winter Soldier* [2014]). In similar
ways, we have seen how far *Black Panther* engaged with the turbulent political climate in which it was produced, although which of
Geoff King's three categories above we should consider most applicable to it is not entirely clear: is it a *product of, shaped by*, or does it
have *resonances with* its times? This is problematized by the fact that
the period in which the film was in the process of pre-production,
production, post-production, and release spanned three presidencies: that of George W. Bush's second term (2005–2009), both terms
of Barack Obama (2009–2017), and the Donald Trump administration (2017–21). Comments by the writer, director, producer, and
overall team responsible for the creation of *Black Panther* indicate
an awareness of these processes although each, without exception,
are careful to be restrained in their observations, perhaps aware that
overly forthright comments on the political nature of a blockbuster

can spread quickly in the internet age and alienate some fans who prefer their experiences to be apolitical, at least in their understanding of the term. Nevertheless, some make interesting reading: as Joe Robert Cole stated,

> We started writing this film a year and a half ago, long before this [Trump reportedly referring to some African countries as "shitholes"]. The themes aren't new concepts or topics. These are things that have existed for decades, such as representation. . . . This current climate may be ripe for it and I'm excited about that because maybe our film can be something that positively adds to the conversation but I don't think we're looking at it as some sort of comment on politics." (quoted in Rock 2018)

Winston Duke, who played M'Baku in the film, said, "After that election [Trump's victory in 2016] it was like, 'What's next?' We went into this movie wondering, 'Oh my God, is the world ready for this film?' Like so many people in the country, I was wondering where I stood—wondering where my narratives stood" (quoted in Miller 2018).

If this is true that both Coogler and Boseman used Barack Obama as an influential figure when constructing the characterization of T'Challa, what is it of Obama that we can discern in the film itself? Is there anything meaningful present or are these connections only superficial ones? Is Boseman's softly spoken portrayal of the character, someone who is "the type of person who can hold his tongue and hold his ground" influenced by Obama's own personality, bearing, and the predicaments of his own presidency? Several writers saw such connections, among them Nicol Turner Lee, who suggested, "It could be argued that since the end of the historic and groundbreaking Obama presidency, black people have been searching for a superhero, or a 'yes we can' leader like T'Challa. For two hours, he becomes more than a comic-book superhero. He transforms into a symbol of hope for African Americans, much like President Obama was during the previous eight years" (2018). This is something that was concurred with by Hamid Dabashi in even more direct terms when he wrote, "This Black Panther is not just Obam-aesque. It is Obama" (2018). Barack Obama was often compared to a superhero by his supporters and, just as frequently, as a supervillain by his opponents. Adilifu Nama explained the desire to see him in such a way as follows: "With his square jawline, a captivating origin story, elegant oratory, lightning quick intelligence, and sleek ath-letic profile, Barack Obama fulfilled the needs of a nation yearning for a superhero persona to confront the multiple challenges fac-ing America" (152). One might consider T'Challa's moral dilemma, that of the future direction of Wakanda, to be very similar to the one Obama was faced with through his own two-term presidency, the results of which have left many Americans divided and some even speculating that the lasting legacy of the Obama years was the election of Donald Trump himself (see Zelizer, ed. 2018; Ashbee and Dumbrell 2018). Prior to the start of his presidency in 2008, Obama stated, "I personally would want to see our tragic history, or the tragic elements of our history, acknowledged" (quoted in Au 2008), in comments that were excoriated by many members of the Republican Party at the time and even by Donald Trump himself, but they seem to accurately encapsulate what T'Challa experiences in *Black Panther*.

As Donald Trump's speech to the United Nations in 2018 offers an interesting contrast to the one delivered by T'Challa in the film, we might turn to Obama's time at the very same podium a few years before, in September 2016, the year in which *Black Panther* was actu-ally written, in what would be his final speech to the United Nations as president of the United States. The speech contains messages and passages which are very similar to T'Challa's and even lines which, I would argue, are almost interchangeable. He repudiated walls three times ("The world is too small for us to simply be able to build a wall and prevent it from affecting our own societies"; "Today, a nation ringed by walls would only imprison itself"), called for a rejection of "fundamentalism, tribalism, aggressive nationalism, and crude populism," and offered a warning for the future: "History shows that strong men are then left with two paths: permanent crackdown, which sparks strife at home, or scapegoating enemies abroad, which

Three leaders speaking in front of the United Nations: Barack Obama in 2016, T'Challa in 2018, and Donald Trump in 2018 (public domain images courtesy of wh.gov).

can lead to war." While he did not use the bridge metaphor in this speech, as T'Challa does, it was one he had frequently returned to in the past, as did those who sought to describe him; indeed, it is considered by many as a metaphor central to his time in office (see Elkatawneh 2016) and was the title of David Remnick's biography of him, *The Bridge: The Life and Rise of Barack Obama* (2010).

It is not entirely coincidental that one of the key chroniclers of the Obama presidency has been Ta-Nehisi Coates, who became a writer of the comic book iteration of Black Panther and whose tenure on that project had a profound influence on Coogler's interpretation of the character. Coates's book *We Were Eight Years in Power: An American Tragedy* (2017) collects eight of his previous articles for *The Atlantic*, adding additional commentary on each with an epilogue concerned with the rise to prominence of Donald Trump. Together they offer a powerful and sometimes painful assessment of the Obama administration, of its many achievements and aspects of its failed promise. Just as interestingly they seem to offer parallels to the thematic motifs we have explored in this book, some of which appear to be critical of what a film or an entertainment product is capable of. He wrote:

> I know now that all people hunger for a noble, unsullied past, that as sure as the black nationalist dreams of a sublime Africa before the white man's corruption, so did Thomas Jefferson dream of an idyllic Britain before the Normans, so do all of us dream of some other time when things were so simple. I know now that that hunger is a retreat from the knotty present into myth and that what ultimately awaits those who retreat into fairy tales, who seek refuge in the mad pursuit to be made great again, in the image of greatness that never was, is tragedy. (10) [18]

In sections of the book, he argues vehemently about what the social role of film and literature should be, stating that art "has no responsibility to be hopeful or optimistic or make anyone feel better about the world. It must reflect the world in all its brutality and beauty, not in hopes of changing it but in the mean and selfish desire to not be enrolled in its lie, to not be co-opted by the television dreams, to not ignore the great crimes all around us" (88). However, when he appeared onstage with Ryan Coogler and the cast in February 2018 chairing a conversation about *Black Panther* at the Apollo Theatre in Harlem, his opinions had undergone something of a transition. During the discussion Coates memorably called the film "*Star Wars* for Black people," "an incredible achievement," and went on to say, "I didn't realize how much I needed the film, a hunger for a myth that [addressed] feeling separated and feeling reconnected"—a contrast to the passage in his book which comes to almost exactly the opposite conclusion.

As we have seen on so many occasions throughout this book, these comments appear paradoxical and hard to reconcile, but they are suggestive of the diverse reactions the film has triggered. Rather than considering any given opinion to be right or wrong, as is often a temptation these days more than ever, it is more valuable to seek to understand why people held such contrasting views about the film and the debates it inspired. In the case of the film's respective relationships to the presidencies of Obama and Trump, it is clear to see that understandings of them both have contributed to what the film has come to mean in the cultural imaginary. Evan Narcisse, the cowriter of the Marvel comic "Rise of Black Panther," argued that *Black Panther* resonated more in 2018, the "Age of Trump," than it would have if it had been released two years earlier in 2016, the "Age of Obama." He suggested, "The fractious atmosphere—Charlottesville, 's—hole'—nowadays harks back to the ways black folks and black spaces were demonized during slavery and Jim Crow.... Pre-Trump, the illusion of progress would've lessened the emotional impact of the Black Panther's ascendancy" (quoted in Bernadin 2018). [19]

It is Adilifu Nama who we turn to once more in order to bring this book to a conclusion. In 2011, Nama wrote that "black superheroes offer some of the most stimulating and ideologically provocative representations of blackness ever imagined" (154), referring at the time only to comic book iterations of these characters, because in 2011 not a single film had been able to bring to the screen a

At the center of *Black Panther* are the two dynamic and vibrant characterisations of the cousins T'Challa and N'Jadaka, here both shown sitting on the throne of Wakanda.

Black superhero which warranted such a description. This book has argued that *Black Panther* is a film that has earned the right to be described in such a way, with Nama's term "provocative" being particularly apt as it is one that has provoked a diverse variety of responses from audiences, commentators and writers all around the globe. Whether *Black Panther* really is a "defining moment for Black America," as Carvell Wallace suggested in the *New York Times Magazine*, or "more than a film. It carries the hopes of the global African diaspora," as Aamna Mohdin and Lynsey Chutel wrote, is not for the author of this book to decide, rather it is to its readers themselves or audience members we should turn to: like the Facebook user LadyRock Maranatha who posted, "I cried for my people and felt immense pride in being Ethiopian and most importantly AFRICAN. We are truly resilient and beautiful" (quoted in anon.

"Fans in Africa react to *Black Panther*") or Sumeya Gasa, who said, "We were humanised, and that matters. It feels so good" (quoted in Oduah 2018), or Dave Verhaagen, who wrote in "Why *Black Panther* Matters to Us All" that the film "has made a difference. It has made my son—and many other Black sons—proud of who they are and where they have come from. The film gives us a reason for optimism and an opportunity for us all to celebrate our common humanity. It is a movie that matters to me and to my son, and also one that matters to us all . . ." (2019, loc. 4138). What is without any doubt is that *Black Panther* was indeed an important cultural artifact in 2018, with an impact rare in contemporary popular culture, but whether it will herald changes in the representation of Africa and African Americans onscreen, both in the superhero genre and outside of it, and whether it will continue to resonate in such a way in years to come, remains to be seen.

Notes

Introduction

1. In addition to this it was the first film screened in Saudi Arabia for thirty-five years (see France-Presse 2018), its Wikipedia entry was the most read article on the site across the globe in the month of February 2018 (see Erhart 2018) and it was, at the time of release, the most tweeted about film ever (see Chuba 2018).

2. In comparison to T'Challa, Tony Stark's wealth was estimated as "only" $12.4 billion (see Davidson 2015). The monetary value of vibranium is not confirmed in the film series, but the comic *Fantastic Four* no. 607 (2012) states that it is worth $10,000 per gram.

3. While this book will primarily refer to him as N'Jadaka, it will use the name he is referred to in the context of any particular scene: for example, while in scenes with Ulysses Klaue, who is unaware of his ancestral heritage, he might be referred to as Erik, but in scenes with his father N'Jobu or those in Wakanda he will be referred to as N'Jadaka. There are moments in the film where this proves challenging, but these emerge as revealing about his own attitude and relationship with those around him.

4. By way of comparison, in 2017 the United States was estimated to be comprised of 61 percent Caucasian, 18 percent Hispanic/Latino, 6 percent Asian, but film audiences in the same year are slightly different with 54 percent being Caucasian, 24 percent being Hispanic/Latino, and 8 percent being Asian. Other examples of American films in this period that drew African American audiences in numbers larger than usual are *Hidden Figures* (2016), which *Deadline* reported had a 37 percent African American audience on its opening weekend in January 2017 (see D'Alessandro 2017a), and *Get Out* (2017), which had a 38 percent African American audience in the month after (see D'Alessandro 2017b).

5. Going back slightly further we have *The Meteor Man* (1993), *Blankman* (1994), *Spawn* (1997), and *Steel* (1997). If we take into account smaller roles we can include the likes of the several Black characters in the X-Men franchise

(2000–), *The Incredibles* (2004), *Suicide Squad* (2016), and *Justice League* (2017), among others.

6. In 2018, the year of the release of *Black Panther*, gains appeared to be made in some areas with sixteen directors out of the top one hundred films being Black. However, only five were women, and the newest report by Dr. Smith and her team contained other disappointing figures concerning the prevalence of white male producers (72.3 percent), white male editors (84.5 percent), white male cinematographers (97 percent), and a variety of others (see Smith et al. 2019).

7. The fact that both Serkis and Freeman had previously appeared in Peter Jackson's *The Hobbit* trilogy (2012–14) led to the joke that they were to be regarded as the film's "Tolkien white guys" (see Kyriazis 2017). When Freeman was asked about the experience of being the only white actor on the set, he answered, "You think, 'Right, this is what black actors feel like all the time'" (quoted in Hodges 2018b).

8. In interviews, Ryan Coogler has been reluctant to comment directly about how the film engages with real-world contemporary politics. In one interview he stated, "When people say, 'This film is a political movie,' well, yeah. Black Panther is a politician. . . . It's the first MCU film about a politician'" (quoted in Boone 2018).

9. Something less widely reported by the news media is the fact that an estimated 10,000 Iraqi civilians were killed in the same year as well as 2,118 Afghan civilians, which Dexter Filkins at the *New York Times* reported was an increase of 40 percent from the previous year (2009).

10. While the name of the character was not directly connected to the revolutionary organization, Jeffrey A. Brown in his *Black Superheroes, Milestone Comics, and Their Fans* (2001) suggested that Lee and Kirby "had been somewhat inspired by the organization, and at the very least the character's name was a hip reference to the struggles of black American culture" (19–20).

11. In this way, *Black Panther* joins a number of films that were too easily connected to the Trump presidency in a process I have described elsewhere as the "ex post facto allegory,"—that is, films that were made prior to Donald Trump's tenure as forty-fifth president of the United States but are regarded as emerging and commenting on it, including *Hidden Figures* (2016), *Rogue One: A Star Wars Story* (2016), *Moana* (2017), *Patriots Day* (2017), *La La Land* (2017), *War for the Planet of the Apes* (2017), *The Boss Baby* (2017), and *Death Wish* (2018), to name just a few (see McSweeney 2019).

12. For books that chart the resonance and impact of *Saving Private Ryan* see Nigel Morris's *The Cinema of Steven Spielberg: Empire of Light* (2007) and Warren Buckland's *Directed by Steven Spielberg: Poetics of the Contemporary Hollywood Blockbuster* (2006).

Chapter One

1. One needs to turn to *Guardians of the Galaxy* (2014) and *Guardians of the Galaxy: Vol. 2* (2017) to go back even further than this. James Gunn's films provide

information as to how the universe actually came into existence and along with it the six Infinity Stones, which provided the name to the first three phases of the Marvel Cinematic Universe: "the Infinity Saga."

2. Two years later, the image was again recreated in Spike Lee's *Da 5 Bloods* (2020), a drama about the experiences of African Americans participating in the Vietnam War and also with Chadwick Boseman.

3. The year 1992 is also significant in ways perhaps not considered by Ryan Coogler: it was in this year that Wesley Snipes unsuccessfully sought to make a film about Black Panther (see Parker and Couch 2018). Six years later, Snipes played another iconic Black superhero in *Blade*.

4. If vibranium is indeed worth $10,000 per gram, this would mean the value of the amount stolen would be somewhere in the region of $2.5 billion.

5. "Motherland" was the film's secret working title, a process often adopted by large scale productions in an effort to disguise themselves from fans and journalists seeking information and "spoilers." Other notable examples within the MCU are *Group Hug* for *The Avengers*, *Eye See You* for *Doctor Strange*, *Freezer Burn* for *Captain America: Winter Soldier*, and *Blue Bayou* for *Black Widow* (2021). Outside of the MCU some memorable ones are *Planet Ice* for *Titanic* (1997), *How the Solar System Was Won* for *2001: A Space Odyssey* (1968), and *Star Beast* for *Alien* (1979).

6. These descriptions of the real-world tribes that influenced *Black Panther* are indebted to the works of Roussos (2018), Wilkins, ed. (2018), and Chutel and Yomi Kazeem (2018).

7. As one might expect, lines like these are often frowned upon by some Christian writers (see Bryant 2018; Perry 2018). Outside of the MCU in *Deadpool: The Super Duper Cut* (2018), the title character calls himself "merely a vessel for the lord" and later suggests he is a god.

8. *Black Panther* actually has a character called Griot, an artificial intelligence played by South African comedian Trevor Noah, who contributes his voice to the film.

9. Later, when the film moves into Jabari territory, they are shown to be a tribe which has eschewed the technological advances provided by vibranium: M'Baku's throne room sits on the edge of a snow-capped cliff, seemingly held up by a statue of a giant gorilla and is constructed entirely from wood and other natural resources.

10. Interestingly, the charismatic Duke adopts a conspicuous Igbo accent rather than the Xhosa that most of the Wakandans can be heard to use, a choice which saw him embraced by many Nigerians. Duke said, "I do more of a Nigerian Igbo. . . . It's not Igbo, but it's influenced by Igbo because the rest of the cast is doing South African Xhosa. We wanted something that had its own personality and had its own beauty. So we referenced Igbo, and that helped" (quoted in Orubo 2018).

11. Sekhmet is another god of Ancient Egyptian origin like Bast but is not mentioned in *Black Panther*. Additionally, T'Challa informs Black Widow that "my father thought so [that the afterlife was real]. I am not my father," a line which anticipates the central thematic motif of *Black Panther* two years before it was released.

Chapter Two

1. The animated six-episode television series *Black Panther* (2010, BET) has Agent Ross describe Wakanda as a "rogue state" that possesses a "warrior spirit that makes the Vietnamese look like . . . well, French" (1.01).

2. New countries are still formed from time to time: on July 9, 2011, South Sudan declared its independence from Sudan after a civil war that saw millions die (see Johnson 2004). Other new countries to have emerged since the turn of the new millennium are East Timor in 2002, Montenegro and Serbia in 2006, and Kosovo in 2008. Just two years before in *Captain American: Civil War*, its location had been slightly different, bordering Uganda, Kenya, and South Sudan. This shift has been a frequent occurrence in the comics too which has seen it move around the region sharing borders with countries both real and fictional, as in *Marvel Atlas 2* (Moreels et al. 2008), where it was shown to have borders with Niger, Burundi, Chad, and Nigeria, but also Rudyarda. There are some complications to this: to avoid contentious politics the comic book Wakanda has been traditionally shown to interact with other fictional African countries like Niganda, Canaan, Azania, and Mohannda. The other most notable fictional country in the MCU is Sokovia from *Avengers: Age of Ultron* (2015), coded by the film as being reminiscent of Kosovo, circa 1991–2001.

3. At a lunch with African leaders in New York in the year before Donald Trump gave a speech during which he referred to "Nambia" instead of "Namibia," not once but twice (see Karimi 2017).

4. Later in the film, Ross will try to talk to M'Baku in his throne room but is forced into silence by the chief's loud shouting noises directed at him. At a screening in Nairobi, Kenya, according to Larry Madowo, the scene was clapped at loudly by the audience (see Madowo 2018).

5. We might consider that another *planet* is afforded this privilege in the MCU, Asgard in *Thor* and *Thor: The Dark World*. However, Asgard too was read by many as very American in the way it was constructed (see Gaine 2015).

6. Among these seventeen were the Democratic Republic of Congo (shown as having a border with Wakanda in the film), Nigeria, and South Africa, both connected to *Black Panther* and the MCU.

7. See also John Winthrop's sermon "A Model of Christian Charity" (1630). In his address to the nation on the day after 9/11, George W. Bush stated that "America was targeted for attack because we're the brightest beacon for freedom and opportunity in the world. And no one will keep that light from shining."

8. Marvel's official tie-in comic book, called *Black Panther Prelude* (2017), tells the story of how T'Challa and Okoye met ten years before and their first mission together. It also shows that the first time he became the Black Panther was in 2008 as he is shown watching Tony Stark reveal that he is Iron Man at the climax of *Iron Man*.

9. In *Daredevil* (Netflix, 2015–18), the episode "Kinbaku" (2.05) reveals that Frank Castle, aka The Punisher, enlisted in the military after 9/11.

10. There is a rich history of Xhosa poets and novelists like D. L. P. Yali-Manisi, S. E. K. Mqhayi, Nontsizi Mgqwetho, Sindiwe Magona, and Godfrey Mzamane. These writers are largely unknown outside of Africa (see Opland 2017).

11. Despite the extent to which the film went to create a believable, multilayered African nation and having the cast speak Xhosa, not everyone was impressed. Criticizing the use of Xhosa which started in *Captain America: Civil War*, Rachel Strohm wrote, "It's the equivalent of having Queen Elizabeth chatting to Prince Charles in Russian" (2016).

12. In the "Notes on a Scene" video produced by *Vanity Fair*, Ryan Coogler comments that for him "the color blue represented colonization," pointing out that in the scenes in Busan Klaue is dressed in blue and the color blue is a key part of the *mise en scene* in the sequence in the Museum of Great Britain (anon. 2019).

13. While this is not new (see *Rope* [1948], which has long takes of ten minutes), advances in digital technology allow for more complicated uses of the cinematic technique.

14. Only two films spent longer than two weeks at number one in 2018: *Avengers: Infinity War* and *Bohemian Rhapsody*.

15. The film only received a limited release outside China and made just $2.7 million at the US box office.

16. There are certainly depictions of the CIA that are not positive as in those in *The Quiet American*, *Three Days of the Condor*, Nathan D. Muir in *Spy Game*, and the characters in the Bourne franchise (2002–), but they tend to feature rogue characters rather than the agency itself being at fault as an institution.

Chapter Three

1. The soundtrack has songs that can be considered as being taken from the points of view of both T'Challa and N'Jadaka. The song "Black Panther" features the lines "king of the past, present, future, my ancestors watchin," which clearly refer to T'Challa. Kendrick Lamar's work has featured repeated motifs connected to African American identity, resistance, and rebellion: a song on his third album, *To Pimp a Butterfly* (2015), "Mortal Man," features the lyrics "next time it's a riot there's gonna be bloodshed for real . . . it's gonna be like Nat Turner, 1831, up in this muthafucka." Spencer Kornhaber saw the content of the *Black Panther* album more closely affiliated to Killmonger than T'Challa with the film portraying "the same conflicts that animate Lamar's career" (2018).

2. In particular, the clothes Killmonger is wearing in this sequence seem very similar to those worn by Tupac's character of Bishop in *Juice*.

3. Another Smithsonian museum had been memorably featured in *Captain America: Winter Soldier*, the National Air and Space Museum, with an exhibit dedicated to Steve Rogers/Captain America entitled "Living Legend and Symbol

of Courage" situated among other icons of American cultural history like Charles Lindbergh's *Spirit of St. Louis* and the X-15, the fastest aircraft ever made.

4. In 2018, billionaire Stephen Schwartzman, co-founder and CEO of Blackstone, donated $1 billion to MIT (see Adams 2018).

5. When Todd Phillips's *Joker* was released in 2019 and won the Golden Lion at Venice, some reviewers worried that the film provided too much for viewers to empathize with (see Kelly, "Is *Joker* a Danger to Society?").

6. When Donald Trump pulled out of the Paris Climate Agreement, his response was similar to T'Challa's comment that he "was elected to represent the citizens of Pittsburgh, not Paris."

7. The number of scars is impossible to count, but the FX artist responsible, Joel Harlow, said there were more than 3,000 (see Dillon 2018).

8. The scene is prefigured in unexpected ways by Shuri's lament that "we didn't even get to bury him," as a similar fate befell her uncle N'Jobu back in 1992.

Chapter Four

1. This seems to be confirmed in one of the film's deleted scenes called "UN Meet and Greet," where Ross tells T'Challa at the UN, "What you guys have is gonna scare a lot of people in that room," suggesting that he chose to tell no one the truth about Wakanda.

2. In recent years the term has often been used in connection to terrorism (see Pfaff 2005), Iran (see Heath 2006), or Osama bin Laden (see Scheer 2011), as well as in a range of other contexts.

3. These places are also not chosen at random and are three cities with historic connections to colonialism: Geraint Smith wrote, "Slavery is as the heart of the wealth of London" (199, 1); the New York Historical Society's "Slavery in New York" exhibition (October 2005–March 2006) featured the text "Though it is barely mentioned in school textbooks, slavery was a key institution in the development of New York, from its formative years." For an analysis of how the colonial legacy of Hong Kong is still felt in the modern era, see Ban Wang's *Illuminations from the Past: Trauma, Memory, and History in Modern China* (2004).

4. In Jeremy Scahill's *The Assassination Complex: Inside the Government's Secret Drone Warfare Program* (2017), the author writes, "According to a former drone operator for the military's Joint Special Operations Command, the National Security Agency often identifies targets for drone strikes based on controversial metadata analysis and cell phone tracking technologies—an unreliable tactic that results in the deaths of innocent or unidentified people. Rather than confirming a target's identity with operatives or informants on the ground, the CIA or the US military orders a strike based on the activity and location of the mobile phone a person is believed to be using" (96).

5. The film's editor, Michael Shawver, said in an interview that N'Jadaka had an extra line of dialogue that was removed from the final film for being too explicitly connected to these themes. The line was: "It's beautiful, but what are you going to do for everybody in the world who can't see this?" (quoted in Sharf 2019).

Chapter Five

1. We must also here include the director of the museum featured in one of the film's early scenes who is poisoned.

2. In the televisual world of the MCU, we can see examples like Ruth Negga's Raina in *Marvel's Agents of S.H.I.E.L.D.*, Simone Missick's Misty Knight in *Luke Cage*, and Rosario Dawson's Claire Temple in *Daredevil* first then in various other Netflix Marvel television shows.

3. This is very different to the history of the character in the comic books. Nakia was introduced in *Black Panther*, vol. 3, no. 1 (November 1998) as a woman who became obsessed with and was then spurned by T'Challa before ultimately siding with Erik Killmonger and becoming a villain named Malice.

4. We might add to this list Joe Russo's comments about his decision to feature (and play) a gay character in *Avengers: Endgame* about which he said, "It was important to us as we did four of these films, we wanted a gay character somewhere in them. We felt it was important that one of us play him, to ensure the integrity and show it is so important to the filmmakers that one of us is representing that. It is a perfect time, because one of the things that is compelling about the Marvel Universe moving forward is its focus on diversity" (quoted in Kelly 2019).

Conclusion

1. A rare superhero film to win outside of technical awards is *The Dark Knight* for Heath Ledger's performance in the category of Best Supporting Actor which was followed by Joaquin Phoenix's Best Actor Academy Award for the same character in *Joker*. Disney pushed for twenty-six different nominations for Academy Awards in sixteen different categories for *Black Panther* (see Clark 2018). Ultimately, it was nominated for six and won three (Best Original Music Score, Best Costume Design, and Best Production Design).

2. The most interesting covers however might have been the ones which were *not real* and created by Darian Robbins. He completed one for *Time* ("The Wakanda Issue"), *Wired* ("This Metal Will Change the World: VB, Vibranium"), and *Military History Today* ("The Battles of the Dora Milaje"). Aspiring graphic designer Robbins commented, "I chose these covers because I was thinking about

how to bridge the gap of fiction to reality to help world building and character introduction" (quoted in Kuchera 2015).

3. The MTV sketch jokes about Vodka vibranium and stays at the Wakanda Sheraton. That night, *Black Panther* won Best Picture, Best Performance in a Movie (Chadwick Boseman), Best Hero (Chadwick Boseman), and Best Villain (Michael B. Jordan).

4. About a year before, Jimmy Kimmel had featured a segment on his show about Wakanda called "Lie Witness News," in which he asked people on the street about the crisis in Wakanda. Many of those featured seemed to think the country was real. One said: "I think we need a strong presence there, I definitely support our troops . . . they have a reason to be there." When another was asked, "Why does Donald Trump hate the Wakandans so much?" one unnamed woman replied, "Should I say it? Because they are not his color!" (*Jimmy Kimmel Live* [2018], February 23, 2018).

5. Whether the project had any discernible impact is impossible to determine. The turnout for Black voters in the midterm elections in November 2018 was said to be up 174 percent, according to Ben Ray Luján, chairman of the Democratic Congressional Campaign Committee (DCCC) (quoted in Gambino 2017).

6. For more information, see https://www.amnesty.org/en/countries/africa/.

7. The piece is a fascinating one and includes a remarkable sentence that I am quite sure no one else would have written about the film, one which embodies Žižek's idiosyncratic approach to film scholarship. About *Black Panther* he writes, "Reading the film in the way Leo Strauss read Plato's and Spinoza's work, as well as Milton's *Paradise Lost* [1667], we can recover this apparently foreclosed potential."

8. In the same year, for the first time ever, a remarkable six out of the top ten earning films of the year featured superheroes: *Avengers: Infinity War*, *Black Panther*, *Incredibles 2*, *Venom*, *Deadpool 2*, and *Aquaman* (with *Ant-Man and the Wasp* just outside, at number eleven). However, of these only *Black Panther* made more in the US than it did abroad, one of only three films in the top twenty to do so (the others being *Dr. Seuss' The Grinch* and *A Star is Born*).

9. The South African journalist Adekeye Adebajo called it "racial therapy in the Trump era" (2018).

10. To these, we might add cinematic icons of the twentieth century like Rambo, Rocky, Indiana Jones, and that powerful signifier that is "John Wayne," each of whom have been held up of representative of what it means to be American in compelling ways.

11. Siddhant Adlakha reads this expression in the following way: "The king only smiles, for he knows the answer is possibility" (2018). In the opinion of the author, J. Scott Jordan and Daniel Jun Kim take this a little too far when they interpret T'Challa's lack of answer here as "The king of Wakanda smiles as if to say, 'The answer, young friend, is the story of my life, and of all lives ever lived'" (loc 1575: 2019).

12. There are several exceptions to this pattern, including *Avengers: Infinity War*, which only contains the distress signal being sent to Captain Marvel;

Avengers: Endgame has no mid- or post-credit scenes; and *Guardians of the Galaxy, Vol. 2* has five scenes spread across its credits.

13. Agent Ross can be seen in the background here but in the deleted scene "UN Meet and Greet" says to T'Challa, "It's not my place to say but man I really don't think you should do this," before adding, "I'll do my best to keep them off your back." At this point, he attempts to offer a phrase in Wakandan/Xhosa, which is translated as: "Good luck and many shoelaces."

14. This sequence also ends with an unanswered question, this time from the French ambassador to the United Nations who asks, "With all due respect King T'Challa, what can a nation of farmers offer to the rest of the world?"

15. As we have seen so often, aspects about the film which were praised by some were criticized by others. Andrews argues that this scene shows T'Challa channeling "his inner Obama and gives the most tepid, post-racial speech possible in the situation, declaring that Wakanda will reach out to the world who after all are just one tribe" (Andrews n.d.).

16. In the same interview, Boseman also said, "That idea of Wakanda was written in the 1960s so again this story is, you know, uh, we're just trying to fulfill the needs of this story and if Wakanda hasn't been conquered and other people haven't got in, then you have to ask yourself what it's been doing. It isn't like we were trying to point to Trump" (quoted in Gilbey 2018).

17. In a highly publicized visit to Trump's White House in 2018, rapper Kanye West met the president while wearing a red MAGA cap and told him, "There was something about when I put this hat on; it made me feel like Superman. . . . You made a Superman. That's my favorite superhero. You made a Superman cape for me" (quoted in Quinn 2018).

18. Making a similar argument he also points out that "Black people are not the descendants of kings. We are—and I say this with big pride—the progeny of slaves. If there's any majesty in our struggle, it lies not in fairy tales but in those humble origins and the great distance we've traveled since. Ditto for the dreams of a separate but noble past" (26).

19. The film's connections to Obama persist: *Black Panther* featured in the former president's annual list of favorite films, and Michelle Obama tweeted about the film: "Because of you, young people will finally see superheroes that look like them on the big screen. I loved this movie and I know it will inspire people of all backgrounds to dig deep and find the courage to be heroes of their own stories." When asked what the theme of the film was, Coogler suggested on more than one occasion: "Am I my brother's keeper?" (see Minnow 2018; Paige-Kirby 2018). Obama's Foundation is called My Brother's Keeper Alliance, launching in February 2014. Michael B. Jordan and Ryan Cooglar have both participated in the foundation's events and its motto is: "We believe that every young person deserves the opportunity to achieve their dreams, regardless of their race, gender, or socioeconomic status." Indeed, Obama visited Oakland about a year after the film's release with Jordan and Coogler in attendance. Their talk was called "Changing the Narrative: The Story We Tell, and Who Tells the Story."

Select Filmography

12 Years a Slave (Steve McQueen, 2013)
42 (Brian Helgeland, 2013)
2001: A Space Odyssey (Stanley Kubrick, 1968)

Abar: The First Black Superman (Frank Packard, 1977)
Alien (Ridley Scott, 1979)
Aliens (James Cameron, 1986)
Ant-Man (Peyton Reed, 2015)
Ant-Man and the Wasp (Peyton Reed, 2018)
Apocalypto (Mel Gibson, 2006)
Aquaman (James Wan, 2018)
Atomic Blonde (David Leitch, 2017)
Avatar (James Cameron, 2009)
The Avengers (Joss Whedon, 2012) [in the UK, *Avengers Assemble*]
Avengers: Age of Ultron (Joss Whedon, 2015)
Avengers: Infinity War (Russo Brothers, 2018)
Avengers: Endgame (Russo Brothers, 2019)

Back to the Future (Robert Zemeckis, 1985)
Batman (Tim Burton, 1989)
Batman Begins (Christopher Nolan, 2005)
Batman Returns (Tim Burton, 1992)
Batman & Robin (Joel Schumacher, 1997)
Batman v. Superman: Dawn of Justice (Zack Snyder, 2016)
Beasts of the Southern Wild (Benh Zeitlin, 2012)
Birdman (Alejandro G. Iñárritu, 2014)
The Birth of a Nation (D. W. Griffith, 1915)
The Birth of a Nation (Nate Parker, 2016)
Black Panther (BET, 2010)

Black Panther (Ryan Coogler, 2018)
Black Widow (Cate Shortland, 2021)
Blade (Stephen Norrington, 1998)
Blade II (Guillermo del Toro, 2002)
Blade: Trinity (David S. Goyer, 2004)
Blankman (Mike Binder, 1994)
The Boss Baby (Tom McGrath, 2017)
The Bourne Legacy (Tony Gilroy, 2012)
Boyhood (Richard Linklater, 2014)
Boyz n the Hood (John Singleton, 1991)
The Brother from Another Planet (1984)
Brown Girl Begins (Sharon Lewis, 2017)

The Cabinet of Dr. Caligari (Robert Weiner, 1920)
Captain America: Civil War (Russo Brothers, 2016)
Captain America: The First Avenger (Joe Johnston, 2011)
Captain America: The Winter Soldier (Russo Brothers, 2014)
Captain Marvel (Anna Boden and Ryan Fleck, 2019)
Casablanca (Michael Curtiz, 1942)
Casino Royale (Martin Campbell, 2006)
Catwoman (Pitof, 2004)
Children of Men (Alfonso Cuarón, 2006)
Coming to America (John Landis, 1988)
Creed (Ryan Coogler, 2015)

Da 5 Bloods (Spike Lee, 2020)
Dances with Wolves (Kevin Costner, 1990)
Daredevil (Netflix, 2015–)
The Dark Knight (Christopher Nolan, 2008)
Deadpool 2 (David Leitch, 2018)
Deadpool: The Super Duper Cut (David Leitch, 2018)
Death Wish (Eli Roth, 2018)
The Dictator (Larry Charles, 2012)
Django Unchained (Quentin Tarantino, 2012)
Doctor Strange (Scott Derrickson, 2016)

The Empire Strikes Back (Irwin Kershner, 1980)

The Falcon and the Winter Soldier (Disney+, 2021–)
Fruitvale Station (Ryan Coogler, 2013)

La Grande Illusion (Jean Renoir, 1937)
Get on Up (Tate Taylor, 2014)
Get Out (Jordan Peele, 2017)

Gods of Egypt (Alex Proyas, 2017)
Green Book (Peter Farelly, 2018)
Guardians of the Galaxy (James Gunn, 2014)
Guardians of the Galaxy: Vol. 2 (James Gunn, 2017)

Hancock (Peter Berg, 2008)
The Help (Tate Taylor, 2011)
Hidden Figures (Theodore Melfi, 2017)
The Hunger Games (Gary Ross, 2012)

The Incredible Hulk (Louis Leterrier, 2008)
The Incredibles (Brad Bird, 2004)
Incredibles 2 (Brad Bird, 2018)
Independence Day: Resurgence (Roland Emmerich, 2016)
Invasion of the Body Snatchers (Don Siegel, 1956)
Iron Man (Jon Favreau, 2008)
Iron Man 2 (Jon Favreau, 2010)
Iron Man 3 (Shane Black, 2013)

JFK (Oliver Stone, 1992)
Joker (Todd Phillips, 2019)
Juice (Ernest R. Dickerson, 1992)
Jungle Fever (Spike Lee, 1991)
Justice League (Zack Snyder, 2017)

La La Land (Damien Chazelle, 2017)
Life of Pi (Ang Lee, 2012)
Lincoln (Steven Spielberg, 2012)
Locks (Ryan Coogler, 2009)
London has Fallen (Babak Najafi, 2016)
Luke Cage (Netflix, 2016–)

Malcolm X (Spike Lee, 1992)
Man of Steel (Zack Snyder, 2013)
Marshall (Reginald Hudlin, 2017)
Marvel's Agents of S.H.I.E.L.D. (ABC, 2013–)
Memento (Christopher Nolan, 2001)
The Meteor Man (Robert Townsend, 1993)
Message from the King (2016)
Miles Ahead (Don Cheedle, 2016)
Mission Impossible: Fallout (Christopher McQuarrie, 2018)
Mo' Better Blues (Spike Lee, 1990)
Moana (Ron Clements and John Musker, 2017)
Moonlight (Barry Jenkins, 2016)

Mudbound (Dee Rees, 2017)

New Jack City (Mario Van Peebles, 1991)

The Office (BBC, 2002–2003)
Oldboy (Park, Chan-Wook, 2003)
Olympus has Fallen (Antoine Fuqua, 2013)

The Passion of the Christ (Mel Gibson, 2004)
Patriot's Day (Peter Berg, 2017)
Psycho (Alfred Hitchcock, 1960)

The Quiet American (Philip Noyce, 2002)

Rashomon (Akira Kurosawa, 1950)
Red Dawn (John Milius, 1984)
Rogue One: A Star Wars Story (2016)
Roots (ABC, 1977)
Rope (Alfred Hitchcock, 1948)

Saving Private Ryan (Steven Spielberg, 1998)
The Searchers (John Ford, 1956)
South Central (Stephen Milburn Anderson, 1992)
Spawn (Mark A. Z. Dippé, 1997)
Spider-Man (Sam Raimi, 2002)
Summer of Sam (Spike Lee, 1999)
Spider-Man: Far from Home (Jon Watts, 2019)
Spider-Man: Homecoming (Jon Watts, 2017)
The Spook Who Sat by the Door (1973)
Spy Game (Tony Scott, 2001)
Steel (Kenneth Johnson, 1997)
Suicide Squad (David Ayer, 2016)
The Sum of all Fears (Phil Alden Robinson, 2002)
Superman (Richard Donner, 1978)
Survivor (James McTeigue, 2015)

Taken (Pierre Morel, 2008)
Thor (Kenneth Branagh, 2011)
Thor: The Dark World (Alan Foster, 2014)
Thor: Ragnarok (Taika Waititi, 2017)
Three Days of the Condor (Sydney Pollack, 1975)
Titanic (James Cameron, 1997)
Top Gun (Tony Scott, 1986)

The Usual Suspects (Bryan Singer, 1995)

Venom (Ruben Fleischer, 2018)

The Walking Dead (AMC, 2010–)
WandaVision (Disney+, 2020–)
War for the Planet of the Apes (Matt Reeves, 2017)
Watchmen (Zack Snyder, 2009)
What's Love Got To Do With It (Brian Gibson, 1993)
Wolf Warrior (Wu Jing, 2015)
Wolf Warrior 2 (Wu Jing, 2017)
Wonder Woman (Patty Jenkins, 2017)
A Wrinkle in Time (Ava DuVernay, 2018)

X-Men (Bryan Singer, 2000)
X-Men 2 (Bryan Singer, 2003)
X-Men: First Class (Matthew Vaughn, 2011)

Zero Dark Thirty (Kathryn Bigelow, 2012)

Works Cited

Abubakar, Atiku. 2018. "*Black Panther*—A Good Film with Many Lessons for Nigeria." *Medium*, March 5. https://medium.com/@atiku/black-panther-a-good -film-with-many-lessons-for-nigeria-448d952c56b (accessed August 11, 2019).

Adebajo, Adekeye. 2018. "*Black Panther*: Racial Therapy in a Trump Era." *Independent Online*, April 29. Available: https://www.iol.co.za/sundayindependent /dispatch/black-panther-racial-therapy-in-a-trump-era-14698965 (accessed August 11, 2019).

Adebeyo, Bukola. 2018. "Nigerian Army Hands over Nearly 200 Boko Haram Child 'Foot Soldiers' to UN." *CNN*, July 10. Available: https://www.cnn.com /2018/07/10/africa/nigerian-army-child-soldiers-released/index.html (accessed August 11, 2019).

Adlakha, Siddhant. 2018. "In 'Black Panther,' American Dreams and American Nightmares Clash." *Village Voice*, February 23. Available: https://www.village voice.com/2018/02/23/in-black-panther-american-dreams-and-american -nightmares-clash/ (accessed October 11, 2019).

Agee, Philip. 1980. "Introduction." In Ellen Ray, William Schaap, Karl Van Meter, and Louis Wolf, eds., *Dirty Work 2: The CIA in Africa*. London: Zed Press, 1–8.

Ahrens, Jan Martínez. 2018. "El superhéroe negro contra el 'supervillano' Donald Trump." *El País*, February 19. Available: https://elpais.com/cultura/2018/02/17 /actualidad/1518883354_889751.html (accessed August 11, 2019).

Alexander, Jeffrey, Ron Eyerman, Bernhard Giesen, Neil J. Smelser, and Piotr Sztompka, eds. 2004. *Cultural Trauma and Collective Identity*. Berkeley, California, and London: University of California Press.

Alford, Matthew, and Tom Secker. 2017. *National Security Cinema: The Shocking New Evidence of Government Control in Hollywood*. Bath: Drum Roll Books.

Allen, Marlene D. 2018. "If You Can See It, You Can Be It: *Black Panther*'s Black Woman Magic." *Africology: The Journal of Pan African Studies* 11, no. 9 (August): 20–22.

Alpern, Stanley B. 1998. *Amazons of Black Sparta: The Women Warriors of Dahomey*. New York: New York University Press.

Anapol, Avery. 2018. 'Black Voter Registration Effort Launched at 'Black Panther' Screenings." *The Hill*. February 16. Available: https://thehill.com/blogs/in-the-know/374343-black-voter-registration-effort-launched-at-black-panther-screenings (accessed August 11, 2019).

Andrews, Kehinde. n.d. "Black Mask, White Movie." *Organisation of Black Unity*. Available: http://www.blackunity.org.uk/make-it-plain/black-mask-white-movie/ (accessed August 11, 2019).

Anon. 2018. "*Black Panther*: un tournant dans la représentation des noirs à l'écran." *LeFigaro*, September 14. Available: http://www.lefigaro.fr/cinema/2018/02/14/03002–20180214ARTFIG00133—black-panther-un-tournant-dans-la-representation-des-noirs-a-l-ecran.php (accessed September 22, 2019).

Anon. 2018. "Every Hero in 'Avengers: Infinity War' Explained by the Russo Brothers." *Wired*, August 14. Available: https://www.youtube.com/watch?v=YU7iBkl3anQ&feature=youtu.be&t=17m45s (accessed August 11, 2019).

Anon. 2018. "Fans in Africa React to *Black Panther*." *CBS News*, February 19. Available: https://www.cbsnews.com/news/fans-in-africa-react-to-black-panther/ (accessed August 11, 2019).

Anon. 2017. "Motion Picture Association of America (MPAA) 'Theme Report' of 2017," n.d. Available: https://www.mpaa.org/wp-content/uploads/2018/04/MPAA-THEME-Report-2017_Final.pdf (accessed September 11, 2019).

Anon. 2018. "Notes on a Scene: *Black Panther*'s Director Ryan Coogler Breaks Down a Fight Scene." *Vanity Fair*, February 7. Available: https://www.youtube.com/watch?v=SNHc2PxY8lY (accessed August 11, 2019).

Anon. 2018. "Philly Audiences Find Deeper Meaning in 'Black Panther.'" *6ABC NEWS*, February 16. Available: https://www.youtube.com/watch?v=b4kEEpnfLrI (accessed September 21, 2019).

Anon. n.d. "Slavery in New York." *New York Historical Society*. Available: http://www.slaveryinnewyork.org/history.htm (accessed August 11, 2019).

Anon. 2017. "Sterling K. Brown on the Power of Representation in *Black Panther*." *Entertainment Weekly*, August 27. Available: https://www.youtube.com/watch?v=jqn2rV17P_c (accessed October 7, 2019).

Anon. 2018. "The Story of BEYNO, That Awesome Font You Saw on Black Panther." *Creative Market*, March 28. Available: https://creativemarket.com/blog/beyno-black-panther (accessed August 11, 2019).

Anon. n.d. "Torture on TV Rising and Copied in the Field," *Human Rights First*. http://secure.humanrightsfirst.org/us_law/etn/primetime/index.asp (accessed September 11, 2019)

Anon. 2018. "Wakanda and Busan." *Ask a Korea*, March 1. Available: http://askakorean.blogspot.com/2018/03/wakanda-and-busan.html (accessed August 11, 2019).

Anon. 2018. "Wakandanomics." *The Economist*, March 31. Available: https://www.economist.com/finance-and-economics/2018/03/31/wakandanomics (accessed August 11, 2019).

Anon. 2018. "Wakandan Technology Today: A CIA Scientist Explores the Possibili-
    ties." *CIA.gov*, August 1. Available: https://www.cia.gov/news-information/featured
    -story-archive/2018-featured-story-archive/wakandan-technology-today-a
    -cia-scientist-explores-the-possibilities.html (accessed August 11, 2019).
Anon. 2018. "What Korean People Think of *Black Panther*." *Asian Boss*, n.d. Avail-
    able: https://www.youtube.com/watch?v=FO6dRbQMPPw (accessed August
    11, 2019).
Anon. 2017. "Your 'Rabidly Intolerant Regime Is a Dismal Failure,' Swazi's King
    Mswati III Told." *Huffington Post*, November 3. Available: https://www.huff
    ingtonpost.co.uk/2017/03/11/your-rabidly-intolerant-regime-is-a-dismal
    -failure-swazis-ki_a_21879872/ (accessed September 13, 2019).
Ashbee, Edward, and John Dumbrell, eds. 2018. *The Obama Presidency and the
    Politics of Change*. London and New York: Palgrave Macmillan.
Ashcroft, Bill, Gareth Griffiths, and Helen Tiffin, eds. 1995. *The Post-Colonial
    Studies Reader*. London and New York: Routledge.
Au, Laurie. 2008. "Obama Notes 'Tragic' Past." *Star Bulletin*, July 28. Available:
    http://archives.starbulletin.com/2008/07/28/news/story05.html (accessed
    September 29, 2019).
Bailey, Issac. 2018. "*Black Panther* is for Film What Barack Obama was for the
    Presidency." *CNN*, February 9. Available: https://edition.cnn.com/2018/02/09
    /opinions/black-panther-black-america-donald-trump-bailey-opinion/index
    .html (accessed September 22, 2019).
Baldwin, James. 1963. *The Fire Next Time*. New York: Dial Press.
Baldwin, James. 1965. "The White Man's Guilt." *Ebony* XX, no. 10 (August): 47–48.
Baldwin, James, Lorraine Hansberry, Langston Hughes, Emile Capouya, Alfred
    Kazin, and Nat Hentoff. 1962. "The Negro in American Culture." *Black World*,
    March: 80–98.
Barthes, Roland. 1957. *Mythologies*. Paris, France: Les Lettres nouvelles.
Bartholomew, James. 2015. "The Awful Rise of 'Virtue Signalling.'" *The Spectator*,
    April 18. Available: https://www.spectator.co.uk/2015/04/hating-the-daily
    -mail-is-a-substitute-for-doing-good/ (accessed August 11, 2019).
Beevor, Antony. 2012. *The Second World War*. New York and London: Back Bay
    Books.
Bell, Breanna. 2019. "Martin Scorsese Compares Marvel Movies to Theme Parks:
    'That's Not Cinema.'" *Variety*, October 4. Available: https://variety.com/2019
    /film/news/martin-scorsese-marvel-theme-parks-1203360075/ (accessed
    October 14, 2019).
Bell, Gabriel. 2017. "Does God Exist in the Marvel Universe?" *Salon*, May 28.
    Available: https://www.salon.com/2017/05/28/does-god-exist-in-the-marvel
    -universe-all-above-one/ (accessed August 11, 2019).
Bernadin, Marc. 2018. "*Black Panther* Writers on Wakanda's Unique Celebration
    of Black Glory." *Variety*, February 5. Available: https://variety.com/2018/film
    /features/black-panther-joe-robert-cole-evan-narcisse-wakanda-1202686413/
    (accessed August 11, 2019).

Bishop, Bryan. 2018. "*Black Panther* is the Grown-Up Marvel Movie We've Been Waiting For." *The Verge*, February 16. Available: https://www.theverge.com/2018/2/6/16977756/black-panther-movie-review-ryan-coogler-marvel-cinematic-universe-chadwick-boseman-michael-b-jordan (accessed August 11, 2019).

Blum, William. 2014. *Killing Hope: US Military and CIA Interventions Since World War II*. London: Zed Books.

Boone, Josh. 2018. "The 'Black Panther' End-Credits Scenes, Explained by Director Ryan Coogler (Exclusive)." *ET Online*, February 16. Available: https://www.etonline.com/the-black-panther-end-credits-scenes-explained-bny-director-ryan-coogler-exclusive-96449.

Bouie, Jamelle. 2018. "*Black Panther* Is a Marvel Movie Superpowered by Its Ideas." *Slate*, February 15. Available: https://slate.com/culture/2018/02/black-panther-the-new-marvel-movie-reviewed.html (accessed August 11, 2019).

Bourne Joel K., Jr. 2019. "Last American Slave Ship is Discovered in Alabama." *National Geographic*, May 22. Available: https://www.nationalgeographic.com/culture/2019/05/clotilda-the-last-american-slave-ship-found-in-alabama/ (accessed August 11, 2019).

Bradner, Eric. 2015. "Donald Trump: 'If I Tank,' I'll Drop Out." *CNN*, October 2. Available: https://edition.cnn.com/2015/10/01/politics/donald-trump-tanking-superman/index.html (accessed October 7, 2019).

Briley, Ron. 2008. "The Dark Knight: An Allegory of America in the Age of Bush?" *History News Network*, n.d. Available: https://historynewsnetwork.org/article/53504 (accessed August 11, 2019).

Brown, Jeffrey. 2001. *Black Superheroes, Milestone Comics, and Their Fans.* Jackson: University Press of Mississippi.

Brown, Jeffrey. 2013. "Panthers and Vixens: Black Superheroines, Sexuality, and Stereotypes in Contemporary Comic Books." In Sheena C. Howard and Ronald L. Jackson II, eds., *Black Comics. Politics of Race and Representation*, 133–49. London and New York: Bloomsbury.

Bryant, Eric. 2018. "The Avengers and Jesus?" *Christian Post*, May 4. Available: https://www.christianpost.com/voice/avengers-jesus-infinity-war.html (accessed August 11, 2019).

Buckland, Warren. 2006. *Directed by Steven Spielberg: Poetics of the Contemporary Hollywood Blockbuster*. London and New York: Continuum.

Budds, Diane. 2018. "The Origin Story of the 'Black Panther' Throne." *Curbed*, February 20. Available: https://www.curbed.com/2018/2/20/17032838/black-panther-wakanda-throne-peacock-chair (accessed October 7, 2019).

Bui, Hoan-Tran. 2018. "'Black Panther' Inspires Disney to Fund a STEM Center in Oakland." *Slash Film*, February 26. Available: https://www.slashfilm.com/disney-stem-center-black-panther/ (accessed October 7, 2019).

Byrd, Ayana, and Lori Tharps. 2002. *Hair Story: Untangling the Roots of Black Hair in America*. New York: St. Martin's Press.

Carter, Sean, and Klaus Dodds. 2014. *International Politics and Film: Space, Vision and Power*. London: Wallflower.

Childs, Joi. 2018. "The Touching 'Black Panther' Hashtag Inspired by a Mother's Eight-Year-Old Son." *Hollywood Reporter*, February 18. Available: https://www.hollywoodreporter.com/heat-vision/whatblackpanthermeanstome-story-behind-black-panther-hashtag-1085869 (accessed August 11, 2019).

Choueiti, Marc, Dr. Stacy L. Smith, and Dr. Katherine Pieper. "Critic's Choice 2: Gender and Race/Ethnicity of Film Reviewers Across 300 Top Films from 2015–2017," September 2018. Available: http://assets.uscannenberg.org/docs/critics-choice-2.pdf.

Chuang, Angie. 2016. "Trump, A Monster of Our Own Making." *Huffington Post*, February 11. Available: https://www.huffingtonpost.com/entry/trump-a-monster-of-our-own-making-he-learned-to-exploit_us_581a56aee4b0570d6d6f0b3c?guccounter=1 (accessed August 11, 2019).

Chuba, Kirsten. 2018. "'Black Panther' Becomes Most Tweeted-About Movie Ever." *Variety*, March 20. Available: https://variety.com/2018/film/news/black-panther-most-tweeted-movie-ever-1202731499/ (accessed August 11, 2019).

Chutel, Lynsey. 2018. "'Black Panther' is Now the Highest Grossing Film Ever in East, West and Southern Africa." *Quartz Africa*, March 21, 2018. Available: https://qz.com/africa/1234258/black-panther-breaks-box-office-records-in-east-west-and-south-africa/ (accessed October 7, 2019).

Chutel, Lynsey, and Yomi Kazeem. 2018. "Marvel's 'Black Panther' is a Broad Mix of African Cultures—Here are Some of Them." *QZ Africa*, February 19. Available: https://qz.com/africa/1210704/black-panthers-african-cultures-and-influences/ (accessed August 11, 2019).

Ciccariello-Maher, George. 2007. "Public Enemy." In Mickey Hess, ed., *Icons of Hip Hop: An Encyclopedia of the Movement, Music, and Culture volume 1*, 169–92. Westport, CT: Greenwood Icons.

Clark, Karla. 2018. "The 'Black Panther' Writing System Subverts Our Expectations of Africa." *Fandom*, February 13. Available: https://www.fandom.com/articles/how-the-black-panther-writing-system-subverts-our-expectations-of-africa (accessed August 11, 2019).

Clark, Travis. 2018. "Disney is Pushing 'Black Panther' in 16 Oscar Categories, and 'Avengers: Infinity War' in Just 1." *Business Insider*, October 20. Available: https://www.businessinsider.com/disney-pushing-black-panther-for-16-oscars-infinity-war-for-1-2018-10?r=US&IR=T (accessed August 11, 2019).

Clarke, Ashley. 2015. "Afrofuturism on Film: Five of the Best," April 2, 2015. https://www.theguardian.com/film/filmblog/2015/apr/02/afrofuturism-on-film-five-best-brooklyn-bamcinematek.

Cleaver, Kathleen, and George Katsiaficas, eds. 2001/2013. *Liberation, Imagination and the Black Panther Party: A New Look at the Black Panthers and Their Legacy*. London: Routledge.

Coates, Ta-Nehisi. 2017. *We Were Eight Years in Power: An American Tragedy.* London: One World Books.

Cobb, Jelani. 2018. "'Black Panther' and the Invention of 'Africa.'" *New Yorker*, February 18. Available: https://www.newyorker.com/news/daily-comment /black-panther-and-the-invention-of-africa (accessed August 11, 2019).

Comolli, Jean-Louis, and Jean Narboni. 1976. "Cinema/Ideology/Criticism." In Bill Nichols, ed., *Movies and Methods*, volume 1, 22–30. Berkeley: University of California Press. Originally printed in *Cahiers du cinema*, no. 216 (October 1969).

Coogan, Peter. 2006. *Superhero: The Secret Origin of a Genre.* Austin: Monkeybrain.

Connolly, N. D. B. n.d. "How 'Black Panther' Taps Into 500 Years of History." *Hollywood Reporter*, February 16. Available: https://www.hollywoodreporter .com/heat-vision/black-panther-taps-500-years-history-1085334 (accessed August 11, 2019).

Controvich, James T. 2015. *African-Americans in Defense of the Nation: A Bibliography.* Lanham, MD: Scarecrow Press.

Costello, Matthew. 2009. *Secret Identity Crisis: Comic Books and the Unmasking of Cold War America.* New York: Continuum.

Coward, Sacha. 2018. 'Who Owns History? Museums in the Wake of 'Black Panther.'" *Royal Museums Greenwich*, March 14. Available: https://www.rmg.co.uk /who-owns-history-museums-wake-black-panther (accessed August 11, 2019).

Cox, Danny. 2018. "Marvel's 'Black Panther' Has A Not-So-Hidden Message For President Donald Trump." *Inquisitr*, February 20. Available: https://www .inquisitr.com/4794611/marvels-black-panther-has-a-not-so-hidden-message -for-president-donald-trump/ (accessed August 11, 2019).

Dabashi, Hamid. 2018. "Watching *Black Panther* in Harlem." *Al Jazeera*, February 27. Available: https://www.aljazeera.com/indepth/opinion/watching-black -panther-harlem-180227091520981.html (accessed August 11, 2019).

D'Alessandro, Anthony. 2017a. "'Hidden Figures' Calculates $27.5M Weekend, 'Rogue' Passes $500M, Other Movies Bomb Over MLK—Box Office Final." *Deadline*, January 17. Available: https://deadline.com/2017/01/patriots-day -sleepless-bye-bye-man-live-by-night-rogue-one-mlk-box-office-1201885490/ (accessed October 7, 2019).

D'Alessandro, Anthony. 2017b. "Jordan Peele's 'Get Out' Jumps to $33.4M Opening—Monday AM Box Office Update." *Deadline*, February 27. Available: https:// deadline.com/2017/02/get-out-collide-rock-dog-lego-batman-fifty -shades-darker-box-office-1201964096/ (accessed October 9, 2019).

Dargis, Manohla. 2018. "Review: 'Black Panther' Shakes Up the Marvel Universe." *New York Times*, February 6. Available: https://www.nytimes.com/2018/02/06 /movies/black-panther-review-movie.html (accessed August 11, 2019).

Davidson, Jacob. 2015. "These Are the 5 Richest Superheroes." *Money.com*, July 9. Available: http://money.com/money/3950362/richest-superheroes-comic -con/ (accessed August 11, 2019).

Dawkins, Jason. 2018. "There is Some Wakanda in All of Us." *Sanford Journal,* April 23. Available: https://www.sanfordjournal.org/sjpp/2018/9/6/there-is -some-wakanda-in-all-of-us (accessed August 11, 2019).

DeGruy, Joy. 2005. *Post Traumatic Slave Syndrome: America's Legacy of Enduring Injury and Healing.* Milwaukee, OR: Upton Press.

Demby, Gene. 2018. "'Black Panther' and the 'Very Important Black Film.'" *NPR,* February 18. Available: https://www.npr.org/2018/02/18/586888497/black -panther-and-the-very-important-black-film (accessed October 9, 2019).

Denison, Rayna, and Rachel Mizsei-Ward, eds. 2015. *Superheroes on World Screens.* Jackson: University Press of Mississippi.

Dery, Mark. 1994. "Black to the Future: Interviews with Samuel A. Delaney, Greg Tate, and Tricia Rose." In Mark Dery, ed., *Flame Wars: The Discourse of Cyberculture,* 179–222. Durham and London: Duke University Press.

Desowitz, Bill. 2018. "'Black Panther': How Wakanda Got a Written Language as Part of its Afrofuturism." *Indiewire,* February 22. Available: https://www .indiewire.com/2018/02/black-panther-wakanda-written-language-ryan -coogler-afrofuturism-1201931252/ (accessed August 11, 2019).

Dicker, Ron. 2018. "Serena Williams' 'Wakanda-Inspired Catsuit' Banned By French Open." *Huffington Post,* August 24. Available: https://www.huff ingtonpost.co.uk/entry/serena-williams-black-panther-catsuit-banned _us_5b80173ae4b0729515126848 (accessed August 11, 2019).

Dillon, Ananda. 2018. "Killmonger's *Black Panther* Scars Were Made from 3,000 Prosthetic Dots." *CBR.com,* May 4. Available: https://www.cbr.com/killmonger -black-panther-scars-prosthetic-dots/ (accessed August 11, 2019).

Dionne, Evette. 2018. "The Women of Wakanda: Nakia is the Real Revolutionary of 'Black Panther.'" *Bitch Media,* February 20. Available: https://www.bitch media.org/article/the-women-of-wakanda-are-the-real-revolutionaries

Dittmer, Jason. 2005. "Captain America's Empire: Reflections on Identity, Popular Culture and Post-9/11 Geopolitics." *Annals of the Association of American Geographers* 95, no. 3: 626–43.

Dittmer, Jason. 2012. *Captain America and the Nationalist Superhero: Metaphors, Narratives, and Geopolitics.* Philadelphia: Temple University Press.

Dixon, Benjamin. 2018. "The Most Important Moment in *Black Panther* No One Is Talking About." *Progressive Army.* Available: http://progressivearmy.com /2018/02/18/important-moment-black-panther/ (accessed August 11, 2019).

Dohlvik, Charlotta. 2006. "Museums and Their Voices: A Contemporary Study of the Benin Bronzes," PhD thesis. Available: https://www.semanticscholar .org/paper/A-CONTEMPORARY-STUDY-OF-THE-BENIN-BRONZES -WRITTEN-Dohlvik/28e6e0520ff058b9a2db77b30c62ab8140395f39 (accessed October 9, 2019).

Domise, Andre. 2018. "Killmonger is Not a Revolutionary, Man." *ByBlacks.com,* February 20. Available: https://byblacks.com/entertainment/film-tv/item /1828-killmonger-is-not-a-revolutionary (accessed August11, 2019).

Donnenfeld, Zachary. 2019. "Drone Strikes a Growing Threat to African Civilians." *ISS Africa,* February 27. Available: https://issafrica.org/iss-today/drone-strikes-a-growing-threat-to-african-civilians (accessed August 11, 2019).

Du Bois, W. E. B. 1903. *The Souls of Black Folk.* New York: New American Library.

Edwards, Breanna. 2018. "#BlackPantherChallenge Raises More Than $300,000 to Send 23,000 Kids to Theaters." *The Root,* February 9. Available: https://the grapevine.theroot.com/blackpantherchallenge-raises-more-than-300–000-to-sen-1822879892 (accessed August 11, 2019).

Eeles, Josh. 2018. "The 'Black Panther' Revolution." *Rolling Stone,* February 18. Available: https://www.rollingstone.com/movies/movie-features/the-black-panther-revolution-199536/ (accessed August 11, 2019).

El-Faizy, Monique. 2018. "'Black Panther' is More than Just a Superhero Movie." *France24,* February 19. Available: https://www.france24.com/en/20180219-black-panther-more-just-superhero-movie (accessed August 11, 2019).

Eliahou, Maya, and Saeed Ahmed. 2018. "Wakanda Heads to Washington: The Smithsonian Adds 'Black Panther' Props to its Collection." *CNN,* June 25. https://edition.cnn.com/2018/06/25/entertainment/black-panther-smithsonian-trnd/index.html (accessed August 11, 2019).

Elkatawneh, Hassan. 2016. "Bridging Theory and Practice Leadership/Barack Obama." *SSRN,* November 11. Available: https://papers.ssrn.com/sol3/papers.cfm?abstract_id=2867772 (accessed October 9, 2019).

Erhart, Ed. 2018. "On Wikipedia, *Black Panther* Won the Olympic Gold." *Wikimedia.org,* March 5. Available: https://blog.wikimedia.org/2018/03/05/wikipedia-black-panther/ (accessed August 11, 2019).

Eyerman, Ron. 2001. *Cultural Trauma: Slavery and the Formation of African American Identity.* Cambridge: Cambridge University Press.

Failes, Ian. 2018. "Why The Craziest Stunt In 'Black Panther' Took 214 Versions." *Cartoon Brew,* February 22. Available: https://www.cartoonbrew.com/vfx/craziest-stunt-black-panther-took-214-versions-156779.html (accessed August 11, 2019).

Faruqi, Osman. 2018. "Why Michael B. Jordan's Killmonger Is the Real Hero of 'Black Panther.'" *Junkee.com,* February 19. Available: https://junkee.com/black-panther-killmonger-hero/147096 (accessed August 11, 2019).

Feblowitz, Joshua. 2009. "The Hero We Create: 9/11 & The Reinvention of Batman." *Inquiries Journal* 1, no. 12. Available: http://www.inquiriesjournal.com/articles/104/the-hero-we-create-911-the-reinvention-of-batman (accessed September 11, 2019).

Filkins, Dexter. 2009. "Afghan Civilian Deaths Rose 40 Percent in 2008." *New York Times,* February 17. Available: https://www.nytimes.com/2009/02/19/world/asia/19afghan.html (accessed August 11, 2019).

Fleming, Mike, Jr. 2014. "Alejandro G. Iñárritu and 'Birdman' Scribes on Hollywood's Superhero Fixation: 'Poison, Cultural Genocide'—Q&A." *Deadline,*

October 15. Available: http://deadline.com/2014/10/birdman-director-alejandro -gonzalez-inarritu-writers-interview-852206/ (accessed March 2, 2016).

Flood, Alison. 2014. "Superheroes a 'Cultural Catastrophe,' Says Comics Guru Alan Moore." *The Guardian*, January 21. Available: https://www.theguardian .com/books/2014/jan/21/superheroes-cultural-catastrophe-alan-moore-comics -watchmen (accessed June 9, 2017).

France-Prese, Agence. 2018. "Saudi Arabia's First Cinema in Over 35 Years Opens with 'Black Panther.'" *The Guardian*, April 20. Available: https://www.the guardian.com/world/2018/apr/20/saudi-arabias-first-cinema-in-over-35-years -opens-with-black-panther (accessed August 11, 2019).

Fuster, Jeremy, and Umberto Gonzalez. 2018. "Marvel Boss Kevin Feige on Ryan Coogler's 'Black Panther': 'Best Movie We've Ever Made.'" *The Wrap*, June 9. Available: June 9. https://www.thewrap.com/kevin-feige-ryan-coogler-black -panther/ (accessed August 11, 2019).

Gaine, Vincent M. 2015. "Thor God of Borders: Transnationalism and Celestial Connections in the Superhero Film." In Rayna Denison and Rachel Mizsei-Ward, eds., *Superheroes on World Screens*, 26–52. Jackson: University Press of Mississippi.

Gambino, Lauren. 2017. "Latino Turnout up 174% in 2018 Midterms Elections, Democrats Say." *The Guardian*, November 14. Available: https://www.the guardian.com/us-news/2018/nov/14/latino-turnout-up-174-in-2018-midterms -elections-democrats-say (accessed August 11, 2019).

Gans, Herbert. 1999. *Popular Culture and High Culture: An Analysis and Evaluation of Taste*. New York: Basic Books.

Gathara, Patrick. 2018. "'Black Panther' Offers a Regressive, Neocolonial Vision of Africa." *Washington Post*, February 26. Available: https://www.washington post.com/news/global-opinions/wp/2018/02/ 26/black-panther-offers-a -regressive-neocolonial-vision-of-africa. (accessed August 11, 2019).

Gay, Anna. 2018. "The Claws are Out: Marvel's *Black Panther* Confronts Museum Authority on Black Heritage." *Heritage & Memory Studies*, March 7. Available: https://heritageandmemorystudies.com/2018/03/07/the-claws-are-out -marvels-black-panther-confronts-museum-authority-on-black-heritage/ (accessed August 11, 2019).

Gerson, Joseph, and Bruce Birchard, eds. 1999. *The Sun Never Sets . . . : Confronting the Network of Foreign U.S. Military Bases*. Boston: South End Press.

Gilbey, Ryan. 2018. "*Black Panther*'s Chadwick Boseman: 'Everybody's Minds are Opening Up.'" *The Guardian*, February 15. Available: https://www.theguardian .com/film/2018/feb/15/black-panther-chadwick-boseman-interview-everybodys -minds-are-opening-up (accessed August 11, 2019).

Gilmore, Corey. 2016. "Is the Superhero Craze Destroying the Movies?" *Indiewire*, May 6. Available: https://www.indiewire.com/2016/05/is-the-superhero-craze -destroying-the-movies-291157/ (accessed August 11, 2019).

Gleason, Aaron. 2018. "'Black Panther' Is Boring as Heck Until the Villain Shows Up." February 19. Available: https://thefederalist.com/2018/02/19/black-panther -boring-heck-villain-shows/ (accessed August 11, 2019).

Goldberg, Matt. 2018. "'Black Panther' Post-Credits Scenes, Explained." *Collider*, February 17. Available: http://collider.com/black-panther-post-credits-scenes -explained/#tchalla-visits-un (accessed August 11, 2019).

Gopep, Jonathan, Dionne Searcey, and Emmanuel Akinwotu. 2018. "Boko Haram's Seizure of 110 Girls Taunts Nigeria, and Its Leader." *New York Times*, March 18. Available: https://www.nytimes.com/2018/03/18/world/africa/boko -haram-dapchi-girls-nigeria.html (accessed August 11, 2019).

Grieder, William. 2009. *Come Home, America: The Rise and Fall (and Redeeming Promise) of Our Country*. Emmaus: Rodale Press.

Grierson, Tim. 2018. "Review." *Screen Daily*, February 6. Available: https://www .screendaily.com/reviews/black-panther-review/5126078.article (accessed August 11, 2019).

Guerrero, Ed. 1993. *Framing Blackness: The African American Image in Film*. Philadelphia: Temple University Press.

Guo, Eileen. 2018. "In China, 'Black Panther' is a Movie about America." *The Outline*, March 11, 2018. Available: https://theoutline.com/post/3704/black-panther -in-china?zd=2&zi=svp5imca (accessed August 11, 2019).

Giroux, Henry, and Grace Pollock. 1999. *The Mouse that Roared: Disney and the End of Innocence*. Lanham, Boulder, and New York: Rowman and Littlefield.

Hall, Stuart. 1980. "Encoding/Decoding." In Stuart Hall, Dorothy Hobson, Andrew Lowe, and Paul Willis, eds., 117–28. *Culture, Media, Language*. Birmingham: Routledge.

Haring, Mike. 2018. "'Black Panther' Princess Letitia Wright Is Ready To Rule If Required," *Deadline*, May 27. Available: https://deadline.com/2018/05/black -panther-princess-letitia-wright-is-ready-to-rule-if-required-1202398768/ (accessed October 13, 2019).

Harris, Aisha. 2018. "*Black Panther* Is the Most Feminist Superhero Movie Yet." *Slate*, February 23. Available: https://slate.com/culture/2018/02/black-panthers -feminism-is-more-progressive-than-wonder-womans.html (accessed August 11, 2019).

Harwood, Richard. 1989. "Hyperbole Epidemic." *Washington Post*, October 1. Available: https://www.washingtonpost.com/archive/opinions/1989/10/01 /hyperbole-epidemic/82fe62b1–7816–4df1–8080–7027abb6911d/?utm_term =.782ce70f8cd5

Hassan, Adeel. 1989/2016. "Hero, Criminal or Both: Huey P. Newton Pushed Black Americans to Fight Back." *New York Times*, August 22. Available: https://www.nytimes.com/interactive/projects/cp/obituaries/archives/huey -newton (accessed August 11, 2019).

Hassler-Forest, Dan. 2012. *Capitalist Superheroes: Caped Crusaders in the Neoliberal Age*. Aylesford: Zero Books.

Haughlin, Casey. 2018. "Why Museum Professionals Need to Talk about *Black Panther*." *Hopkins Exhibitionist*, February 22. Available: https://jhuexhibitionist .com/2018/02/22/why-museum-professionals-need-to-talk-about-black -panther/ (accessed September 11, 2019).

Heath, Allister. 2006. "A Monster of Our Own Making." *The Spectator*, February 11. Available: https://www.spectator.co.uk/2006/02/a-monster-of-our-own -making/ (accessed September 11, 2019).

Hedges-Stocks, Zoah. 2018. "African Audiences are Having a Very Emotional Response to *Black Panther*: 'We Were Humanised, and that Matters.'" *The Telegraph*, February 21. Available: https://www.telegraph.co.uk/films/2018/02/21 /african-audiences-having-emotional-response-black-panther-humanised / (accessed August 11, 2019).

Herbert, Jon, Trevor McCrisken, and Andrew Wroe. 2019. *The Ordinary Presidency of Donald J. Trump*. London & New York: Palgrave Macmillan.

Hewitt, Chris. 2018. "*Black Panther* Empire Podcast Spoiler Special with Ryan Coogler and Nate Moore." *Empire Magazine*, February 20. Available: https:// www.empireonline.com/movies/news/black-panther-empire-podcast-spoiler -special-ryan-coogler-nate-moore/ (accessed August 11, 2019).

Higgins, MaryEllen. 2012. "Introduction: African Blood, Hollywood's Diamonds? Hollywood's Africa after 1994." In MaryEllen Higgins, ed., *Hollywood's Africa After 1994*, 1–4. Athens, Ohio: Ohio University Press.

Hirsch, Marianne. 2008. "The Generation of Postmemory." *Poetics Today,* March 1: 103–128.

Hoberman, J. 2012. "*The Avengers*: Why Hollywood is No Longer Afraid to Tackle 9/11." *The Guardian*, May 11. Available: http://www.guardian.co.uk/film/2012 /may/11/avengers-hollywood-afraid-tackle-9-11 (accessed January 11, 2017).

Hodges, Michael. 2018a. "Jodie Foster: 'My Greatest Strength is What's in My Head.'" *Radio Times*, January 6. Available: https://www.radiotimes.com/news /tv/2018–01–06/jodie-foster-my-greatest-strength-is-whats-in-my-head/ (accessed December 15, 2018).

Hodges, Michael. 2018b. "Andy Serkis and Martin Freeman on *Black Panther*: Movies Like This Have the Power to Change the World." *Radio Times*, February 12. Available: https://www.radiotimes.com/news/film/2018–02–12/black -panther-marvel-andy-serkis-martin-freeman/ (accessed December 15, 2018).

Holmes, Adam. 2018. "*Black Panther* DVD Commentary Reveals an Important Detail About Killmonger." *Cinemablend*, n.d. Available: https://www.cinema blend.com/news/2415132/black-panther-dvd-commentary-reveals-an-important -detail-about-killmonger (accessed August 11, 2019).

Howard, Sheena C., and Ronald L. Jackson II, eds. 2013. *Black Comics: Politics of Race and Representation*. New York and London: Bloomsbury.

Hume, David Hume. 1748 [original 1753]. "Of National Characters." In Thomas Hill Green and Thomas Hodge Gross, eds., *The Philosophical Works*, volume 3, 252, n. 1. Aalen: Scientia Verlag.

Huver, Scott. 2015. "Chadwick Boseman Shares New 'Black Panther' Insight: 'It's a Brainstorming Phase.'" *Comic Book Resources*, February 3. Available: https://www.cbr.com/chadwick-boseman-shares-new-black-panther-insight-its-a-brainstorming-phase/ (accessed August 11, 2019).

Iwanek, Krzysztof. 2018. "How Marvel Failed to Promote Seoul and Busan." *The Diplomat*, March 26. Available: https://thediplomat.com/2018/03/how-marvel-failed-to-promote-seoul-and-busan/ (accessed October 9, 2019).

Izo, David Garret, ed. (2014) *Movies in the Age of Obama*. Lanham, MD: Rowman & Littlefield.

Jeffords, Susan. 1994. *Hard Bodies: Hollywood Masculinity in the Reagan Era*. New Brunswick, NJ: Rutgers University Press.

Jenkins, Henry. 2006. *Convergence Culture: Where Old and New Media Collide*. New York: New York University Press.

Jenkins, Henry. 2018. "What 'Black Panther' Can Teach Us About the Civic Imagination." *Twenty-First Century Global*, May 22. Available: https://www.21global.ucsb.edu/global-e/may-2018/what-black-panther-can-teach-us-about-civic-imagination (accessed August 11, 2019).

Johnson, Chalmers. 2002. *Blowback: The Costs and Consequences of Empire*. London: Time Warner.

Johnson, Douglas. 2004. *The Root Causes of Sudan's Civil Wars—Old Wars and New Wars*. Bloomington: Indiana University Press.

Johnson, Victoria. 2018. "*Black Panther* Writer Reginald Hudlin on T'Challa and the Future of Black Superheroes." *Vulture*, February 13. Available: https://www.vulture.com/2018/02/black-panther-reginald-hudlin-interview.html (accessed August 11, 2019).

Jones, Jonathan. 2014. "The Art World's Shame: Why Britain Must Give Its Colonial Booty Back." *The Guardian*, November 4. Available: https://www.theguardian.com/artanddesign/jonathanjonesblog/2014/nov/04/art-worlds-shame-parthenon-elgin-marbles-british-museums (accessed October 9, 2019).

Jones, Van. 2018. "CNN's Van Jones Calls 'Black Panther' a Revelation." *AP News*, February 17. Available: https://apnews.com/5aceef8737e44f7cae129f4b952fccad (accessed August 11, 2019).

Jordan, J. Scott, and Daniel Jun Kim. 2019. "Who Is the Black Panther? The Self as Embodied Others." In Travis Langley and Alex Simmons, eds., *Black Panther Psychology: Hidden Kingdoms*. New York: Sterling.

Jordon, William. 1897. "The Greatest Nation on Earth." *Ladies' Home Journal* (July): 7–8.; cited in Kaiser (2005).

Kaiser, Kaitlyn. 2005. "Americanizing the American Woman: Symbols of Nationalism in the Ladies Home Journal, 1890–1900," Salve Regina University (thesis): 17, fn. 57, 58.

Kant, Immanuel. 1802. *Lecture on Physical Geography*, 9: 316

Karim, Fariha. 2018. "Colonial Past of Top Art Venues Exposed." *The Times*, April 17. Available: https://www.thetimes.co.uk/article/colonial-past-of-top-art -venues-exposed-cwsdtkdtm (accessed October 9, 2019).

Karimi, Faith. 2017. "Trump Praises Health Care of Nambia, a Nonexistent African Country." *CNN*, September 21. Available: https://edition.cnn.com/2017/09 /21/africa/trump-nambia-un-africa-trnd/index.html (accessed October 9, 2019).

Kaye, Don. 2018. "Black Panther: The Return of Klaw and Andy Serkis." *Den of Geek*, February 15. Available: https://www.denofgeek.com/us/movies/black -panther/271012/black-panther-the-return-of-klaw-and-andy-serkis (accessed September 24, 2019).

Kayode, Bodurin. 2014. "Inside Nigeria's Sambisa Forest, the Boko Haram Hideout where Kidnapped School Girls are Believed To Be Held." *The Guardian*, April 29. Available: https://www.theguardian.com/world/2014/apr/29/nigeria -sambisa-forest-boko-haram-hideout-kidnapped-school-girls-believed-to-be -held (accessed August 11, 2019).

Kazeem, Yomi, Lynsey Chutel, and Abdi Latif Dahir. 2018. "An Impromptu Slack Review of the Politics of 'Black Panther.'" *Quartz Africa*, February 21. Available: https://qz.com/africa/1211240/black-panther-review-by-quartz-africa -reporters/ (accessed August 11, 2019).

Keating, Patrick. 2019. *The Dynamic Frame: Camera Movement in Classical Hollywood*. New York: Columbia University Press.

Keegan, John. 1997. *The Second World War*. London: Pimlico Press.

Kelly, Aoife. 2019. "'Is 'Joker' a Danger to Society—Or Just a Reflection of Times?'" *Independent*, September 4. Available: https://www.independent.ie/opinion /comment/aoife-kelly-is-joker-a-danger-to-society-or-just-a-reflection-of -times-38465275.html (accessed October 9, 2019).

Kelly, Emma. 2019. "Avengers: Endgame Directors Russo Brothers Dragged for their Attempt at LGBTQ+ Representation." *Metro*, April 29. Available: https://metro. co.uk/2019/04/29/avengers-endgame-directors-russo-brothers-dragged -attempt-lgbtq-representation-9335307/?ito=cbshare (accessed October 9, 2019).

Kelly, Tiffany. 2018. "The Best 'Black Panther' Memes on the Internet." *Daily Dot*, June 11. Available: https://www.dailydot.com/unclick/black-panther-memes/ (accessed October 9, 2019).

Kendzior, Sarah. 2016 "Monster of Our Own Making: How Donald Trump Punked America by Manipulating Our Obsession with Useless Polls." *Quartz*, July 28. Available: https://qz.com/743923/how-donald-trump-punked-america-by -manipulating-our-obsession-with-useless-polls/ (accessed August 11, 2019).

King, Geoff. 2016. "Responding to Realities or Telling the Same Old Story? Mixing Real World and Mythic Resonances in *The Kingdom* (2007) and *Zero Dark Thirty* (2012)." In Terence McSweeney, ed., *American Cinema in the Shadow of 9/11*, 49–66. Edinburgh: Edinburgh University Press.

Kornhaber, Spencer. 2018. "The Song of Killmonger." *The Atlantic*, February 29. Available: https://www.theatlantic.com/entertainment/archive/2018/02/black-panther-soundtrack-kendrick-lamar-killmonger/553586/ (accessed August 11, 2019).

Krogstad, Jens Manuel, and Mark Hugo Lopez. 2017. "Black Voter Turnout Fell in 2016, Even as a Record Number of Americans Cast Ballots." *Pew Research*, May 12. Available: http://www.pewresearch.org/fact-tank/2017/05/12/black-voter-turnout-fell-in-2016-even-as-a-record-number-of-americans-cast-ballots/ (accessed August 11, 2019).

Kuchera, Ben. 2015. "Meet the Marvel Fan Energizing *Black Panther* Fans with His Fake Magazine Covers." *Yahoo.com*, June 3. Available: https://www.yahoo.com/news/meet-marvel-fan-energizing-black-163002882.html?guccounter=1&guce_referrer=aHRocDovL2h1ZGxpbmVudGVydGFpbm1lbnQuY29tL3NtZi9pbmRleC5waА_dG9waWM9MTMxNDkuMA&guce_referrer_sig=AQAAAEFqfQp70OanROy6vmjb8yErAUy5zLPLeWJeobiqvPFBjK1MK SEEvnVAF4vMF1u2UBpyzOV-orjG204nTsiPDBtNf-ho-WDHfeBzCD3Db trch-YIAXg68OkG5kx83sAzCIqbpX4CcpLFfeEMng5WISmPByS-jhCoay4I FoWdANSo (accessed August 11, 2019).

Kurtz, Michael L. 2000. "Oliver Stone, *JFK*, and History." In Robert Brent Toplin, ed., *Oliver Stone's USA: Film, History and Controversy*, 166–77. Lawrence: University of Kansas Press.

Kyriazis, Stefan. 2017. "*Black Panther* 'Tolkien WHITE Guys' Comments Go Viral—GOLLUM Is In the Marvel Movie?" *Express*, October 19. Available: https://www.express.co.uk/entertainment/films/868072/Black-Panther-HOBBIT-Martin-Freeman-Andy-Serkis-Bilbo-Gollum-Lord-of-the-Rings (accessed August 11, 2019).

Last, Jonathan V. 2016. "Comic Book Movies Are Killing the Movie Industry." *Weekly Standard*, May 25. Available: https://www.weeklystandard.com/jonathan-v-last/comic-book-movies-are-killing-the-movie-industry (accessed August 11, 2019).

Lawrence, John Shelton, and Robert Jewett. 1977. *The American Monomyth*. New York: Anchor Press/Doubleday.

Lawrence, John Shelton, and Robert Jewett. 2002. *The Myth of the American Superhero*. Grand Rapids, MI: Wm. B. Eerdmans Publishing Company.

LeBron, Christopher. 2018. "'Black Panther' Is Not the Movie We Deserve." *Boston Review*, February 17. Available: http://bostonreview.net/race/christopher-lebron-black-panther (accessed August 11, 2019).

Lee, Nicole Turner. 2018. "*Black Panther*: Lessons in Hollywood Diversity and Black Pride." *Brookings.edu*, February 26. Available: https://www.brookings.edu/blog/up-front/2018/02/26/black-panther-lessons-in-hollywood-diversity-and-black-pride/ (accessed August 11, 2019).

Levin, Sam. 2018. "*Black Panther* Film Fuels Calls for Release of Jailed Political Activists," *The Guardian*, February 16. Available: https://www.theguardian.com/film/2018/feb/16/black-panther-party-marvel-film-jail (accessed August 11, 2019).

Liao, Shannon. 2018. "Chadwick Boseman says T'Challa is the Enemy in *Black Panther*." *The Verge*, February 28. Available: https://www.theverge.com/2018/2/28/17063218/chadwick-boseman-tchalla-enemy-black-panther (accessed September 22, 2019).

Loomba, Ania. 1998. *Colonialism/Postcolonialism*. Routledge: London and New York.

Lopez, Germaine. 2018. "This is One of the Most Racist Remarks a Contemporary Politician Has Made about Drug Policy." *Vox*, January 9. Available: https://www.vox.com/identities/2018/1/9/16866754/marijuana-legalization-racism-alford-kansas-republican (accessed October 14, 2019).

Lopez, Ricardo. 2017. "'Black Panther' Actor Publicly Announces His DACA Status, Lending Voice to Immigration Fight." *Variety*, November 28. Available: https://variety.com/2017/film/news/black-panther-actor-daca-1202624929/ (accessed August 11, 2019).

Loughrey, Clarisse. 2019. "Trevor Noah Trolls Oscars Audience with 'Great Xhosa Phrase.'" *The Independent*, February 26. Available: https://www.independent.co.uk/arts-entertainment/films/news/trevor-noah-xhosa-oscars-2019-phrase-translation-presenter-a8797161.html (accessed August 11, 2019).

Lu, Joanne. 2018. "Why Big Thinkers Can't Stop Talking About 'Black Panther.'" *NPR*, March 2. Available: https://www.npr.org/sections/goatsandsoda/2018/03/02/590216283/why-big-thinkers-cant-stop-talking-about-black-panther?t=1563712077194 (accessed August 11, 2019).

Lussier, Germaine. 2018. "Director Ryan Coogler Explains the Identity Issues at the Heart of *Black Panther*." *IO9*, February 13. Available: https://io9.gizmodo.com/director-ryan-coogler-explains-the-identity-issues-at-t-1822937410 (accessed August 11, 2019).

Madowo, Larry. 2018. "'Black Panther': Why the Relationship between Africans and Black Americans Is So Messed Up." *Washington Post*, February 16. Available: https://www.washingtonpost.com/news/global-opinions/wp/2018/02/16/black-panther-why-therelationship-between-africans-and-african-americans-is-so-messedup/?utm_term=.b6c1751b6d43. (accessed August 11, 2019).

Malik, Kenan. 2018. "*Black Panther* Has a Burden That No Superhero Is Strong Enough to Carry." *The Guardian*, February 18. Available: https://www.theguardian.com/commentisfree/2018/feb/18/black-panther-has-burden-no-superhero-strong-enough-to-carry (accessed August 11, 2019).

Malkin, Marc. 2018. "The Real-Life Possibilities of *Black Panther*'s Wakanda, According to Urbanists and City Planners." *Architectural Digest*, February 28. Available: https://www.architecturaldigest.com/story/the-real-life-possibilities-of-black-panthers-wakanda-according-to-urbanists-and-city-planners (accessed August 11, 2019).

Maloney, Nora. 2018. "Backstage at the *Black Panther* New York Fashion Week Presentation." *Vanity Fair*, February 13. Available: https://www.vanityfair.com/style/2018/02/backstage-at-the-black-panther-new-york-fashion-week-presentation (accessed August 11, 2019).

Markert, John. 2011. *Post-9/11 Cinema: Through a Lens Darkly.* Lanham, MD: Scarecrow Press.

Martin, Ben L. 1991. "From Negro to Black to African: The Power of Names and Naming." *Political Science Quarterly* 106, no. 1 (Spring): 83–107.

Martin, Michael T., ed. 2019. *The Birth of a Nation: The Cinematic Past in the Present.* Bloomington: Indiana University Press.

Mazrui, Ali A. 1978. *Political Values and the Educated Class in Africa.* London: Heinemann.

McCann, Jim. 2018. *Black Panther: A Novel.* Newton Abbot: Centum Books.

McCarthy, Todd. 2013. "Iron Man 3: Film Review." *Hollywood Reporter*, April 23. Available: https://www.hollywoodreporter.com/review/iron-man-3-film-review-444861 (accessed August 11, 2019).

McGregor, Don. 2019. "Foreword: Living Inside the Head of the King of the Wakandans." In Travis Langley and Alex Simmons, eds., *Black Panther Psychology: Hidden Kingdoms.* New York: Sterling.

McKittrick, Katherine. 2006. *Demonic Grounds: Black Women and the Cartographies of Struggle.* Minneapolis: University of Minnesota Press.

McMillan, Graeme. 2018. "How 'Black Panther' Favorite M'Baku Transcends His Comic Book Origins." *Hollywood Reporter*, February 19. Available: https://www.hollywoodreporter.com/heat-vision/black-panther-winston-dukes-mbaku-transcends-comic-book-origins-1086344 (accessed August 11, 2019).

McNary, Dave. 2017. "'Black Panther' Climbs to Top of Social Media Chart With First Trailer." *Variety*, June 12. Available: https://variety.com/2017/film/news/black-panther-social-media-buzz-trailer-1202462910/ (accessed August 11, 2019).

McSweeney, Terence. 2014. *The "War on Terror" and American Film: 9/11 Frames per Second.* Edinburgh: Edinburgh University Press.

McSweeney, Terence. 2018. *Avengers Assemble! Critical Perspectives on the Marvel Cinematic Universe.* London: Wallflower Press.

McSweeney, Terence. 2019. "Political Apathy, the *ex post facto* Allegory and Waldo's Trumpian Moment." In Terence McSweeney and Stuart Joy, eds., *Through the Black Mirror: Reflections on 'the Side Effects' of the Digital Age,* 83–94/ London and New York: Palgrave Macmillan.

Mendelson, Scott. 2018. "'Black Panther': The Key Lesson Hollywood Refuses To Learn." *Forbes*, February 22. Available: https://www.forbes.com/sites/scottmendelson/2018/02/22/black-panther-the-key-box-office-lesson-that-hollywood-refuses-to-learn/#4698da3a159c (accessed 1August 11, 2019).

Mhlambi, Innocentia J. 2016. "Wena ungubani (Who are You)?: Post-1994 Identity and Memory through Ukuthakazela in the 'New' Media Blog." *South African Journal of African Languages* 36, no. 1: 109–122.

Mignolo, Walter D. 2011. *The Darker Side of Western Modernity: Global Futures, Decolonial Options.* Durham and London: Duke University Press.

Mikael-Debass, Milena. 2018. "What Afrofuturists Think of 'Black Panther.'" *Vice*, February 12. Available: https://news.vice.com/en_us/article/59k9k8/what-is-afrofuturism-in-marvels-black-panther (accessed August 11, 2019).

Miller, Matt. 2018. "Winston Duke Had Marvel's Greatest Introduction." *Esquire*, February 21. Available: https://www.esquire.com/entertainment/movies/a18 199538/winston-duke-black-panther-m-baku-interview/ (accessed August 11, 2019).

Minnow, Steve. 2018. "We Hung Onto It: Ryan Coogler on *Black Panther*." *RogerEbert.com*, February 13. Available: https://www.rogerebert.com/interviews /we-hung-onto-it-ryan-coogler-on-black-panther (accessed August 11, 2019).

Mirrlees, Tanner. 2014. "How to Read Iron Man: The Economics, Politics and Ideology of an Imperial Film Commodity." *Cineaction: Canada's Leading Film Studies Journal* 92, no. 1: 4–11.

Mitchell, Sean lxg. 2018. *How Do We Build a Real Wakanda?* Fort Washington, MD: ALB Management and Publishing.

Mithaiwala, Mansoor. 2018. "*Black Panther*'s Opening Scene Was Added After Test Screenings." *Screenrant*, February 21. Available: https://screenrant.com /black-panther-opening-scene/ (accessed August 11, 2019).

Mkhabela, Sabelo. 2018. "How IsiXhosa Became the Official Language of Wakanda on 'Black Panther.'" *Okay Africa*, February 19. Available: http://www .okayafrica.com/black-panther-isixhosa-language/ (accessed August 11, 2019).

Mock, Brentlin. 2018. "'Black Panther' Marks Milestone in Black Culture's Impact on Hollywood." *NBC News*, February 11. Available. https://www.nbcnews.com /pop-culture/movies/black-panther-marks-milestone-black-culture-s-impact -hollywood-n846891 (accessed August 11, 2019).

Mohdin, Aamna, and Lynsey Chutel. 2018. "'Black Panther' is More than a Film. It Carries the Hopes of the Global African Diaspora." *Quartz*, February 2. Available: https://qz.com/quartzy/1196551/black-panther-is-more-than-a-film-it -carries-the-hopes-of-the-global-african-diaspora/ (accessed August 11, 2019).

Mokoena, Dikeledi A. 2018. "*Black Panther* and the Problem of the Black Radical." *Pambazuka News*, March 9. Available: https://www.pambazuka.org/arts -books/black-panther-and-problem-black-radical (accessed October 9, 2019).

Moral, Pedro. 2018. "'Black Panther': Una película para cambiar el mundo." *Cinemania*, April 25. Available: https://cinemania.20minutos.es/noticias/repaso -marvel-lo-que-debes-saber-de-black-panther/ (accessed August 11, 2019).

Morgan, Jo Ann. 2014. "Huey P. Newton Enthroned—Iconic Image of Black Power." *Journal of American Culture* 37: 129–48.

Moreels, Eric J., Stuart Vandal, Anthony Flamini, and Michael Hoskin. 2008. *Marvel Atlas 2*. New York: Marvel Press.

Morris, Nigel. 2007. *The Cinema of Steven Spielberg: Empire of Light*. London and New York: Wallflower.

Morse, Brandon. 2018. "*Black Panther* Is a Good Movie with Both Fresh and Tired Political Overtones." *RedState.com*, February 19. Available: https://www .redstate.com/brandon_morse/2018/02/19/black-panther-good-movie-fresh -tired-political-overtones/ (accessed August 11, 2019).

Mpofu, Blessing. 2018. "Ungabani? Who Are You?" *One Africa*, n.d. Available: https://www.1africa.tv/ungubani/ (accessed August 11, 2019).

Mudd, Philipp. 2019. *Black Site: The CIA in the Post-9/11 World*. London and New York: Liveright Publishing.

Murdock, Deroy. 2018. "President Trump Displays Commanding Leadership at U.N." *National Review*, September 28. Available: https://www.nationalreview .com/2018/09/president-trump-displays-commanding-leadership-at-un/ (accessed October 9, 2019).

Musere, Jonathan, and Shirley C. Byakutaga. 1998. *African Names and Naming*. Los Angeles: Ariko Publications.

Musila, Grace A. 2018. "Chimamanda Adichie: The Daughter of Postcolonial Theory." *Al-Jazeera*, February 4. Available: https://www.aljazeera.com/indepth /opinion/chimamanda-adichie-burden-representation-180204094739657 .html (accessed August 11, 2019).

Mwakikagile, Godfrey. 2000. *Africa and the West*. Huntington, NY: Nova Science Publishers.

Mwakikagile, Godfrey. 2001. *Military Coups in West Africa Since the Sixties*. Huntington, NY: Nova Science Publishers.

Nama, Adilifu. 2011. *Super Black: American Pop Culture and Black Superheroes*. Austin: University of Texas Press.

Nava, Gabriela. 2018. "Esta es la escena de *Black Panther* que hará que los mexicanos aplaudan de pie." *Vix*, n.d. Available: https://www.vix.com/es/cultura -pop/197432/esta-es-la-escena-de-black-panther-que-hara-que-los-mexicanos -aplaudan-de-pie (accessed August 11, 2019).

Neumann, Osha. 2018. "A White Guy Watches 'The Black Panther.'" *Counterpunch*, February 23. Available: https://www.counterpunch.org/2018/02/23/a -white-guy-watches-the-black-panther/ (accessed October 9, 2019).

Newkirk, Van, II. 2018. "The Provocation and Power of *Black Panther*." *The Atlantic*, February 14, 2018. Available: https://www.theatlantic.com/entertainment /archive/2018/02/the-provocation-and-power-of-black-panther/553226/ (accessed August 11, 2019).

Newport, Frank. 2015. "Percentage of Christians in U.S. Drifting Down, but Still High." *Gallup*, December 24. Available: https://news.gallup.com/poll/187955 /percentage-christians-drifting-down-high.aspx (accessed August 11, 2019).

Nikolov, Nikolay. 2019. "'X-Men' Finally Gives Its Most Powerful Characters, Women, a Chance to Fix Past Mistakes." *Mashable*, n.d. Available: https:// me.mashable.com/entertainment/5245/x-men-finally-gives-its-most-power ful-characters-women-a-chance-to-fix-past-mistakes (accessed October 9, 2019).

Nochimson, Martha P. 2011. *World on Film: An Introduction*. Oxford and Chichester: Wiley-Blackwell.

Nolte, John. 2018. "'Black Panther' Review: The Movie's Hero is Trump, the Villain is Black Lives Matter." *Breitbart.com*, February 16. Available: https://www .breitbart.com/entertainment/2018/02/16/black-panther-review-great-actors -make-failure-launch/ (accessed August 11, 2019).

Obikili, Nonso. 2018. "Toxic Economics and Politics: The *Black Panther* Edition." *Nonso Obikili*, February 23. Available: https://nonsoobikili.wordpress .com/2018/02/23/toxic-economics-and-politics-the-black-panther-edition/ (accessed August 11, 2019).

O'Brien, Daniel. 2017. *Black Masculinity on Film: Native Sons and White Lies*. London: Palgrave Macmillan.

Oduah, Chika. 2018. "Audiences Across Africa Hail *Black Panther* for Humanizing Black Characters." *The Root*, February 20. Available: https://www.theroot .com/audiences-across-africa-hail-black-panther-for-humanizi-1823155921 (accessed August 11, 2019).

Opland, Jeff. 2017. *Xhosa Poets and Poetry*. Pietermaritzburg: University of KwaZulu-Natal Press.

Orr, Christopher. 2018. "*Black Panther* Is More Than a Superhero Movie." *The Atlantic*, February 16. Available: https://www.theatlantic.com/entertainment /archive/2018/02/black-panther-review/553508/ (accessed August 11, 2019).

Orubo, Daniel. "Nigerians Are Convinced 'Black Panther' Scene-Stealer, M'Baku Is Actually Igbo." *Konbini*, February 19. Available: https://www.konbini.com /ng/entertainment/cinema/nigerians-are-convinced-black-panther-scene -stealer-mbaku-is-actually-igbo/ (accessed August 11, 2019).

Outlaw, Kofi. 2018. "'Black Panther' Cast Reacts to Donald Trump's Reported Comment About Africa." *Comicbook.com*, January 31. Available: https://comic book.com/marvel/2018/01/31/black-panther-cast-donald-trump-africa-shit hole-countries/ (accessed August 11, 2019).

Paige-Kirby, Kristen. 2018a. "For Ryan Coogler, 'Black Panther' is About the Big Picture." *Washington Post*, February 15. Available: https://www.washingtonpost .com/express/wp/2018/02/15/for-ryan-coogler-black-panther-is-about-the-big -picture/?noredirect=on&utm_term=.04ac8b5ca21c (accessed August 11, 2019).

Paige-Kirby, Kristen. 2018b. "*Black Panther* is More Than a Name. It's an Identity." *Washington Post*, February 16. Available: https://www.washingtonpost.com /express/wp/2018/02/16/black-panther-is-more-than-a-name-its-an-identity /?utm_term=.d5f4d5a8091b (accessed August 11, 2019).

Paramore, Lyne Stuart. 2018. "Why Does a White CIA Agent Play the Hero to Killmonger's Villain in 'Black Panther'?" *NBC News*, March 11. Available: https://www.nbcnews.com/think/opinion/why-does-white-cia-agent-play -hero-killmonger-s-villain-ncna855401 (accessed August 11, 2019).

Parker, Ryan. 2018. "Francis Ford Coppola Screened an Early Cut of 'Black Panther.'" *Hollywood Reporter*, May 4. Available: https://www.hollywoodreporter .com/heat-vision/black-panther-early-cut-was-screened-francis-ford-coppola -1108741 (accessed August 11, 2019).

Parker, Ryan, and Aaron Couch. 2018. "Wesley Snipes Reveals Untold Story Behind His 'Black Panther' Film." *Hollywood Reporter*, January 30. Available: https://www.hollywoodreporter.com/heat-vision/black-panther-wesley-snipes -reveals-untold-story-behind-90s-film-1078868 (accessed August 11, 2019).

Pearson, Ben. 2018. "Director Ryan Coogler Talks 'Black Panther's Unbroken Casino Fight Shot, Obama's Influence, and More [Interview]." *Slashfilm.com*, February 15. Available: https://www.slashfilm.com/black-panther-interview/ (accessed August 11, 2019).

Perry, Kevin EG. "Senegalese Singer Baaba Maal on Being the Sound of *Black Panther*'s Wakanda." *NME*, March 21. Available: https://www.nme.com/music-interviews/baaba-maal-soundtracking-black-panthers-wakanda-2270695#trLhCutXBWrrpH15.99 (accessed August 11, 2019).

Perry, Travis. 2018. "The Metaphysics of Marvel's Avengers: Infinity War." *Speculative Faith*, May 3. Available: http://speculativefaith.lorehaven.com/the-metaphysics-of-marvels-infinity-war/#comments (accessed August 11, 2019).

Pitts, Leonard, Jr. 2018. "'Black Panther' a Watershed in Cultural History of African Americans." *Miami Herald*, February 15. Available: https://www.miamiherald.com/opinion/opn-columns-blogs/leonard-pitts-jr/article200350754.html (accessed August 11, 2019).

Pfaff, William. 2005. "A Monster of Our Own Making." *The Guardian*, August 21. Available: https://www.theguardian.com/uk/2005/aug/21/july7.terrorism (accessed August 11, 2019).

Powell, Kevin. 2018. "Michael B Jordan on *Black Panther*: 'We're Giving Black People Power.'" *GQ Magazine*, February 26. Available: https://www.gq-magazine.co.uk/article/black-panther-michael-b-jordan-cover (accessed August 11, 2019).

Powell, Mark. 2018. "The Radical Politics of *Black Panther*." *The Spectator*, February 26. Available: https://www.spectator.com.au/2018/02/the-radical-politics-of-black-panther/ (accessed August 11, 2019).

Prouix, Natalie. 2018. "Is 'Black Panther' a 'Defining Moment' for the United States—and Particularly for Black America?" *New York Times*, March 1. Available: https://www.nytimes.com/2018/03/01/learning/is-black-panther-a-defining-moment-for-the-united-states-and-particularly-for-black-america.html.

Quinn, Melissa. 2018. "Kanye West: MAGA Hat Made Me 'Feel like Superman.'" *Washington Examiner*, October 11. Available: https://www.washingtonexaminer.com/news/kanye-west-maga-hat-made-me-feel-like-superman (accessed October 9, 2019).

Radford, Bill. 2007. "Marvel Stays True to Superhero Characters in Transition to Big Screen." *The Gazette*, February 8. Available: https://web.archive.org/web/20070216043834/http://www.fortwayne.com/mld/newssentinel/living/16652105.htm (accessed August 11, 2019).

Rees, Jasper. 2016. "Arts Feature 'Do Black Movies Really Not Sell?': Don Cheadle on Miles Ahead." *The Spectator*, April 16. Available: https://www.spectator.co.uk/2016/04/do-black-movies-really-not-sell-don-cheadle-on-miles-ahead/ (accessed August 11, 2019).

Remnick, David. 2010. *The Bridge: The Life and Rise of Barack Obama*. New York: Borzoi Books.

Rhiannon, Alexis. 2018. "These Female 'Black Panther' Stars Think Wakanda Is Super Feminist & Hollywood Should Really Take Note." *Bustle.com*, October 10. Available: https://www.bustle.com/p/these-female-black-panther-stars-think -wakanda-is-super-feminist-hollywood-should-really-take-note-12212868 (accessed August 11, 2019).

Riley, Rochelle. 2019. "Why America Can't Get Over Slavery, Its Greatest Shame." *USA Today*, February 8. Available: https://eu.usatoday.com/story/news /nation-now/2018/02/08/column-why-america-cant-get-over-slavery-its -greatest-shame/1000524001/ (accessed August 11, 2019).

Robb, David L. 2004. *Operation Hollywood: How the Pentagon Shapes and Censors the Movies*. New York: Prometheus Books.

Robbins, Jacob. 2018. "'Black Panther' Is a Watershed Moment in Pop Culture." *The Eagle*, February 16. Available: https://www.theeagleonline.com/blog /silver-screen/2018/02/black-panther-watershed-moment-in-pop-culture (accessed August 11, 2019).

Robinson, Tasha. 2018. "Akon Wants to Found a 'Real-Life Wakanda' Based around His Cryptocurrency Akoin." *The Verge*, June 20. Available: https:// www.theverge.com/2018/6/20/17480674/real-life-wakanda-cryptocurrency -akoin-akon-crypto-city-senegal" (accessed August 11, 2019).

Rock, Lucy. 2018. "'This is the Movie I wish I'd Had to Look Up To': Joe Robert Cole on Co-Writing *Black Panther*." *The Guardian*, February 13. Available: https://www.theguardian.com/film/2018/feb/13/black-panther-joe-robert -cole-black-superhero-interview (accessed August 11, 2019).

Rojek, Chris. 2001. *Celebrity*. London & Chicago: Reaktion.

Rose, Steve. 2016. "Black Films Matter—How African American Cinema Fought Back Against Hollywood." *The Guardian*, October 13. Available: https://www. theguardian.com/film/2016/oct/13/do-the-right-thing-how-black-cinema -rose-again.

Rose, Steve. 2018. "Does the Marvel Epic Solve Hollywood's Africa Problem?" *The Guardian*, February 3. Available: https://www.theguardian.com/film/2018/feb /03/marvel-black-panther-chadwick-boseman-michael-b-jordan (accessed August 11, 2019).

Rosenbaum, Jonathan. 2002. *Movie Wars: How Hollywood and the Media Limit what Films We Can See*. London: Wallflower Press.

Rothe, Anne. 2011. *Popular Trauma Culture: Selling the Pain of Others in the Mass Media*. New Brunswick, NJ: Rutgers University Press.

Roussos, Eleni. 2018. *The Art of Marvel Studios: Black Panther*. New York: Marvel Press.

Rozsa, Matthew. 2018. "The Powerful Politics of Killmonger." *Salon.com*, February 23. Available: https://www.salon.com/2018/02/23/the-powerful-politics-of -killmonger/ (accessed August 11, 2019).

Rüsen, Jörn. 2010. "Holocaust Experience and Historical Sense Generation from a German Perspective." In Mamadou Diawara, Bernard Lategan, and Jörn

Rüsen, eds., *Historical Memory in Africa: Dealing with the Past, Reaching for the Future in an Intercultural Context*, 165–85. New York, London, and Oxford: Berghahn.

Sal. 2018. "Black Panther Movie Is Anti Black American (Character Review)." February 18. Available: https://www.youtube.com/watch?v=itai2nPG_Jo&t=29s (accessed August 11, 2019).

Salami, Minna. 2019. "*Black Panther* Deserves an Oscar—But Is It a Feminist Film? No Way." *The Guardian*, February 18. Available: https://www.theguardian .com/commentisfree/2019/feb/18/black-panther-oscar-feminist-film-wakanda (accessed August 11, 2019).

Sanghio, John. 2018. "How *Black Panther* Betrays Dr. King's Dream." *Voices*, April 8. Available: https://voices.uchicago.edu/religionculture/2018/04/08/how -black-panther-betrays-dr-kings-dream/ (accessed August 11, 2019).

Scahill, Jeremy. 2016. *The Assassination Complex: Inside the Government's Secret Drone Warfare Program*. New York: Simon & Schuster.

Scheer, Robert. 2011. "Osama bin Laden: A Monster of Our Own Creation." *The Nation*, May 4. Available: https://www.thenation.com/article/osama-bin-laden -monster-our-own-creation/ (accessed August 11, 2019).

Schneiker, Andrea. 2018. "Telling the Story of the Superhero and the Anti-Politician as President: Donald Trump's Branding on Twitter." *Political Studies Review* 17, no. 3: 210–23.

Schou, Nicolas. 2016. "How the CIA Hoodwinked Hollywood." *The Atlantic*, July 14. Available: https://www.theatlantic.com/entertainment/archive/2016/07/ operation-tinseltown-how-the-cia-manipulates-hollywood/491138/ (accessed October 9, 2019).

Schwerdtfeger, Conner. 2018. "Is Michael B. Jordan's Killmonger Marvel's Best Villain Yet?" *Cinemablend*. Available: https://www.cinemablend.com/news/2312522/is-mi chael-b-jordans-killmonger-marvels-best-villain-yet (accessed August 11, 2019).

Scott, Ian, and Henry Thompson. 2016. *The Cinema of Oliver Stone: Art, Authorship and Activism*. Manchester: Manchester University Press.

Segrave, Kerry. 2014. *Foreign Films in America: A History*. Jefferson, NC, and London: McFarland & Company.

Secker, Tom. 2019. "ClandesTime 178—*Black Panther* vs. *Django Unchained*." *Spyculture.com*, April 28. Available: https://www.spyculture.com/clandestime -178-black-panther-vs-django-unchained/ (accessed August 11, 2019).

Serwer, Adam. 2018. "The Tragedy of Erik Killmonger." *The Atlantic*, February 21. Available: https://www.theatlantic.com/entertainment/archive/2018/02/black -panther-erik-killmonger/553805/ (accessed August 11, 2019).

Sexton, Jared. 2017. *Black Masculinity and the Cinema of Policing*. London: Palgrave Macmillan.

Sharf, Zack. 2019. "Ryan Coogler Retooled 'Black Panther' Ending by Cutting Killmonger's Big Line." *Salon.com*, January 16. Available: https://www.salon .com/2019/01/16/ryan-coogler-retooled-black-panther-ending-by-cutting -killmongers-big-line_partner/ (accessed August 11, 2019).

Simmons, Alex. 2019. "Introduction: What You Wish For." In Travis Langley and Alex Simmons, eds., *Black Panther Psychology: Hidden Kingdoms.* New York: Sterling.

Singer, Marc. 2002. "Black Skins and White Masks: Comic Books and the Secret of Race." *African American Review* 36, no. 1 (Spring): 107–119.

Slater, Alice. 2018. "The US Has Military Bases in 80 Countries. All of Them Must Close." *The Nation*, January 24. Available: https://www.thenation.com/article/the-us-has-military-bases-in-172-countries-all-of-them-must-close/ (accessed August 11, 2019).

Smith, Geraint. 1993. *Evening Standard*, June 24. Found in Seán Mac Mathúna, "Slavery and London," *Fantompowa*, n.d. Available: http://www.fantompowa.net/Flame/slavery_in_london.html (accessed September 11, 2019).

Smith, Jamil. 2018. "The Revolutionary Power of *Black Panther*." *Time*, February 11. Available: http://time.com/black-panther/ (accessed August 11, 2019).

Smith, Ronald. 2018. *Black Panther: The Young Prince.* New York and Los Angeles: Marvel.

Smith, Stacy L., Marc Choueiti, Katherine Pieper, Ariana Case, and Angel Cho. 2018. "Inequality in 1,100 Popular Films: Examining Portrayals of Gender, Race/Ethnicity, LGBT & Disability from 2007 to 2017." Available: http://assets.uscannenberg.org/docs/inequality-in-1100-popular-films.pdf (accessed August 11, 2019).

Smith, Stacy L., Marc Choueiti, Katherine Pieper, Ariana Case, and Angel Cho. 2019. "Inequality in 1,200 Popular Films: Examining Portrayals of Gender, Race/Ethnicity, LGBTQ & Disability from 2007 to 2018." Available: file:///C:/Users/teren/Documents/NEWEST%20STACEY%20SMITHaii-inequality-report-2019–09–03.pdf (accessed October 1, 2019).

Snyder, Brian. 2015. "How the Legacy of Slavery Affects the Mental Health of Black Americans Today." *The Conversation*, July 27. Available: https://theconversation.com/how-the-legacy-of-slavery-affects-the-mental-health-of-black-americans-today-44642 (accessed August 11, 2019).

Spengler, Sam, and Zoe Sayler. 2018. "The New Director of the Smithsonian's African Art Museum Reflects on the Look and Fashion of *Black Panther*." *Smithsonian.com*, February 20. Available: https://www.smithsonianmag.com/smithsonian-institution/new-director-smithsonians-african-art-museum-reflects-look-and-fashion-emblack-pantherem-180968212/#ggSTX0R8dypfWSlc.99 (accessed August 11, 2019).

Stockwell, John. 1978. *In Search of Enemies: A CIA Story.* New York: W. W. Norton & Co.

Stork, Matthias. 2014. "Assembling the Avengers: Reframing the Superhero movie through Marvels' Cinematic Universe." In James N. Gilmore and Matthias Stork, eds., *Superhero Synergies*, 77–95. Lanham, MD: Rowman and Littlefield.

Strohm, Rachel. 2016. "Where is Wakanda?" *RachelStrohm.com*, May 28. Available: https://rachelstrohm.com/2016/05/28/where-is-wakanda/ (accessed August 11, 2019).

Subrick, J. Robert. 2018. "The Political Economy of *Black Panther*'s Wakanda." *SSRN*, March 2. Available: https://papers.ssrn.com/sol3/papers.cfm?abstract_id=3129750 (accessed August 11, 2019).

Tapley, Christopher. 2015. "Yes, that Dazzling Boxing Sequence in *Creed* Really Was One Shot." *Variety*, December 1. Available: https://variety.com/2015/film/awards/yes-that-dazzling-boxing-sequence-in-creed-really-was-one-shot-1201650969/ (accessed August 11, 2019).

Taylor, A. J. P. 1961. *The Origins of the Second World War*. London: Hamish Hamilton.

Teutsch, Matthew. 2018. "*Black Panther*, What Now?" *Interminable Rambling*, February 19. Available: https://interminablerambling.wordpress.com/2018/02/19/9778/ (accessed August 11, 2019).

Thomas, Dexter. 2015. "Why Everyone's Saying 'Black Girls are Magic.'" *Los Angeles Times*, September 9. Available: https://www.latimes.com/nation/nationnow/la-na-nn-everyones-saying-black-girls-are-magic-20150909-htmlstory.html (accessed August 11, 2019).

Thomas, Nicholas. 2018. "Should Colonial Art be Returned Home?" *Financial Times*, December 7. Available: https://www.ft.com/content/6c61c6e6-f7ed-11e8-af46-2022a0b02a6c (accessed October 9, 2019).

Thompson, Anne. 2018. "Ryan Coogler Changed the Rules of Hollywood with *Black Panther*—Indiewire Honours." *Indiewire*, November 1. Available: https://www.indiewire.com/2018/11/ryan-coogler-hollywood-black-panther-indiewire-honors-1202016749/ (accessed August 11, 2019).

Thrasher, Steven. 2018. "There Is Much to Celebrate—and Much to Question—About Marvel's *Black Panther*." *Esquire*, February 20. Available: https://www.esquire.com/entertainment/movies/a18241993/black-panther-review-politics-killmonger/ (accessed August 11, 2019).

Timmons, Heather. 2018. "Trump's UN Speech was Bold, Isolationist, and Full of Outright Lies." *Quartz*, September 25. Available: https://qz.com/1401423/unga-trumps-speech-rejects-globalism-embraces-nationalism/ (accessed October 9, 2019).

Travis, Ben. 2018. "11 *Black Panther* Secrets from Ryan Coogler and Nate Moore." *Empire*, March 1. Available: https://www.empireonline.com/movies/features/11-black-panther-secrets-ryan-coogler-nate-moore/ (accessed August 11, 2019).

Travers, Peter. 2018. "Marvel's History Making Superhero Movie's a Masterpiece." *Rolling Stone*, February 6. Available: https://www.rollingstone.com/movies/movie-reviews/black-panther-review-marvels-history-making-superhero-movies-a-masterpiece-198071/ (accessed August 11, 2019).

Tumarkin, Maria. 2005. *Traumascapes: The Power and Fate of Places Transformed by Tragedy*. Melbourne: Melbourne University Publishing.

Turner, Matthew. 2018. "*Black Panther* Review: Marvel's African Superhero Could be a Watershed Moment for Hollywood." *I.N News*, February 13. Available: https://inews.co.uk/culture/film/black-panther-review/ (accessed August 11, 2019).

Turse, Nick. 2017. "The War You've Never Heard Of." *Vice*, May 18. Available: https://news.vice.com/en_us/article/nedy3w/the-u-s-is-waging-a-massive -shadow-war-in-africa-exclusive-documents-reveal (accessed August 11, 2019).

Tyson, Alec, and Shiva Maniam. 2016. "Behind Trump's Victory: Divisions by Race, Gender, Education." *Pew Research*, November 9. Available: https://www .pewresearch.org/fact-tank/2016/11/09/behind-trumps-victory-divisions-by -race-gender-education/ (accessed August 11, 2019).

Upton, Bryn. 2014. *Hollywood and the End of the Cold War: Signs of Cinematic Change*. New York: Rowan and Littlefield Publishers.

Valentine, Douglas. 2016. *The CIA as Organized Crime: How Illegal Operations Corrupt America and the World*. Atlanta: Clarity Press.

Verhaagen, Dave. 2019. "Why *Black Panther* Matters to Us All." In Travis Langley and Alex Simmons, eds., *Black Panther Psychology: Hidden Kingdoms*. New York: Sterling

Vescia, Monique. 2019. *The Culture of Scarification*. New York: Rosen Publishing Group.

Villaverde, Noah. 2018. "Ryan Coogler Explains 'Black Panther' End Credits Scenes." *Heroic Hollywood*, February 16. Available: https://heroichollywood. com/ryan-coogler-black-panther-end-credits/ (accessed August 11, 2019).

Vishnevetsky, Ignatiy (2018) "The Entertaining and Ambitious *Black Panther* Breaks from the Marvel Formula." *A.V. Club*, February 14. Available: https:// www.avclub.com/the-entertaining-and-ambitious-black-panther-breaks-fro -1822976016 (accessed August 11, 2019).

Wallace, Carvell. 2018. "Why *Black Panther* is a Defining Moment for Black America." *New York Times Magazine*, February 12. Available: https://www .nytimes.com/2018/02/12/magazine/why-black-panther-is-a-defining-moment -for-black-america.html (accessed August 11, 2019).

Wang, Ban. 2004. *Illuminations from the Past: Trauma, Memory, and History in Modern China*. Stanford, CA: Stanford University Press.

Webster, Peter. 2015. *White Dust Black Death: The Tragedy of Asbestos Mining at Baryulgil*. Manchester: Trafford Publishing.

Weston, Kellie. 2018. "*Black Panther* Review: An Electrifying, Afrofuturist Super-hero Movie." *Sight and Sound*, March 15. Available: https://www.bfi.org.uk /news-opinion/sight-sound-magazine/reviews-recommendations/black -panther-electrifying-afrofuturist-superhero-movie (accessed August 11, 2019).

Wilkins, Jonathan, ed. 2018. *Black Panther: The Official Movie Companion*. London: Titan Magazines.

Williams, Délice. 2018. "Three Theses about *Black Panther*." *Africology: The Journal of Pan African Studies* 11, no. 9 (August): 27–30.

Williams, Stereo. 2017. "Ta-Nehisi Coates's *Black Panther*: A Powerful Symbol for the Black Lives Matter Generation." *Daily Beast*, July 12. Available: https:// www.thedailybeast.com/ta-nehisi-coatess-black-panther-a-powerful-symbol -for-the-black-lives-matter-generation (accessed August 11, 2019).

Wilson, Julee. 2016. "The Meaning of #BlackGirlMagic, and How You Can Get Some of It." *Huffington Post*, January 12. Available: https://www.huffingtonpost.co.uk/entry/what-is-black-girl-magic-video_n_5694dad4e4b086bc1cd517f4 (accessed August 11, 2019).

Wilt, James. 2018. "How *Black Panther* Liberalizes Black Resistance for White Comfort." *Canadian Dimension*, February 21. Available: https://canadiandimension.com/articles/view/how-black-panther-liberalizes-black-resistance-for-white-comfort (accessed August 11, 2019).

Wiltz, Teresa. 2013. "'Shopping while Black' is Still an Issue—At Barneys and Elsewhere." *The Guardian*. Available: https://www.theguardian.com/commentisfree/2013/oct/28/barneys-racial-profiling-shopping-while-black (accessed August 11, 2019).

Wittmer, Carrie. 2018. "The Top 22 Marvel Cinematic Universe Villains, Ranked from Worst to Best." *Business Insider*, July 23. Available: https://www.businessinsider.com/marvel-cinematic-universe-villains-ranked-from-worst-to-best-2018-2?r=US&IR=T (accessed August 11, 2019).

Womack, Ytasha. 2013. *Afrofuturism: The World of Black Sci-Fi and Fantasy Culture*. Chicago: Lawrence Hill Books.

Wynn, Neil. 2010. *The African American Experience during World War II*. New York: Rowman & Littlefield.

Yandolli, Krystie Lee. 2018. "Director Ryan Coogler Surprised Fans at a 'Black Panther' Screening In His Hometown." *Buzzfeed.com*, February 16. Available: https://www.buzzfeednews.com/article/krystieyandoli/director-ryan-coogler-surprised-fans-at-a-black-panther (accessed August 11, 2019).

Yang, Linda. 2018. "'Black Panther' Could Have Depicted the First Queer Romance in a Marvel Movie." *Vice*, February 13. Available: https://broadly.vice.com/en_us/article/a343pa/black-panther-first-queer-romance-in-a-marvel-movie (accessed August 11, 2019).

Young, Cathy. 2016. "The Totalitarian Doctrine of 'Social Justice Warriors.'" *The Observer*, February 2. Available: https://observer.com/2016/02/the-totalitarian-doctrine-of-social-justice-warriors/ (accessed August 11, 2019).

Zelizer, Julian, ed. 2018. *The Presidency of Barack Obama: A First Historical Assessment*. Princeton: Princeton University Press.

Ziabari, Kourosh, and Akil Houston. 2019. "Being Black in America." *Fair Observer*, January 9. Available: https://www.fairobserver.com/region/north_america/racism-america-black-african-american-culture-news-latest-world-news-today-20126/ (accessed August 11, 2019).

Zipes, Jack. 2006. *Fairy Tales and the Art of Subversion. The Classical Genre for Children and the Process of Civilisation*, second edition. New York and London: Routledge.

Žižek, Slavoj. 2018. "Quasi Duo Fantasias: A Straussian Reading of 'Black Panther.'" *Los Angeles Review of Books*, March 3. Available: https://lareviewofbooks.org/article/quasi-duo-fantasias-straussian-reading-black-panther/ (accessed August 11, 2019).

Zoller Seitz, Matt. 2017. *The Oliver Stone Experience*. New York: Abrams Books.

Index

Page numbers in *italics* refer to illustrations.

About the Author

Photo courtesy of the author

Terence McSweeney is senior lecturer in film and television studies at Solent University. He is the author of *The "War on Terror" and American Film: 9/11 Frames Per Second* and *Avengers Assemble! Critical Perspectives on the Marvel Cinematic Universe*.